Knowledge Studies in Higher Education

Volume 18

Series Editors

Jung Cheol Shin, Seoul National University, Seoul, Korea (Republic of)
Hugo Horta, The University of Hong Kong, Hong Kong SAR, China

Editorial Board Members

Ulrich Teichler, University of Kassel, Kassel, Germany
Loet Leydesdorff, Amsterdam School of Communications Research, Amsterdam, The Netherlands
Simon Marginson, UCL Institute of Education, London, UK
Keun Lee, Seoul National University, Seoul, Korea (Republic of)
Gary Rhoades, University of Arizona, Arizona, USA

AF823274

Scope of the Series
Even though knowledge is the main content of teaching and universities are key knowledge producers, scholars have only recently begun to actively explore research on knowledge studies in higher education. As this field of study has grown, it has increasingly overlapped with the research focus of other fields, namely research and science policy, and information studies. However, these three fields have developed independently with little interaction between them, causing our understanding of knowledge to be limited, compartmented, and lacking a multidimensional perspective. This book series is designed to improve knowledge studies in higher education by stimulating interactions between these different approaches.

Coverage in this series includes:

- University and knowledge production
- R & D funding systems
- Education reforms
- Innovation systems for emerging regions
- School curriculum and knowledge
- Social utility of knowledge production
- University research and in-house research
- Research collaborations.

With its comprehensive overview and multidisciplinary perspective, this series provides scholars and policymakers with the theory and data they need to make more informed decisions regarding knowledge research in higher education.

Kathleen M. Brennan • Kimberly S. Gorman
Editors

A University-Wide Approach to Changing Campus Cultures of Mental Illness Stigma

Springer

Editors
Kathleen M. Brennan
Department of Anthropology and Sociology
Western Carolina University
Cullowhee, NC, USA

Kimberly S. Gorman
Division of Student Affairs
Western Carolina University
Cullowhee, NC, USA

ISSN 2566-7106 ISSN 2566-8315 (electronic)
Knowledge Studies in Higher Education
ISBN 978-3-031-86495-7 ISBN 978-3-031-86496-4 (eBook)
https://doi.org/10.1007/978-3-031-86496-4

© The Editor(s) (if applicable) and The Author(s), under exclusive license to Springer Nature Switzerland AG 2025

This work is subject to copyright. All rights are solely and exclusively licensed by the Publisher, whether the whole or part of the material is concerned, specifically the rights of translation, reprinting, reuse of illustrations, recitation, broadcasting, reproduction on microfilms or in any other physical way, and transmission or information storage and retrieval, electronic adaptation, computer software, or by similar or dissimilar methodology now known or hereafter developed.
The use of general descriptive names, registered names, trademarks, service marks, etc. in this publication does not imply, even in the absence of a specific statement, that such names are exempt from the relevant protective laws and regulations and therefore free for general use.
The publisher, the authors and the editors are safe to assume that the advice and information in this book are believed to be true and accurate at the date of publication. Neither the publisher nor the authors or the editors give a warranty, expressed or implied, with respect to the material contained herein or for any errors or omissions that may have been made. The publisher remains neutral with regard to jurisdictional claims in published maps and institutional affiliations.

This Springer imprint is published by the registered company Springer Nature Switzerland AG
The registered company address is: Gewerbestrasse 11, 6330 Cham, Switzerland

If disposing of this product, please recycle the paper.

Kathleen dedicates this volume to Eric, Molly Frances, and Shaney.
Kim dedicates this volume to the memory of her parents, Jim & Agnes Sandford.

Preface

Nearly 10 years ago, we began our journey of collaboration and consultation. Our partnership started when we asked the question "is it possible to….?" Since then, we have answered that question in the affirmative many times. Our research partnership has delved into the presence and impact of mental illness stigma on our campus while considering the representations of stigma reflected in the larger body of research. As we engaged in our scholarship, we had ongoing conversations about how the silos inherent in academia and university settings make systemic change in higher education difficult, if not impossible. We discussed finding ways to bridge academic affairs (Kathleen's silo) and student affairs (Kim's silo) to change mental illness stigma on our campus and other campuses, underscoring the importance of communication between academics and higher education decision-makers. Our practice and advocacy partnerships have put us in front of several groups on our campus to enact steps toward changing stigma. As such, we have utilized a tridirectional approach centered in the interrelationship of research, practice, and administrative decision-making. The current volume reflects an effort to build and cross that bridge on a broader scale.

This volume focuses on changing campus cultures of mental illness stigma with preemptive, evidence-based solutions reflecting the involvement of stakeholders across campus. This approach is an improvement over more traditional methods (e.g., reactive, one-off responses used by single groups) used on many campuses. Each chapter reflects a different segment of the university and the ways that mental illness stigma is present within it. Each chapter also provides examples and/or suggestions to address the stigma within the subculture and/or segment of the university and beyond. We have developed this volume as a guide for campuses wishing to address mental illness stigma in a strategic, systemic manner. We also hope readers will use the chapters as a guide to change their individual practice.

Cullowhee, NC, USA

Kathleen M. Brennan
Kimberly S. Gorman

Acknowledgments

We wish to acknowledge the students, faculty, and staff at Western Carolina University (WCU) who have supported our efforts in myriad ways. They have participated in our research projects, they have listened to our presentations about mental illness stigma, they have engaged in conversations and provided examples of how stigma has impacted them, and they have actively worked to change mental illness stigma on our campus. We wish to explicitly thank the administrators at WCU who have recognized and supported our partnership and have recognized our work with awards, grants, and publicity.

Kathleen: Thank you to my students who, over the years, have showed me the many ways higher education excludes people with mental illness, but also the many ways to be resilient and inclusive in this cultural context. You have helped me improve as a professor and a person. Thank you to my colleagues and academic mentors who have challenged me and built me up. Thank you to Kim Gorman, my dear friend and colleague, who has fueled my professional and personal growth over the last decade. And finally, I thank my spouse, Eric, and our children, Molly Frances and Eily, for their unconditional love and support. No matter what, I have you, and that is what matters most to me.

Kim: Thanks to those who grew and nurtured me into the feminist psychologist that I have become and helped me to understand the intricate and inevitable intersection of culture, politics, and mental illness: Pam & Rory Remer, Sue Stock, and Jay Zimmerman. A big thank you to Kathleen Brennan, my colleague, my research partner and my friend who models kindness and fierceness with every breath. You are truly amazing. A big thank you to my late parents, Jim & Agnes Sandford, who demonstrated what it means to love without bounds. And finally, thanks to my life partner, Frank Gorman, for loving me through everything.

Contents

List of Figures

List of Tables

Chapter 1
Addressing Campus Cultures of Mental Illness Stigma: An Introduction

Kathleen M. Brennan and Kimberly S. Gorman

Abstract Cultural ideas, values, and norms that reflect taken-for-granted assumptions about how institutions of higher education should operate situate these practices as "normal," while concurrently situating mental illness in opposition to cultural rules. In this context, mental illness and those who experience it become viewed as threats to the social order defined by local cultural beliefs. Thus, university strategies must address cultures of stigma on individual campuses to reduce mental illness stigma in higher education. In this chapter, we introduce the volume by discussing its contributions related to sources of mental illness stigma on university campuses and working models and/or tests of practical solutions to these stigma sources that may be implemented by campus leaders at their institutions.

Keywords Mental illness · Stigma culture · University campuses · Anti-stigma strategies · Practical examples

Student mental health concerns have increased in the last decade, leading universities to prioritize campus mental health (Chessman & Taylor, 2019; Orygen, 2020). Amidst the pandemic, U.S. universities used additional funding, reallocated funds, and invested significant amounts of staff and faculty time to address student mental health concerns to improve student success; these commitments of time and funds have continued (U.S. Department of Education, 2021). While this is a positive and important step, the effectiveness of these efforts will be limited if mental illness

---

The authors have no conflicts of interest to declare that are relevant to the content of this chapter.

K. M. Brennan (✉)
Department of Anthropology and Sociology, Western Carolina University, Cullowhee, NC, USA
e-mail: kbrennan@wcu.edu

K. S. Gorman
Division of Student Affairs, Western Carolina University, Cullowhee, NC, USA

© The Author(s), under exclusive license to Springer Nature Switzerland AG 2025

K. M. Brennan, K. S. Gorman (eds.), *A University-Wide Approach to Changing Campus Cultures of Mental Illness Stigma*, Knowledge Studies in Higher Education 18, https://doi.org/10.1007/978-3-031-86496-4_1

stigma, a key barrier to student help-seeking, is not addressed (Gaddis et al., 2018; Gorman & Brennan, 2023b).

Mental illness stigma has been studied across a variety of academic disciplines, including psychology, sociology, social work, education, public health, medical and health sciences, marketing, communication studies, and anthropology. Despite differences in theoretical frame and methodological approach, this body of research largely confirms the persistence and pervasiveness of mental illness stigma in a variety of forms across demographic groups, social institutions, and societies. Likewise, the research confirms stigma is formed and reproduced within social contexts and acts as a barrier to treatment-seeking and other behaviors that positively influence recovery and minimize disease progression (Aguirre Velasco et al., 2020; Brennan & Gorman, 2022; Clement et al., 2015; Javed et al., 2021). These findings are important for understanding the cultural hold mental illness stigma has on individuals, especially when anecdotal claims about decreasing stigma rates are increasingly made by institutional decision-makers and members of the public.

The context of higher education presents an interesting case for the study of mental illness stigma. Stigma research in this context is robust, with decades of investigation into the prevalence of mental illness, stigma, and treatment-seeking, as well as the associations between them in university student populations. Much of this research is framed with academic student success in mind, given the negative associations found between mental illness and retention and degree completion. The scant research that examines the role of treatment in student success finds mental health treatment use and, more specifically, number of sessions attended are positively associated with retention and completion (Gorman & Brennan, 2023a). In the United States, retaining already enrolled students at universities has become critical with the drop in the college-age population, and consequent university enrollment, expected to begin in 2025 (Adams, 2020; Grawe, 2018). Addressing factors to facilitate student success in this population is key.

Findings regarding the prevalence of mental illness, stigma, and treatment-seeking in student populations offer universities a starting point in helping accomplish the goal of preparing students, regardless of mental illness status, for lifetime success. But this body of research falls short in several ways. Primarily, it rarely ventures beyond assessing mental illness stigma prevalence in university student populations when the pervasiveness of stigma is only one part of a larger cultural problem within institutions of higher education. Higher education, like all social contexts, reifies stigmas through its unique cultural arrangements, meaning the devalued mark, condition, or status of mental illness is culturally constructed (Goffman, 1963). The stigmatization process reflects the ways those touched by mental illness, whether personally or through their relationships with others, are negatively affected due to this devaluation (Pescosolido & Martin, 2015). In university settings, this manifests as those with mental illness being defined and labeled as different from other community members. This difference is then associated with negative designations and stereotypes which lead those with mental illness to be separated from the "normal" members of the campus community. The related status loss results in unfair treatment toward those with mental illness, which affects their life chances (Link & Phelan, 2001; Pescosolido & Martin, 2015), most notably through degree incompletion.

Separation and unfair treatment toward students with mental illness is demonstrated in myriad ways such as university policies that do not allow those with in-patient histories to live on campus, faculty asking for students to be removed from classes after a suicidal statement or a self-injurious event, lack of academic accommodations such as flexible deadlines or absence policies, insufficient mental health services or long waiting times for treatment, or lack of staff and faculty training on how to recognize and support students with mental illness. For employees with mental illness, this may manifest, for instance, as lack of attention given to mental health care in discussions about benefits or during the onboarding process, lack of supervisor training on how to recognize and support mental well-being in team members, discouraging employees from openly discussing mental illness, or dissuading them from taking time off for mental health-related challenges. These negatively affect employees' organizational integration and success and students' future educational and career opportunities (Hatzenbuehler et al., 2013).

These policies and practices are symbolic of "institutional schemas that shape actors' taken-for-granted ideas about how an institution does and should operate" (Amenta & Polletta, 2019, p. 281). The supporting cultural ideas, values, and assumptions that define these practices as acceptable and routine (i.e., "normal") in the context of higher education concurrently define mental illness in opposition to cultural rules. In this context, mental illness may indeed be a threat to the social order defined by local cultural beliefs (Walsh & Foster, 2021). An example in U.S. higher education is the broadening use of the term "mental health," which has created more fear and uncertainty for staff and faculty in assisting students. According to Gorman et al. (2024):

> The term 'mental health' is being used more ubiquitously by students to communicate distress at any level (CCMH, 2021). While this may indicate a comfort in talking about mental health, the paradox is that as it is used so broadly, faculty and staff have become more heightened and reactive when students mention their mental health and immediately refer or escort the student to counseling services. (p. 8)

An unintended consequence of this shifting cultural understanding of mental health among students is stigma creation among those with influence on university campuses: staff and faculty. In this way, the normative cultural expectations for the context of higher education form the basis for mental illness stigma, socially constructing stigma as normative and reinforcing it through the various relationships (e.g., faculty/student, administrator/staff, student/student) developed on campus (Amenta & Polletta, 2019; Pescosolido & Martin, 2015; Pescosolido et al., 2008).

Stigma is embedded in a cultural context that influences the way different groups accept, reject, or modify dominant cultural belief, and it persists in higher education, even as some of the cultural ascriptions that underlie the stigmatization process change (Pescosolido & Martin, 2015). For instance, even though the U.S. public is more knowledgeable about mental illness, which means mental illness is identified sooner and makes it possible for more young adults to attend college (Auerbach et al., 2018), public stigma has remained stable in the U.S. adult population (Best & Arseniev-Koehler, 2023; Pescosolido et al., 2021). Also, even though universities in the United States have embraced an approach that pairs mental health with well-being to decrease mental illness stigma (Brewster & Cox, 2022), public stigma continues to be prominent on university campuses (Gaddis et al., 2018; Lipson et al., 2019). Likewise, even though more college students report they do not personally hold stigmatizing views toward persons with mental illness, they expect others in the higher education community to hold stigmatizing views (Healthy Minds Network, 2020). These patterns point to the transformation of mental illness stigma into a more obscure form, invoking the need for more extensive anti-stigma approaches.

Clair and colleagues (2016) note, "reducing public stigma requires the broad resonance of new constructions in the general population, which is typically slow and may transform into hidden forms of bias" (p. 229). This highlights the need to challenge mental illness stigma beyond the level of the individual. At the collective level, representations of stigma must be challenged within the institution of higher education, its spoken and unspoken norms, its policies and practices, and its interpersonal interactions (Clair et al., 2016; Orygen, 2020; Pescosolido et al., 2008). Campus community networks that connect students and employees offer an important means to weaken cultural stereotypes that reinforce cultural aspects of the stigma complex (Pescosolido & Martin, 2015). This is particularly important in the case of groups labeled "at risk," such as students with mental illness, who are often symbolically believed to threaten the social order of higher education due to the implication of noncompletion (Walsh & Foster, 2021). This volume calls for all campus constituents—students, faculty, and staff—to come together to challenge and disempower campus cultures of mental illness stigma.

Volume Definitions

Throughout this volume, authors reference several common concepts utilized in the mental illness stigma literature. We offer the definitions of these terms here to decrease repetition and to standardize the use of the language throughout this volume.

- Mental illness refers to conditions that impact a person's cognitive, behavioral, or emotional regulation and is usually associated with distress or impairment in one or more areas of functioning (World Health Organization, 2022).
- Stigma involves "the situation of the individual who is disqualified from full social acceptance" due to a characteristic that is negatively perceived by others (Goffman, 1963, p. 3).
- Mental illness stigma refers to the negative attitudes, beliefs, and behaviors directed toward individuals who experience mental illness (Centers for Disease Control and Prevention, n.d.).

- Public stigma comprises the stereotypes, prejudice, and discrimination endorsed by the general population toward a person or group who holds some type of discrediting attribute (Corrigan, 2000; Pescosolido & Martin, 2015).
- Self-stigma involves the negative cognitions, including internalized shame, people have about their own condition (American Psychiatric Association, n.d.; Corrigan et al., 2005).

We note these definitions underscore the preponderance of the social science viewpoint reflected across the disciplinary backgrounds of the volume contributors. Predictably, the volume focus on *cultures* of mental illness stigma is more likely to draw scholars from disciplines that examine social group meanings, practices, and expressions. However, we are aware the diversity of views on the nature of mental illness extends beyond those of the social sciences, and we recognize the value in these views. Their absence in the volume was dictated by its overarching theme and space limitations. The solutions we offer within this reduced scope to the complex issues of mental illness and related stigma are not straightforward or easy and necessitate complex solutions. For substantive change to occur, stakeholders must be willing to take the time to unpack these complexities, including the consideration of multiple perspectives, when formulating responses to mental illness and its stigma.

Volume Contributions

While cultural context is widely acknowledged as shaping individual experiences and life chances, the cultural context of higher education that shapes mental illness stigma has not been adequately studied to pinpoint the sources of devaluation. This volume contributes to the literature on mental illness stigma, generally and specifically in the context of higher education, by providing empirical evidence of some of the cultural roots of stigma demonstrated in the groups, programs, and services on university campuses. Taken together, the chapters demonstrate the intersectionality of mental illness stigma represented in the confluence of various parts of university culture and the inequality and oppression associated with each as well as in combination with others. Each chapter identifies and discusses cultural sources of this devaluation then offers practical solutions—many of which have been tested in university contexts and found effective—for reducing or eliminating stigma.

In this way, the volume further contributes to the literature on mental illness stigma in the context of higher education, which sometimes emphasizes discovery at the expense of practice. While offering a comprehensive view of the presence of stigma and its consequences, the literature is underdeveloped regarding discussion of working models or tests of practical solutions (Pescosolido & Martin, 2015; Walsh & Foster, 2021). To be sure, many studies offer finding-specific responses for things universities *could and should* do to address stigma, including enhancing mental health services, creating mental health awareness campaigns, implementing training for faculty and staff to respond to mental health challenges, and starting peer support programs. These approaches certainly make sense on the surface, being historically tried and true pathways for addressing a variety of campus issues related to mental health concerns. However, the research literature typically lacks specific guidance for their effective enactment within the general higher education framework, as well as for how to consider the nuances of individual campus cultures as a part of the implementation. Best methods for executing solutions may not be obvious to campus leaders, even when the resources to do so are available. One-off approaches implemented without adequate cultural understandings and planning may not prove effective, and may sometimes even result in unintended, negative consequences (Pescosolido et al., 2008; Walsh & Foster, 2021), given the intersectional nature of mental illness stigma reflected by the convergence of different aspects of university culture.

For this reason, we view the applied nature of this volume as making a particularly salient contribution to guide the work of challenging stigma in higher education. Our intent is for this volume to be accessible to campus leaders at all levels, from program directors to presidents, and those in between. We offer specific, evidence-based, guided examples they may use as models for their campus and/or their departments and divisions. We intentionally included chapters that represent a variety of academic affairs and student affairs contexts, which we hope will be useful for addressing mental illness stigma systemically. And, while the examples in the volume largely represent those used in the United States, they reflect broader global themes that may be considered within the unique cultural contexts of higher education institutions outside of the United States. This new approach is timely, as college and university presidents recognize attempts to address the intersection of lower student success rates and mental illness on campus, such as hiring more counselors, have not been sufficient (Chessman & Taylor, 2019).

This volume also adds to the literature on mental illness stigma in the context of higher education by expanding the discussion beyond undergraduate students, the main population of focus in this body of research. Chapter contributors consider the role of and/or impact to staff, faculty, administrators, and graduate students in the stigmatization process. This focus is important since stigma is shaped and reshaped by everyone on campus. And everyone on campus—students, faculty, staff, and administrators—who experiences mental illness is a recipient of stigmatizing processes. Currently, there is a dearth of research on mental illness stigma in higher education employees; this limits our understanding of how this population contributes to an overall campus culture of mental illness stigma. Stigmatization is enacted only through social relations (Goffman, 1963), and these groups have the power and ability to stratify knowledge and resources related to both mental health and degree completion (Link & Phelan, 2001). Thus, these groups play a key role when it comes to engaging in anti-stigma efforts to alter campus cultures of mental illness stigma. Additionally, the COVID-19 pandemic highlighted the role of mental health in employee success, so it is critical to address how cultures of stigma negatively affect graduate students, staff, faculty, and administrators who experience mental illness (National Association of Student Affairs Professionals, 2022).

In sum, stigma matters because it is intimately related to and compromises a person's ability to cope with mental illness by producing stress and exposing individuals to additional illness-producing conditions (Link & Phelan, 2001). While campuses continue to find treatment solutions to address the mental health needs of students (Gorman et al., 2024), they need to also consider and address the insidious ways stigma is complicating those efforts. The influence of cultural context on health and well-being is widely acknowledged, but the empirical literature on the cultural nature of mental illness stigma in general and in the context of higher education remains underdeveloped. By exploring the cultural dimensions of stigma in the context of higher education, this volume provides insights into tailoring anti-stigma efforts and offers specific pathways for creating more inclusive and supportive educational communities with successful outcomes for all community members, regardless of mental health status.

Volume Organization and Themes

The volume begins by introducing core concepts, theories, and models that lay the groundwork for understanding the nature and complexity of mental illness stigma in higher education. From there, each of the volume chapters identifies challenges related to mental illness stigma in the context of higher education and the ways those challenges have been addressed on specific campuses or could be addressed on campuses to promote positive outcomes. These include actionable interventions universities can implement to reduce stigma as well as more comprehensive, systemic strategies for addressing stigma across campus communities. Chapters reflect one or more of the following four themes: (1) The identification of specific cultural sources of mental illness devaluation rooted in groups, programs, and/or services on campus; (2) The intersectionality of stigma and its implications for systemic anti-stigma policies and practices; (3) Practical solutions for decreasing mental illness stigma with guidance for effective enactment; and (4) A focus on campus community groups other than, in addition to, or in concert with undergraduate students.

Theme One

The first theme, cultural contexts of higher education that produce and shape mental illness stigma, is addressed in Chapters 2, 5, 6, 10, and 11. In Chapter 2, Brennan and Gorman discuss why mental illness stigma persists and how it gets translated into the cultural context of higher education in terms of values and norms that mark students (and other community members) with mental illness as different. They offer a case study documenting the culture of mental illness stigma on their campus and discuss its roots and implications for campus community members as well as some ways the campus has responded to it. Finally, they consider evidence pointing to contexts in which persons with mental illness thrive and discuss their applicability to the context of higher education.

In Chapter 5, Blake reflects on the effects of his decision to publicly disclose having bipolar disorder. He discusses the risks of this decision, related both to the precarity of his position as an early career Black scholar in academia and the racialized stigma of mental illness facing African American communities. He also discusses how this decision led him, as a higher education scholar, to critically analyze the ways the field implicitly perpetuates ableism and mental illness stigma by largely neglecting the presence of people with mental illnesses in the academy. He contextualizes his experiences by briefly synthesizing literature on race and mental illness, particularly how mental illness diagnoses have been weaponized against African American communities, resulting in a unique form of stigma. He also discusses how attending to the intersections of race and mental health is essential to racial equity.

In Chapter 6, Gorman discusses an important, yet neglected, source of mental illness stigma in higher education: the training of mental health professionals. She focuses her discussion on how stigma is introduced and reinforced by mental health graduate programs and related faculty in counseling, psychology, and social work. She discusses the impact stigma has on the development of skills and the use of language by students training to be mental health professionals. She proposes ways to alter curriculum development and delivery to challenge stigma.

In Chapter 10, Dunn, Boulden, and Cheifetz discuss the shift occurring on campuses reflecting decreased alcohol consumption and increased substance misuse. They highlight ways stigma influences campus policies and cultures surrounding substance use and advocate for a paradigm shift away from moralistic judgments to a strength-based approach that focuses on safety and emphasizes recovery. They argue this compassionate approach, which dismantles stigma, can promote lasting change on campuses.

In Chapter 11, Macbeth and Shelton review the mental health experience of students who participate in collegiate athletics, how mental illness stigma operates within the system of athletics, and stigma's effect on access to mental health care for students who are athletes. They provide research-based recommendations for college athlete mental health support.

Theme Two

The second theme, the intersectionality of stigma and its implications for systemic anti-stigma action, is reflected in the collaborative approaches highlighted in Chapters 4, 5, and 7. These chapters emphasize the greater risk of mental health struggles by individuals who embody multiple marginalized identities and the importance of involving a variety of internal and external campus stakeholders. In Chapter 4, Copeland-Hayes and Remedios argue challenging mental illness stigma necessitates attention to the intersectional stigma students from minoritized backgrounds experience. They discuss the ways institutions ignore students' lived experiences, calling attention to inadequate and culturally ignorant practices on campuses. They call for universities to incorporate intersectionality theory to address mental illness stigma and offer an example of an institution making progress toward this goal. Likewise, in Chapter 5, Blake discusses historical representations of intersectional stigma related to mental illness outside and within the academy, as well as his experience with intersectional stigma as a faculty member who holds multiple marginalized identities.

In Chapter 7, Pescosolido describes the implementation and effectiveness of the University Bring Change to Mind (UBC2M) program, a collaboration between Indiana University and the non-profit Bring Change to Mind. She highlights the unique characteristics of this program model, including the involvement of a variety of on- and off-campus stakeholders, the focus on success for *all* enrolled students, the fact that it is student-led, and that its continued success is based in evidence. Pescosolido emphasizes this model offers a range of mental health-related efforts in which students may choose to engage, which is empowering for students. Last, she offers effective aspects of the program that could be adopted by other campuses.

Theme Three

The volume's third theme highlights the ways universities have increased awareness of and attention to mental illness stigma and changed their practices to facilitate positive institutional outcomes. Most volume chapters include at least one applied example of a practical solution for readers' campuses to emulate, with discussion surrounding successful implementation. Chapters 7, 8, 9, and 10 offer tested solutions for changing campus stigma cultures that are preemptive and evidence-based as an improvement over more traditional methods—that is, reactive responses—currently used on many campuses.

In Chapter 8, Maranzan and her colleagues study the negative impact self-stigma has on the self-esteem, empowerment, and hope of students who experience mental distress by undermining functioning through the "why try" effect and dissuading students from seeking out or fully engaging with social supports and participating in society to their full potential. They discuss an anti-stigma reduction strategy focusing on disclosure that has been used on university campuses in the United States and Canada called Honest, Open, Proud-College (HOP-C) and offer implementation strategies specific to university campuses. Similarly, in the previously discussed chapters U Bring Change to Mind (Chapter 7), and Solidarity, Substance Use, and Stigma (Chapter 10), the authors offer suggestions for changing "moral" conversations about student mental illness and substance use disorders into tangible action.

In Chapter 9, Yeh evaluates the potential of social marketing campaigns for reducing mental illness stigma on campuses. She outlines steps for creating effective campaigns to change mental illness stigma cultures on college campuses and offers a case study demonstrating how the steps can be used to assess, target, and implement a comprehensive social marketing campaign to reduce mental illness stigma. Importantly, Yeh acknowledges the mixed outcomes of these types of campaigns when used in isolation and emphasizes their effectiveness on campus will be contingent on involvement of a variety of campus stakeholders, and especially students.

Theme Four

The fourth and last theme in the volume addresses how campus community groups other than undergraduate students contribute to and are affected by mental illness stigma. Graduate students (regardless of university employment status), staff, faculty, and/or administrators are the focus of this theme, as represented in Chapters 2, 3, 5, 6, and 11. In Chapter 3, Dias and RW explore the model of stigma communication to understand how stigmatizing messages about mental illness are created and perpetuated on college campuses. They offer recommendations for countering stigmatizing messages in higher education, with an emphasis on campus communication in the contexts of the college classroom and student training programs.

Additionally, in the previously discussed Chapters 2, 5, 6, and 11, the authors discuss how mental illness stigma in employee populations spill over into student populations, and/or how specific employee populations with mental health challenges are negatively influenced by mental illness stigma present in the workplace culture.

Volume Gaps

Even with these important contributions to the literatures on mental illness stigma and related higher education practice, the volume embodies several gaps in both realms. Most notably, it is not comprehensive in terms of identifying challenges related to mental illness stigma in the context of higher education, pinpointing its many cultural representations of stigma, or offering numerous ways those challenges have been addressed or could be addressed on campuses to promote positive mental health outcomes across community groups. For instance, as stigma is inextricably linked to institutional power structures, it is imperative to consider how university governance, policy-making bodies, and leadership could actively dismantle and be held accountable for stigmatizing practices. This is touched on in several volume chapters but needs more attention in future work. Nonetheless, we hope the coherence provided by the volume themes offers a highly accessible and easy to use guide for university leaders to single out chapter content that applies to specific issues on their campuses, to begin thinking about the many ways university cultures produce and reproduce stigma, or to see possible solutions for issues on their campus. As the first volume of its kind, we hope it encourages the continued sharing of similar content, whether in open access form via organizational websites and reports, special issues of journals, or through additional edited volumes.

To that end, we acknowledge the contributors in this volume are mostly writing about those who have experienced stigma and centering the expertise related to mental illness and related stigma on academic training instead of lived experience. Only two of the authors acknowledged their lived experience of mental illness; we wonder how many authors made the decision to not disclose their own. Likewise, most authors are writing about students rather than writing with them. We note the power dynamics built into the culture of academia and academic publishing that not only prioritizes credentials over lived experience in determining expertise but also positions lived experience as a potential threat to credentialed expertise. As editors, we were in a position of power to pull together representatives from offices across campus to discuss stigma's impact in all corners of the university. Calls for staff and student participation mostly went unanswered, likely due to a cultural understanding that faculty are the experts. Thus, we fell back on credentialed expertise. Our hope is, now that these problems are named, future volumes will have contributions from those who have been afraid to talk about their experiences because of their lack of power to do so.

In addition to the concentrated nature of the volume, it is important to keep in mind cultures of stigma in the context of higher education may present differently compared to cultures of stigma in other social contexts. As such, the findings and suggestions represented in this volume may not be appropriate to apply to contexts outside of higher education. Likewise, because the volume contributors largely operate from a western approach to higher education and mental illness, readers must consider how to translate these findings and suggestions to the cultural contexts in which they are embedded. Still, this volume offers a real start to answering the question of what cultures of stigma in higher education entail for appropriate responses to be identified and effectively enacted.

A last volume gap to consider is the influence of the COVID-19 era on stigma in general and, more pointedly, on university cultures of mental illness stigma. It is unknown whether the documented increase in psychological distress and clinically significant anxiety and depression in response to the pandemic and its highlighted disparities (Center for Collegiate Mental Health, 2021; Julius et al., 2024; Twenge & Joiner, 2020) reinforced stigmatizing beliefs around mental illness or decreased stigmatization via intensified empathy toward others with mental health struggles. Immediately preceding the pandemic, a study assessing trends in public stigma of mental illness in U.S. adults from 1996–2018 found evidence of both stability and change in public stigma (Pescosolido et al., 2021). During the latter half of the period, significant and substantial decreases in stigma were demonstrated toward major depressive disorder alone, while regressive shifts in stigma were found for schizophrenia and alcohol dependence (Pescosolido et al., 2021). As stigma is deeply ingrained and can take time to change, it is important to understand the cultural shifts that led to this change if decreases in stigma toward major depressive disorder are to be sustained. Ongoing efforts are required to sustain and expand the positive changes observed during this time. While cursory discussions of the pandemic are included in several chapters in the volume, this is not a volume focus.

Despite these gaps, we anticipate this volume could be used as a guide for any institution of higher education wishing to address mental illness stigma on their campus in a strategic, systemic manner. We also anticipate that individuals working in higher education can use chapters as guides to change their individual practice. It is important to remember that mental illness stigma can change but must be addressed collectively in terms of issues at stake in local cultural settings (Corrigan, 2011; Orygen, 2020; Schomerus & Angermeyer, 2021; Walsh & Foster, 2021, Yang et al., 2007).

References

Adams, M. (2020, May 28). The demographic cliff is already here, and it is about to get worse. *Educational Advisory Board.* https://eab.com/insights/expert-insight/enrollment/the-demographic-cliff-is-already-here-and-its-about-to-get-worse/

Aguirre Velasco, A., Cruz, I. S. S., Billings, J., Jimenez, M., & Rowe, S. (2020). What are the barriers, facilitators and interventions targeting help seeking behaviours for common mental health problems in adolescents? A systematic review. *BMC Psychiatry, 20*(1), 293. https://doi.org/10.1186/s12888-020-02659-0

Amenta, E., & Polletta, F. (2019). The cultural impacts of social movements. *Annual Review of Sociology, 45*(1), 279–299. https://doi.org/10.1146/annurev-soc-073018-022342

American Psychiatric Association. (n.d.). Stigma, prejudice and discrimination against people with mental illness. Retrieved December 8, 2024, from https://www.psychiatry.org/patients-families/stigma-and-discrimination#:~:text=Self%2Dstigma%20refers%20to%20the,have%20about%20their%20own%20condition

Auerbach, R. P., Mortier, P., Bruffaerts, R., Alonso, J., Benjet, C., Cuijpers, P., Demyttenaere, K., Ebert, D. D., Green, J. G., Hasking, P., Murray, E., Nock, M. K., Pinder-Amaker, S., Sampson, N. A., Stein, D. J., Vilagut, G., Zaslavsky, A. M., & Kessler, R. C. (2018). WHO world mental health surveys international college student project: Prevalence and distribution of mental disorders. *Journal of Abnormal Psychology, 127*(7), 623–638. https://doi.org/10.1037/abn0000362

Best, R. K., & Arseniev-Koehler, A. (2023). The stigma of diseases: Unequal burden, uneven decline. *American Sociological Review, 88*(5), 938–969. https://doi.org/10.1177/00031224231197436

Brennan, K. M., & Gorman, K. S. (2022). Altering the landscape of mental illness stigma on university campuses. *Stigma & Health, 7*(3), 358–369. https://doi.apa.org/doiLanding?doi=10.1037%2Fsah0000398

Brewster, L., & Cox, A. M. (2022). Taking a 'whole-university' approach to student mental health: The contribution of academic libraries. *Higher Education Research & Development, 42*(1), 33–47. https://doi.org/10.1080/07294360.2022.2043249

Center for Collegiate Mental Health. (2021, February 2). Part 1 of 5: COVID-19 impact on college student mental health. https://ccmh.psu.edu/index.php?option=com_dailyplanetblog&view=entry&year=2021&month=02&day=01&id=9:part-1-of-5-covid-19-impact-on-college-student-mental-health

Centers for Disease Control and Prevention. (n.d.). *Mental health stigma.* Retrieved December 8, 2024, from https://www.cdc.gov/mental-health/stigma/index.html#:~:text=1,4C

Chessman, H., & Taylor, M. (2019, August 12). College student health and Well-being: A survey of presidents. Higher Education Today*:* A Blog by American Council on Education. https://www.higheredtoday.org/2019/08/12/college-student-mental-health-well-survey-college-presidents/

Clair, M., Daniel, C., & Lamont, M. (2016). Destigmatization and health: Cultural constructions and the longterm reduction of stigma. *Social Science & Medicine, 165*, 223–232. https://doi.org/10.1016/j.socscimed.2016.03.021

Clement, S., Schauman, O., Graham, T., Maggioni, F., Evans-Lacko, S., Bezborodovs, N., Morgan, C., Rüsch, N., Brown, J. S. L., & Thornicroft, G. (2015). What is the impact of mental health-related stigma on help-seeking? A systematic review of quantitative and qualitative studies. *Psychological Medicine, 45*, 11–27. https://doi.org/10.1017/S0033291714000129

Corrigan, P. W. (2000). Mental health stigma as social attribution: Implications for research methods and attitude change. *Clinical Psychology: Science and Practice, 7*(1), 48–67. https://doi.org/10.1093/clipsy.7.1.48

Corrigan, P. W. (2011). Strategic stigma change (SSC): Five principles for social marketing campaigns to reduce stigma. *Psychiatric Services, 62*, 824–826. https://doi.org/10.1176/ps.62.8.pss6208_0824

Corrigan, P. W., Kerr, A., & Knudsen, L. (2005). The stigma of mental illness: Explanatory models and methods for change. *Applied and Preventive Psychology, 11*(3), 179–190. https://doi.org/10.1016/J.APPSY.2005.07.001

Gaddis, S. M., Ramirez, D., & Hernandez, E. L. (2018). Contextualizing public stigma: Endorsed mental health treatment stigma on college and university campuses. *Social Science & Medicine, 197*, 183–191. https://doi.org/10.1016/j.socscimed.2017.11.029

Goffman, E. (1963). *Stigma. Notes on the management of spoiled identity*. Simon and Schuster.

Gorman, K. S., & Brennan, K. M. (2023a). More sessions make a difference: University counseling centers and student retention. *Journal of Student Affairs Research and Practice, 61*(4), 1–13. https://doi.org/10.1080/19496591.2023.2201453

Gorman, K. S., & Brennan, K. M. (2023b). Mental illness public stigma and treatment seeking among university students. *Journal of College Student Psychotherapy, 37*(1), 52–70. (Published online March 8, 2021). https://doi.org/10.1080/87568225.2021.1891006

Gorman, K. S., Walden, D., Braun, L., & Hotaling, M. (2024). Navigating a path forward for mental health services in higher education. *Journal of College Student Mental Health, 38*(4), 1–19. https://doi.org/10.1080/28367138.2023.2298647

Grawe, N. D. (2018). *Demographics and the demand for higher education*. Johns Hopkins Press.

Hatzenbuehler, M. L., Phelan, J. C., & Link, B. G. (2013). Stigma as a fundamental cause of population health inequalities. *Journal of American Public Health, 103*(5), 813–821. https://doi.org/10.2105/AJPH.2012.301069

Healthy Minds Network. (2020, August). College student mental health action toolkit on mental health data and statistics. https://healthymindsnetwork.org/wp-content/uploads/2020/09/CollegeStudentMentalHealthActionToolkit.pdf

Javed, A., Lee, C., Zakaria, H., Buenaventura, R. D., Cetkovich-Bakmas, M., Duailibi, K., Ng, B., Ramy, H., Saha, G., Arifeen, S., Elorza, P. M., Ratnasingham, P., & Waqar Azeem, M. (2021). Reducing the stigma of mental health disorders with a focus on low- and middle-income countries. *Asian Journal of Psychiatry, 58*, 102601. https://doi.org/10.1016/j.ajp.2021.102601

Julius, B., Putteeraj, M., & Somanah, J. (2024). A systematic review of university students' mental health in sub-Saharan Africa. *Transformation in Higher Education, 9*, a316. https://doi.org/10.4102/the.v9i0.316

Link, B. G., & Phelan, J. C. (2001). Conceptualizing stigma. *Annual Review of Sociology, 27*, 363–385. https://doi.org/10.1146/annurev.soc.27.1.363

Lipson, S. K., Lattie, E. G., & Eisenberg, D. (2019). Increased rates of mental health service utilization by U.S. college students: 10-year population-level trends (2007–2017). *Psychiatric Services, 70*(1), 60–63. https://doi.org/10.1176/appi.ps.201800332

National Association of Student Affairs Professionals. (2022). *The compass report: Charting the future of student affairs.* Retrieved June 4, 2023, from https://naspa.org/about/future-of-student-affairs-report/the-compass-report-charting-the-future-of-student-affairs

Orygen. (2020). Australian university mental health framework report. https://www.orygen.org.au/Orygen-Institute/University-Mental-Health-Framework/Framework/University-Mental-Health-Framework-full-report

Pescosolido, B. A., Halpern-Manners, A., Luo, L., & Perry, B. (2021). Trends in public stigma of mental illness in the US, 1996–2018. *JAMA Network Open, 4*(12), e2140202. https://doi.org/10.1001/jamanetworkopen.2021.40202

Pescosolido, B. A., & Martin, J. K. (2015). The stigma complex. *Annual Review of Sociology, 41*(1), 87–116. https://doi.org/10.1146/annurev-soc-071312-145702

Pescosolido, B. A., Martin, J. K., Lang, A., & Olafsdottir, S. (2008). Rethinking theoretical approaches to stigma: A framework integrating normative influences on stigma (FINIS). *Social Science & Medicine, 67*(3), 431–440. https://doi.org/10.1016/j.socscimed.2008.03.018

Schomerus, G., & Angermeyer, M. C. (2021). Blind spots in stigma research? Broadening our perspective on mental illness stigma by exploring 'what matters most' in modern Western societies. *Epidemiology and Psychiatric Sciences, 30*(e26), 1–6. https://doi.org/10.1017/S2045796021000111

Twenge, J. M., & Joiner, T. E. (2020). Mental distress among U.S. adults during the COVID-19 pandemic. *Journal of Clinical Psychology, 76*(12), 2170–2182. https://doi.org/10.1002/jclp.23064

U.S. Department of Education. (2021, August 25). *Higher education emergency relief fund*. Retrieved June 4, 2023, from https://www2.ed.gov/programs/heerf/index.html

Walsh, D., & Foster, J. (2021). A call to action. A critical review of mental health related anti stigma campaigns. *Frontiers in Public Health, 8*, 569539. https://doi.org/10.3389/fpubh.2020.569539

World Health Organization. (2022, June 8). *Mental disorders*. Retrieved December 8, 2024, from https://www.who.int/news-room/fact-sheets/detail/mental-disorders

Yang, L., Kleinman, A., Link, B., & Phelan, J. (2007). Culture and stigma: Adding moral experience to stigma theory. *Social Science & Medicine, 64*, 1524–1535. https://doi.org/10.1016/j.socscimed.2006.11.013

Kathleen M. Brennan, Ph.D., is Professor of Sociology and Director of the Sociology Program at Western Carolina University, USA. For more than a decade, she has used quantitative methodologies to collaboratively examine mental illness stigma in the context of higher education. She has co-presented these research findings to professional audiences and co-authored papers in higher education, health, and other disciplinary publications. Additionally, she regularly teaches about and provides consultation on the sociology of mental health and illness on campus and in the regional community.

Kimberly S. Gorman, Ph.D., is Associate Vice Chancellor for Health & Wellness in the Student Affairs Division at Western Carolina University, USA. Dr. Gorman's primary research interests are related to collegiate mental health and mental illness stigma in the college population. She has co-authored several papers about the impacts of mental illness and its related stigma in college students. She is a licensed psychologist who has worked in the higher education setting for more than two decades. She has served on the governing board of the Association for University and College Counseling Center Directors and on the advisory board for the Center for Collegiate Mental Health.

Chapter 2
(De)Constructing Cultures of Mental Illness Stigma in Higher Education

Kathleen M. Brennan and Kimberly S. Gorman

Abstract In response to the persistence of mental illness stigma, scholars have begun to focus on the cultural contexts in which stigma is embedded with the understanding that changing culturally created meanings of mental illness is key to collectively defining people with mental illness as valued community members. With respect to the cultural context of higher education, this chapter aims to serve two audiences who do not talk to each other enough: (1) mental illness scholars and practitioners and (2) higher education decision-makers. In the interest of scholars and practitioners, we discuss the social origins of mental illness stigma, consider the ways meanings surrounding mental illness are transmitted to and uniquely represented in the context of higher education, and examine the implications of stigmatization for higher education community members. In the interest of higher education decision-makers, we offer a case study illustrating a campus culture of mental illness stigma and review actions taken to address the sources of this stigma. We end the chapter by considering evidence pointing to contexts in which persons with mental illness thrive and discuss their applicability to the context of higher education in general.

Keywords Mental illness · Public stigma · Higher education · Culture · Meaning · Norms · Values · Power

The authors have no conflicts of interest to declare that are relevant to the content of this chapter.

K. M. Brennan (✉)
Department of Anthropology and Sociology, Western Carolina University, Cullowhee, NC, USA
e-mail: kbrennan@wcu.edu

K. S. Gorman
Division of Student Affairs, Western Carolina University, Cullowhee, NC, USA

© The Author(s), under exclusive license to Springer Nature Switzerland AG 2025

K. M. Brennan, K. S. Gorman (eds.), *A University-Wide Approach to Changing Campus Cultures of Mental Illness Stigma*, Knowledge Studies in Higher Education 18, https://doi.org/10.1007/978-3-031-86496-4_2

Despite evidence of a decline in college students' personal endorsement of mental illness stigma (Healthy Minds Network, 2020), research indicates stigma persists at notable levels at many institutions of higher education (Dare et al., 2023; Gaddis et al., 2018, 2020; Gallego et al., 2020; Schueth, 2022; Stuart et al., 2015; Tilli & Villar, 2024) and continues to negatively influence student outcomes related to treatment-seeking (Abassi et al., 2021; Baklola et al., 2024; Brennan & Gorman, 2022; Chen et al., 2016; Clement et al., 2015; Dare et al., 2023; Gaddis et al., 2018, 2020; Gorman & Brennan, 2023a; Julius et al., 2024; Li et al., 2024; Loong et al., 2024; Tilli & Villar, 2024), academic success (Eisenberg et al., 2009; Gallup & Lumina Foundation, 2024; Gannon et al., 2024; Julius et al., 2024; Wada et al., 2019), and social interaction (Billings, 2021; Campbell et al., 2022; Dare et al., 2023; Funkhouser et al., 2017; Gallup & Lumina Foundation, 2024; Loong et al., 2024; Wada et al., 2019).[1] The persistence of stigma is perplexing and discouraging, considering the decades-long efforts made by researchers and practitioners to understand mental illness stigma and offer recommendations for addressing it in higher education and other social contexts. Only recently have stigma scholars responded to stigma persistence by recognizing the shortcomings of common research practices and evaluating the effectiveness of programmatic anti-stigma efforts for advancing long-term change (Best & Arseniev-Koehler, 2023; Pescosolido & Martin, 2015; Wada et al., 2019; Walsh & Foster, 2021, 2022). Scholars are concentrating on the specific social contexts in which stigma is embedded, their interrelated meanings for mental illness that contribute to the stigma process, and their various influences on mental health behaviors (Best & Arseniev-Koehler, 2023; Gaddis et al., 2018; Walsh & Foster, 2021). Focusing on these contextual structures and cultures that shape social relationships offers more effective solutions for decreasing stigma (Pescosolido & Martin, 2015).

While this approach to stigma is relatively new, it is not novel to the context of higher education. For years, higher education research has provided evidence that university environments differentially influence students, with those in marginalized or historically underrepresented social identity groups at greater risk for negative health and educational outcomes (Abrica et al., 2023). This research underscores the realities of social forces on individual's lives, making clear that patterns of exclusion operate above and beyond students' efforts to successfully integrate into college contexts (Abrica et al., 2023).[2] These findings translate to the experiences of students with mental health challenges; they are less likely to graduate from college due to rigid and narrowly defined expectations of and routes to success (Baik et al., 2018). A holistic approach to understanding and supporting mental health in higher education must account for and address the campus cultures and structures that contribute to mental illness stigma while simultaneously promoting protective factors that buffer and, more importantly, reduce stigma on university campuses.

[1] Refer to Chapter 1 for a list of common terms and definitions related to stigma.

[2] For an extended discussion of the stigmatization of marginalized groups in higher education, refer to the chapters on intersectionality (Copeland-Hayes & Remedios) and disclosure (Blake) included in this volume.

Scholars have contended illness violates normative expectations for the way we are supposed to behave, think, and feel (Parsons, 1951; 1958), and mental illness is extraordinary in this respect. In their seminal work on the stigma of diseases in U.S. culture, Best and Arseniev-Koehler (2023) underscore the heightened stigma found in health conditions for which the symptoms themselves reflect nonnormative behaviors. In the context of mental health conditions, this means the accompanying behaviors (e.g., impulsivity) are considered deviant irrespective of a mental illness diagnosis since these behaviors are associated with stereotypes of immorality and/or negative personality traits. Best and Arseniev-Koehler's (2023) large-scale study documented a cultural shift over nearly 40 years (1980–2018) from negative meanings surrounding disease in general to decreased stigma related to physical illness, but continued judgment tied to mental health conditions (as well as infectious diseases). They found that ideas about and meanings of mental illness were notably strong and lasting when they were aligned with the interests of those who hold power (Best & Arseniev-Koehler, 2023). Mental illness stigma persists because it facilitates and enhances economic and political power differentials (Hatzenbuehler et al., 2013; Link & Phelan, 2001).

Mental illness stigma has remained remarkably stable over time (Pescosolido et al., 2010; Pescosolido et al., 2021; Schnittker, 2008; Schomerus et al., 2012). While damaging cultural meanings tied to mental illness have been resistant to change (e.g., "people with mental illness are dangerous"), public stigma can be changed by using an approach that addresses its most problematic aspects, adjusts to different contexts, and targets those who can help impact long-term change (Pescosolido et al., 2021). Targeting cultural contexts is increasingly recognized as offering the best opportunity for lasting, positive change related to mental illness stigma (Best & Arseniev-Koehler, 2023; Clair et al., 2016; Lamont, 2018; Pescosolido et al., 2013; Pescosolido et al., 2021; Walsh & Foster, 2021). Changing contextual cultural meanings of mental illness is key to collectively defining people with mental illness as valued community members (Lamont, 2018).

In this chapter, we discuss the social construction of mental illness stigma, with the term social construction loosely reflecting the idea that human beings, in their everyday interactions, actively produce and reproduce societal ideas and values. We aim to serve two audiences with this chapter, and we encourage them to interact more often to reduce mental illness stigma in higher education: (1) mental illness scholars and practitioners and (2) higher education decision-makers. In the interest of scholars and practitioners, we discuss the social and acutely cultural origins of mental illness stigma. For scholars, practitioners, and higher education decision-makers, we consider the ways meanings surrounding mental illness are transmitted to and uniquely represented in the context of higher education, and we examine the implications of stigmatization for higher education community members. In the interest of higher education decision-makers, we offer a case study illustrating a campus culture of mental illness stigma and review actions taken to address the sources of this stigma. For both audiences, we end the chapter by considering evidence from the literature pointing to contexts in which persons with mental illness thrive and discuss their applicability to the context of higher education in general.

The Formation and Persistence of Stigma Cultures

Cultural values are widely distributed and have an enduring influence on society (Pescosolido et al., 2008). In the context of stigma, cultural values matter because they "… shape public views (endorsed stigma), provide frameworks for discrimination (enacted stigma), and transmit messages about the stigma people can expect to face (perceived stigma)" (Best & Arseniev-Koehler, 2023, p. 961). Stigma arises when core social values are threatened in situations that matter most in specific cultural settings (Pescosolido et al., 2008; Schomerus & Angermeyer, 2021; Yang et al., 2007). Thus, successful attempts to reduce stigma must consider and involve local cultural settings and the issues at stake within them (Pescosolido et al., 2008; Walsh & Foster, 2021).

Institutional systems support standard, public expectations for social identities (e.g., woman, athlete) by restricting how community members view them, and how stigmatized group members experience and respond to those views (Lamont, 2018). Cultural repertoires, or "tools available to individuals to make sense of the reality they experience," are unevenly available across social contexts (Lamont, 2018, p. 423). Additionally, what is viewed as mattering most in a cultural context differs by group membership, and what matters most to a group in one context may not matter most in another (Schomerus & Angermeyer, 2021). Cultural systems also reflect access to power, and as such, people with power can disproportionately shape cultural meanings transmitted about the social world such that they more heavily influence societal narratives (Pescosolido et al., 2008; Walsh & Foster, 2021). For instance, rather than funding programs to support individuals with substance use disorders, politicians make public statements that those individuals make poor decisions and we should not help pay for their mistakes. The weighted influence of power translates into macrolevel stigma that surpasses individual beliefs (Best & Arseniev-Koehler, 2023). Notably, the stigma is expressed and circulated in documented text (e.g., emails, contracts, handbooks, news publications, social media posts, or webpages), giving it a more impactful and enduring effect compared to stereotypes expressed by individuals in social interaction. This translates into a public consensus on defining marginalized groups as "other" (Best & Arseniev-Koehler, 2023; Burns et al., 2022; Rhydderch et al., 2016; Walsh & Foster, 2021). Thus, targeting macrolevel, public cultures of stigma offers an advanced approach for dismantling obstinate forms of stigma.

Public cultures of stigma are particularly enduring because they express expectations for how individuals should behave, think, and feel in social interactions, whether presented as commonly understood or codified in organizational policies or laws. Additionally, because context determines resource availability and tolerance for acting on cultural biases (Pescosolido et al., 2008), community members may act according to these prejudicial cultural meanings without self-conscious reflection or to avoid social punishment, even if they do not personally endorse them (Cialdini, 2007; Clair et al., 2016). These responses serve only to reinforce the institutional structure of stigma in everyday contexts in which social interaction takes place (Walsh & Foster, 2021).

Cultures of Mental Illness Stigma

Mental illness stigma results when people with mental illness appear to or actually threaten core values in a specific social context (Yang et al., 2007). Walsh and Foster (2021) emphasize:

> … especially when close attention is paid to the contexts considered to be the "backbone" of mental health related stigma, common-sense thinking about mental health and illness are expressed through a wide constellation of contextually defined affects, rituals, images, narratives, and gestures, whose meanings are often embodied in the process of everyday life. (p. 7)

In this way, the "common-sense" values and norms reflected in everyday social practices can be subversive toward people with mental illness when the values and norms do not allow for diagnosis disclosure, active symptomatology, or even the possibility of mental illness. Individuals who disclose or express mental illness symptoms in these cultures experience notable consequences due to being labeled "different" (Link & Phelan, 2001). How mental illness stigma emerges will depend on the specific norms, values, and beliefs reflected in specific social contexts. These cultural elements are sometimes unspoken and unclear, and are often complicated by the many ways individuals are connected to their environments and the different forms of information reflected in and across them (Walsh & Foster, 2021).

Mental health conditions are found to be consistently marked by judgment across time (Best & Arseniev-Koehler, 2023; Pescosolido et al., 2021). People with mental illness are framed as "at risk" to themselves and others by experts and the lay public. Mental illness has most frequently and persistently been associated with unpredictability and dangerousness, and these views have been sustained through the belief that the actions of those with mental illness are "beyond conscious awareness" and thus beyond their control due to being entrenched in genetics or neurology. Additionally, this biological frame perpetuates the view that mental illness is unrecoverable, and thus a fixed and socially contaminated identity. As such, people with mental illness are situated as a significant threat to the social order (Walsh & Foster, 2021).

Walsh and Foster (2021) emphasize the societal frame for mental illness is "remarkably historically and cross-culturally consistent, [but] the content involved is always particular to the context in which it is practiced" (p. 8). In the context of higher education, campus cultures surrounding mental illness can be complicated by their convergence with academic and professional cultures. In the next section, we discuss the cultural constructions taken for granted within academia that work together with public cultures of mental illness stigma to reify specific forms of implicit bias toward people with mental illness in the context of higher education.

Cultures of Mental Illness Stigma: Higher Education in the United States

In the context of higher education, the combination of environmental stressors and cultural norms works against those with mental illness in distinct ways.[3] In the United States, research has shown that the cultural norms of hard work and competition operate at the expense of well-being in the university context (Baik et al., 2018; Billings, 2021; Sallee, 2016; Turosak & Siwierka, 2021; Wada et al., 2019). These norms are reflected in the promotion of above average achievement as the only reasonable path to success. In an environment that already involves a significant workload and high time demands, success is narrowly defined as performance that exceeds expectations, elevated productivity, and the pursuit of ever-increasing extracurricular accomplishments.

In this constructed cultural environment, community members are discouraged from resting or from seeking less than extraordinary outcomes, and those who prioritize work over other obligations are valued (Sallee, 2016). For those with mental illness, who, by definition, are experiencing distress and having difficulty managing personal functions (World Health Organization, 2021), these cultural meanings may translate into failure when they feel compelled to take on excessive workloads and fall behind or call attention to the workload difficulties they are experiencing. Research has found students with mental illness anticipate being viewed as lazy or weak by others for even small academic transgressions and that those who identify as high achieving experience cognitive dissonance under these circumstances (Turosak & Siwierka, 2021; Wada et al., 2019). These students avoid seeking out accommodations and even treatment to adhere to the norm of self-sufficiency and avoid the label "other."

Relatedly, research has also identified the values of independence, individual agency, and self-reliance—what Lamont (2018, p. 424) refers to as "the privatization of risk"—in relation to success in the context of academia (Baik et al., 2018; Billings, 2021; Turosak & Siwierka, 2021; Wada et al., 2019). These values are reflected in the meritocratic view that individual capabilities and virtues are the drivers of success in academia, which fits well with the societal view of education as a path to individual advancement (Billings, 2021; Kim & Choi, 2017). Notably, what constitutes meritorious conduct in this cultural context is one's organizational production (via constructive competition) and contributions held in high esteem; these contributions indicate individuals' ability to act on (the perception of) equality of opportunity and reinforce individuals' fit with community culture (Kim & Choi, 2017; Wada et al., 2019). Additionally, one's virtuousness in this context is reinforced by a self-presentation that communicates accomplishments come easy and are enjoyable to fulfill (Billings, 2021).

In this cultural environment, community members who are not visibly active, energetic, or engaged are viewed as inadequate or incapable. For those with mental

[3] It is important to remember that cultures of stigma in the context of higher education will not look the same across nations—or even across institutions within the same nation—due to unique historical and cultural stigma processes represented.

illness, these cultural meanings often translate into self-blame (for not being self-sufficient) and estrangement (to avoid others seeing a less than able self) (Billings, 2021; Wada et al., 2019). Research has shown that students with mental illness are hesitant to seek help due to concerns that help-seeking is an admission of lacking ability (Wada et al., 2019). Likewise, they may not disclose their mental health concerns due to fear of being judged and treated as if they do not belong in college (Billings, 2021; Wada et al., 2019). In this way, mental illness stigma becomes a barrier to students making and sustaining relationships. Postponing treatment and social isolation are both associated with negative academic outcomes (Campbell et al., 2022; Gorman & Brennan, 2023a, 2023b; Wada et al., 2019), which perpetuates the belief that people with mental illness are not equipped to cope with academia and therefore do not belong there.

For students, the classroom setting and interactions with faculty represent the higher education contexts in which cultures of stigma are most immediately felt. Research indicates academic teachers play a key role in supporting student well-being (Baik et al., 2018; JED Foundation, 2022; Turosak & Siwierka, 2021; Wada et al., 2019), with some research demonstrating faculty-student interactions are as important for well-being as psychosocial interventions and professional treatment (Baik et al., 2018). At the same time, faculty often encourage mental illness stigma through their reinforcement of the aforementioned stigmatizing norms and values, especially when they support the view that students with mental illness are not properly engaged academically and, worse yet, view mental illness as akin to a conduct problem (Storrie et al., 2010).

Research has revealed the degree to which faculty members are informed about the issues students are dealing with and the breadth of resources available to students can mean the difference between reinforcing or reducing stigma in the academic context (Baik et al., 2018; Turosak & Siwierka, 2021). For instance, faculty often behave toward students as if there are no other stresses or time demands other than those related to the student role (Baik et al., 2018; Sallee, 2016; Turosak & Siwierka, 2021). Additionally, faculty and staff often expect too much from on-campus mental health resources while overlooking the helpfulness of other individuals on campus and services off campus (Gorman et al., 2024; Storrie et al., 2010). These views limit faculty understanding of and advocacy for available and effective treatment prospects for students. They also reinforce the belief that students are to blame when mental health challenges persist despite their use of campus wellness services (Storrie et al., 2010).

Faculty unwillingness to openly communicate about mental health in the classroom and to accommodate students experiencing mental health difficulties is also associated with stigma cultures in higher education settings (Baik et al., 2018; Sallee, 2016; Turosak & Siwierka, 2021).[4] This is evident in several ways. Faculty

[4] For an extended discussion of the ways in which faculty and staff communication is associated with mental illness stigmatization, refer to the chapters on stigma communication (Dias & RW), graduate mental health programs (Gorman), and college athletes (Macbeth & Shelton) included in this volume.

often avoid speaking openly about mental health in the classroom. Some do not acknowledge that students may experience mental health challenges during the class enrollment period. Some will not talk candidly with students they know are experiencing mental health challenges. Finally, they avoid addressing the explicit ways students may negotiate conflicts between faculty's academic expectations and students' mental health challenges, leaving students to figure it out on their own (Baik et al., 2018; Sallee, 2016; Turosak & Siwierka, 2021).

In this cultural construction, doubt is cast on the viability of community members who demonstrate potentially lasting difficulty with the student role. For those with mental illness, these cultural meanings reinforce the public stigma that mental health related behavior is out of one's control and impossible to overcome (Walsh & Foster, 2021). These meanings also convey the risk involved in disclosing mental health challenges. Research has documented disclosure-related concerns in college student populations (Corrigan et al., 2016; Gannon et al., 2024; Turosak & Siwierka, 2021). However, research has also shown that students do not know how to appropriately talk with their professors about their mental health challenges and would like faculty to openly state their expectations for mental health related communication (Baik et al., 2018; Turosak & Siwierka, 2021). Additionally, students would like faculty to overtly state their approach to accommodating students with mental health concerns alongside discussion of accommodations for students with physical health concerns (Baik et al., 2018; Turosak & Siwierka, 2021). In addition to offering an example to emulate in the development of professional communication skills for students' future employment, these types of faculty communication—in the syllabus *and* in verbal form to the entire class—aid in the normalization of mental illness in the context of higher education. Research has shown that students best learn about university work expectations through faculty transmission of academic values and norms (Sallee, 2016), which could include communication about the compatibility of academics and mental illness.

In summary, research documents that mental illness contests the values and norms of higher education culture. In this constructed context, mental health and academic and professional competence are intricately linked (Wada et al., 2019). The capacity to gain valuable experiences, build professional connections, and make quantifiable progress toward degree completion represent core ways college students participate in their immediate social milieu and work toward becoming credentialed to obtain a satisfying and well-paying professional career. But mental illness stigma in higher education reflects its ability to invalidate the moral worth of students with mental illness by threatening two things most proximally at stake for students: their ability to experience a sense of belonging and their ability to earn a valued degree (Yang et al., 2007; Wada et al., 2019).

Identifying cultures of stigma in the context of higher education and on individual university campuses is a key step for understanding, addressing, and reducing stigma's harmful mechanisms. In the next section, we offer an example of how we analyzed and began to address the culture on our campus. We compare patterns of endorsement of multiple mental illness public stigma items in a student sample and an employee sample at our university. We discuss the roots of these patterns by centering the specific campus context related to intimate relationships, differentials in power, and group vulnerability to understand how community groups maintain a view of mental illness as "different" (Walsh & Foster, 2021). Finally, we discuss the implications of similar patterns of stigma endorsement for the groups, while recognizing the limitations of measuring individual attitudes for understanding public cultures of stigma.

A Higher Education Culture of Mental Illness Stigma Case Study

Public stigma endorsement is associated with specific contextual climates. We examined 28 individual items comprising eight dimensions of public stigma related to mental illness in the student and employee populations at our university to determine which are reflected on our campus. These dimensions represent social distance, traditional prejudice, exclusionary sentiments, negative affect, disclosure spillover, treatment carryover, perceptions of dangerousness toward oneself, and perceptions of dangerousness toward others (Pescosolido et al., 2013). See Appendix 2.1 for more information about the 28 items and the eight mental illness stigma dimensions they represent.

Method

IRB approval and participant consent were obtained prior to data collection. An electronic survey focusing on mental illness stigma, experience, and treatment was distributed via email to two groups 2 years apart: (1) graduate and undergraduate students enrolled full-time in campus-based programs during the fall 2018 semester (n = 941, response rate = 10.6%); and (2) full-time, permanent employees during the fall 2020 semester (n = 435, response rate = 27.1%).[5] For each of the 28 stigma items, we asked participants to read a statement that incorporated a general referent to someone with mental illness as defined in the Diagnostic and Statistical Manual of Mental Disorders (fifth ed.; DSM-5; APA, 2013): "Disorders generally characterized by dysregulation of mood, thought, and/or behavior." We then asked them to indicate either their level of agreement, willingness, or perceived likelihood related to each statement. We converted the Likert-type response categories for each item to a 0 or 1 score, with 0 reflecting no stigma endorsement and 1 reflecting stigma endorsement. To document a campus culture of mental illness stigma, we assessed three things: (1) which stigma items were endorsed by 20% or more of the respondents in at least one of the samples, based on the stigma level margin reflected in Pescosolido et al.'s (2013) international study identifying the global core of public

---

[5] Our samples are roughly proportionate to the university's point-in-time student and employee population demographics, with a slightly higher proportions of cisgender females for the student population and administrators for the employee population. See Brennan and Gorman (2022) for more information about the use of a census sampling approach and the reliability of estimates in data collection circumstances with large sampling frames (>500) and lower response rates.

prejudice associated with mental illness; (2) whether the samples endorsed stigma items at the same level; and (3) whether the samples' stigma item endorsement followed a similar order.

Results

As indicated in Table 2.1, at least one-fifth of each sample endorsed six stigma items *and* both samples endorsed the same six prejudicial beliefs: that people with mental illness (1) are likely to be dangerous to others and (2) to their self, (3) are unpredictable, (4) are more creative than normal, and (5) will lose friends and (6) have limited opportunities due to receiving treatment. We tested mean differences between the samples' endorsement of these items and found significant differences in the expectation that people with mental illness will be unpredictable, more creative, and dangerous to themselves and others. In each instance, more students than employees endorsed stigma for the item, although Cohen's d indicated small effect size differences for all but anticipated self-danger, which had a notably large effect size for the difference in endorsement by the samples. Students and employees endorsed these stigma items in the same rank order. Taken together, these findings provide preliminary support for a culture of mental illness stigma that emphasizes social rejection and devaluation related to anticipated self-threat, treatment disclosure, and "uneasiness about how to interact with or whether to fear violence from people with mental health problems" (Pescosolido et al., 2013, p. 857).

Application

These results are noteworthy in that the same six of the 28 stigma items were endorsed by both samples and in the same order, with treatment-related items endorsed at the same level of stigmatization. This evidence within and across samples suggests a culture of stigma with several features. First, the well-documented pattern of judgment that people with mental illness are a risk to the social order via unpredictability and dangerousness has been found (Walsh & Foster, 2021),

Table 2.1 Stigma item endorsement

Stigma item	Employees M (SD)	Students M (SD)	t (p)	Cohen's *d*
Danger to self	0.43 (0.50)	0.75 (0.43)	−12.308 (0.001)	0.70
Treatment limits opportunities	0.43 (0.50)	0.42 (0.49)	0.333 (NS)	–
Treatment will lose friends	0.39 (0.49)	0.37 (0.48)	0.666 (NS)	–
More creative	0.36 (0.48)	0.63 (0.48)	10.39 (0.001)	0.39
Unpredictable	0.21 (0.41)	0.33 (0.47)	6.00 (0.001)	0.18
Danger to others	0.20 (0.40)	0.31 (0.46)	−4.400 (0.001)	0.26

although the level of endorsement of these stigmatizing expectations for the general referent of someone with mental illness in both campus groups tends to be somewhat lower than that previously found in the U.S. adult public for depression and schizophrenia, specifically (Pescosolido et al., 2013). Conversely, student and employee endorsements of stigmatizing expectations for treatment disclosure are greater than (e.g., depression) or on par with (e.g., schizophrenia) previously documented stigmatizing endorsements by the U.S. adult public (Pescosolido et al., 2013). Finally, the samples endorsed a moderate level of stigma for the belief that people with mental illness are more creative than "normal," supporting the recurring stereotype of the "mad genius," which appears positive on the surface but is negatively associated with treatment use and therefore harmful to those it affects (Reddy et al., 2018). Each of these features of stigma is rooted in the view of people with mental illness as "different" and is perpetuated within the context of higher education through modes of contact such as intimate relationships, differentials in power, and/or group vulnerability (Walsh & Foster, 2021).

Stigma via Faculty

On our campus, faculty reflect one potential source of stigma perpetuated through intimate relationships and differentials in power. Endorsement of the view that treatment impacts opportunities is sustained in interactions that take place in the classroom and faculty offices, particularly with faculty advisors and mentors. In these types of close, ongoing professional relationships, students are overtly aware of faculty power over the assignment of grades, implementation of accommodations, disclosure of professional opportunities, and recommendations for internships, paid employment, and graduate school admission. Likewise, student perceptions of faculty bias related to mental illness in professional contexts are exacerbated by lack of open classroom communication about mental illness and ambiguity about or reluctance to accommodate students with mental health challenges (Baik et al., 2018; Sallee, 2016; Turosak & Siwierka, 2021).

For instance, some faculty are hesitant to work with students on flexibility of attendance and assignment accommodations facilitated through the relevant university office due to the perception that students are not held appropriately accountable for missed class time and work. To complicate matters, the related university paperwork uses language stating the student has a "documented disorder with symptoms that are episodic and unpredictable in nature" that could be (and likely is) interpreted in a stigmatizing way by faculty, thus reinforcing unease regarding how to act toward people with mental illness, a demonstrated feature of the culture of mental illness stigma on our campus. Upon further investigation, we found the paperwork language lingered from its original purpose, the accommodation of physical impairments (e.g., Crohn's disease). While the accommodation was not intended for mental health disability, students are increasingly requesting this accommodation for that purpose. This circumstance provides an excellent example of how cultures of mental illness are unintentionally perpetuated through stereotypes expressed and circulated in institutional texts.[6] Alteration of the paperwork to remove the stereotype would be impactful, especially when done in concert with changes to language (that is, removing stigmatizing language or adding destigmatizing language) in related university documents (e.g., forms, policies, syllabi).

Stigma via Students

In addition to faculty, students perpetuate stigma through intimate relationships with other students. Endorsement of the view that treatment impacts friendships is sustained in interactions that take place between students in the classroom, residence halls, off-campus living spaces, and any spaces where student groups congregate on or off campus. Research has documented university settings are embedded with immense pressure to thrive academically and mentally. In this context, students may be encouraged to adopt stigmatizing views toward mental illness, especially at elite institutions where meritocracy and agency are overemphasized, creating a cultural norm of perfection that is in opposition to the lived experience of people with mental illness (Billings, 2021). Likewise, understanding mental illness can be difficult for those without lived experience because of its intangible nature and status as an unseen disability (Turosak & Siwierka, 2021). We see this playing out in student microaggressions around mental illness (e.g., avoiding talking to another student) and conflation of psychological distress with mental illness (Brewster & Cox, 2022; Turosak & Siwierka, 2021).

For instance, on our campus, it is common to hear students say things such as "that's insane," "I'm addicted," or "that's so OCD." These comments may not be intended to stigmatize students with mental illness, but they nonetheless invalidate and minimize their experiences (Turosak & Siwierka, 2021). Moreover, the use of this stigmatizing language communicates the underlying assumption that people with mental illness are not present to hear it, which reflects the associated stigma that people with mental illness must not be present because they do not belong in the university context (Billings, 2021; Wada et al., 2019).[7]

Concurrently, students use the term "mental health" more commonly to communicate any level of distress (Gorman et al., 2024) and universities have broadened official language related to mental health support beyond diagnosed conditions to a more generalized "well-being" that includes the range of human emotion (Brewster & Cox, 2022). This well-intentioned effort has become problematic in terms of faculty and staff's heightened response to student references to their mental health and students being directed toward the wrong resources for the issues they are presenting (Brewster & Cox, 2022; Gorman et al., 2024).

[6] For an extended discussion of strategies for destigmatizing mental illness-related communication in the university context, refer to Dias and RW's chapter on stigma communication included in this volume.

[7] For an extended discussion of the ways cultures of stigma in higher education perpetuate the invisibility of community members, refer to the chapter on stigma surrounding substance misuse (Dunn et al.) included in this volume.

To address concerns related to the perceived consequences of mental illness and treatment disclosure among students, universities can build empathy by encouraging students to support one another in their academic pursuits and personal care. This type of nurturing environment could lessen isolation and build self-compassion, assisting students with mental illness in disclosing challenges in a manner that facilitates their success (Campbell et al., 2022; Wada et al., 2019). Along these lines, our university engaged in a year-long campus theme that focused on mental health and wellness to build empathy and belongingness and to advocate for and normalize help-seeking. Moreover, the campus theme committee provided funding for campus-wide training that prepared campus community members to assist people experiencing mental health challenges. The marketing department also focused its annual magazine on stigma to align with the campus theme.[8] This volume highlighted the problem of the presence of stigma and included personal narratives from students and staff about their mental health challenges and the ways treatment benefitted them. Finally, also as part of the campus theme, the common reader for the year was a book focused on the impact of stigma on those who experienced mental health challenges and the importance of reorienting how we think about these challenges to provide a culture of support.

Other Actions Taken

Multiple efforts were simultaneously undertaken to address the specific stigma features and their contexts arising from our surveys, including the previously described actions. An elemental step was to name and disseminate the types of stigma present. This was done through presentations to the student government organization, the faculty and the staff senates, as well as at divisional and departmental meetings. These presentations and ensuing discussions involving various campus stakeholders led to the decision to embark on the campus theme and its related events mentioned above. Additionally, to address the stigma that individuals with mental illness are unpredictable and dangerous, we began to focus on the use and impact of language for individuals who have suicidal thoughts. In trainings provided by Student Affairs departments to help faculty/staff/students recognize and respond to someone experiencing distress, the language changed from the phrase "suicidal students" or "a student whose conduct is dangerous" to terms such as "a student who needs immediate assistance for medical or mental health." These changes were made in written materials, including a printed guide for helping students as well as online materials available to the public, and reinforced with verbal communication in one-on-one consultations with faculty/staff and early intervention team members. An additional focus has been on decoupling mental illness and suicide (see Gorman & Brennan, 2024) and talking about these as separate concerns during the trainings referenced

[8] For an extended discussion of using social marketing as part of a larger campus strategy for reducing mental illness stigma, refer to Yeh's chapter on social marketing tactics included in this volume.

with faculty, staff, and students. These strategies were derived from identifying and understanding the specific types of stigma operative on this campus.

A Consideration

These examples are not exhaustive, but they illustrate patterns of stigma present in accordance with the unique cultural elements embedded on our campus. It is important to note that the information referenced in this case study involved assessing all members of the campus rather than focusing simply on stigma among students. In so doing, this cross-sectional analysis indicated that stigma is similar across populations; thus, interventions need to be developed for and across these populations. In keeping with developments in the literature, it is important to note that surveying individuals to summarize public culture can be misleading if performed in isolation (Best & Arseniev-Koehler, 2023; Walsh & Foster, 2021). Ideally, campus-level data reflecting formally circulating ideas about mental illness, such as the previously discussed flexibility of attendance and assignment accommodations paperwork, should be collected for consideration alongside individual-level survey data since these ideas reflect those with clout on campus and are influential for campus community members' beliefs (and actions) related to mental illness (Best & Arseniev-Koehler, 2023). In the following section, we discuss additional insights about cultural contexts of higher education in which students with mental illness thrive.

Moving Forward

Knowledge of an institution's cultural landscape is essential for pinpointing not only the origins and perpetuation of mental illness stigma on that campus but also the junctures at which effective interventions may occur (Amenta & Polletta, 2019). Nevertheless, changing stigma is difficult, as decades-worth of anti-stigma campaigns and cultural climate assessments have demonstrated. Although popular, these go-to approaches can be problematic due to an emphasis on individual influences at the expense of structural influences, the omission of marginalized group member knowledge, and the implementation of interventions with mixed and/or unintended outcomes (Abrica et al., 2023; Walsh & Foster, 2022). These approaches also tend to address issues of well-being and inclusion in an oversimplified, linear manner that assumes greater awareness will fix higher education problems (Abrica et al., 2023; Walsh & Foster, 2022). Additionally, they rely on an essentialized view of categorical identities that neglect the subtleties surrounding the process of assigning stigmatizing characteristics to people from marginalized groups (Abrica et al., 2023; Walsh & Foster, 2022). These shortcomings underscore the need to develop new, multifaceted approaches that more judiciously study and begin to deconstruct the structural and cultural influences on individual norms and values surrounding mental illness on university campuses.

Campus Mental Health Cultures that Promote Student Success

In this section, we offer select, broad suggestions highlighted in research for promoting student success related to mental illness. Along with the many other recommendations offered in the chapters in this volume, we offer this information with the caveat that individual institutions must first understand the specific ways mental illness stigma is embedded in their campus(es) to best determine how to implement the recommendations in an effective manner for their campus. An evidence-based approach must be taken, followed by an evaluation of the effectiveness of actions taken, and a routine reassessment of campus anti-stigma strategies (Abelson et al., 2023; Julius et al., 2024; Orygen, 2020).

Creating a Broader Culture of Support

When students perceive an inclusive and/or supportive mental health culture on campus, they are more likely to have positive academic and social outcomes and are more likely to use mental health services on and off campus (Baik et al., 2018; Sontag-Padilla et al., 2018; Turosak & Siwierka, 2021). This is especially the case when leaders prioritize student mental health on campuses and expect community members to be prepared to assist with student mental health (Turosak & Siwierka, 2021). Students enrolled at institutions that do not reflect this kind of campus culture report wanting a culture of support surrounding mental health that reflects inclusion, empathy, understanding, and tolerance among all members of the campus community, from administrators to other students (Baik et al., 2018; Turosak & Siwierka, 2021). Relatedly, research suggests student identification of environmental stressors and protective factors in the academic and social contexts of higher education is key to developing a supportive and inclusive campus culture (Baik et al., 2018). Students are experts in the student experience and, while knowing how to cope with stress is important, it is more effective to address and deconstruct fundamental causes of the problem. Baik et al. (2018) argue, "… it is only by changing the student experience that we will ultimately see improvements in student mental wellbeing" (p. 685).

Calling out the Taken for Granted

Billings (2021) notes the taken for granted cultural values and norms surrounding mental illness stigma "help [universities] mask their institutional role in maintaining and widening social inequalities" (p. 248). As such, what is taken for granted must be identified for institutions to take responsibility for and act on the mental illness stigma present on their campuses (Walsh & Foster, 2021). To start the de-stigmatization process, universities must deconstruct stigma by asking: What are the interests of stigmatizers in the context of higher education? What are the higher education norms and values that reflect these interests? What are the effects on the stigmatized? What policies or practices will diminish them? Research on mental illness in college student populations has documented the effects on the stigmatized, but answers to the other questions are lacking. Importantly, we must not forget that cultural constructions related to mental illness are likely to vary across campuses and thus what is presented in the literature regarding impacts on those who are stigmatized may or may not be true for all campuses.

Campus members without mental illness reap the benefits of stigmatizing cultural constructions whether they intentionally or unintentionally function as stigmatizers. Inclusive climates reflect the adoption and enactment of positive constructions by and among stigmatizers (Clair et al., 2016; Lamont, 2018), particularly those in powerful positions who disproportionately shape cultural meanings. The adoption of new constructions of mental illness by community members with status and visibility gives credibility to the constructions and reflects the "linked fate of the stigmatized and dominant groups" (Clair et al., 2016, p. 223). One example of the adoption and enactment of an inclusive cultural construction is the hiring of a permanent, full-time university staff member to oversee student-led initiatives for reducing mental illness stigma.[9] This dedication of university resources demonstrates commitment to changing stigmatizing aspects of university culture and helps to normalize mental illness on campus, especially if the staff position is well-connected across campus.

However, too much diffusion of responsibility for negative cultural constructions reinforces institutional inaction (Abrica et al., 2023); this is tricky because diffusion of power is necessary to remove prejudicial and discriminatory constructions from stigmatized group members (Walsh & Foster, 2021). Chief among these constructions is the lack of portrayal of people with mental illness in everyday spaces such as university campuses (Walsh & Foster, 2021). Thus, it is important to create a campus environment that promotes the strengths of mental illness while delegitimating misconceptions (Turosak & Siwierka, 2021). The involvement of stigmatized group members in the generation of expert knowledge and identification of interventions is key to motivating positive constructions in campus interactions, policies, and practices (Brewster & Cox, 2022; Clair et al., 2016; Lamont, 2018; Schomerus & Angermeyer, 2021).[10]

[9] For an extended discussion of the importance of this type of staff position, refer to Pescosolido's chapter on UBC2M included in this volume.

[10] For an extended discussion of why it is important to involve stigmatized group members in the destigmatization process, refer to the chapters on HOP-C (Maranzan et al.) and UBC2M (Pescosolido) included in this volume.

Advancing Student Empowerment

Related to the previous recommendation, research has shown that student participation in the design and implementation of university mental health communications, programs, and services is essential to their effectiveness (Baik et al., 2018; Tilli & Villar, 2024) and, in the case of peer support programs, reduces stigma (Funkhouser et al., 2017; Sontag-Padilla et al., 2018). Therefore, it follows that students should be involved in addressing campus cultures of mental illness stigma from the beginning. In addition to acknowledging the expertise of students with mental illness (Baik et al., 2018), this inclusion gives value to student voice (Turosak & Siwierka, 2021), recognizes the limitations of administration, staff, and faculty knowledge, and empowers students as campus community members (Baik et al., 2018; Turosak & Siwierka, 2021). It also helps to engage those with mental illness in mainstream university culture while at the same time retaining a strong, positive group identity, which has been found to foster subjective well-being over time (Lamont, 2018). Moreover, it strengthens community on campus via partnerships between students and other institutional actors (Baik et al., 2018) that challenge "ideological silos" defining the campus and public spheres (Lamont, 2018, p. 434). Campus identity centers may be fruitful in this regard to facilitate broader reach, address intersectional stigma, and provide strong ties between student affairs and academic affairs units.[11] Last, involving students in the process from start to finish can help to create positive constructions of mental illness that should result in positive group outcomes and strengthen positive associations in the campus community over time.

Constructing Alternative Paths to Cultural Membership

Compared to stigmatization, the recognition process is "a social act by which an individual's or group's relative positive social worth is affirmed or acknowledged by others" (Lamont, 2018, p. 423). The very idea of naming that a group exists is an important path to promoting a sense of belongingness. Recognition is positively associated with multiple forms of well-being and is believed to positively affect collective well-being in communities. Recognition gaps, on the other hand, indicate group disparities in cultural membership that are reinforced by narrowly defined cultural repertoires and thus weaken cohesion between stigmatized and mainstream groups (Lamont, 2018). In discussing how equivalences may be drawn between groups, Lamont (2018) stated, "… mobilizing institutions and cultural repertoires in crafting messages about worth can affect recognition gaps and extend cultural membership to the largest number … allow[ing] a wider range of people to be viewed as worthy" (p. 427).

---

[11] For an extended discussion of the important role campus identity centers can play in the reduction of stigma, refer to Copeland-Hayes and Remedios' chapter on intersectional stigma included in this volume.

In addition to recognizing the presence and value of campus members with mental illness, recognition in the context of higher education can be accomplished through widening narrowly defined cultural repertoires. For instance, one way this could be accomplished is through community member recognition that competent academic performance (e.g., earning a C grade) means a student is proficient/qualified/skilled in the subject matter covered, rather than the typical cultural interpretation that the student's skill is wanting. This recognition could improve students' ability to meet academic and social challenges, thus decreasing some environmental stress and serving as one institutional buffer for potential mental health issues. Similarly, community member recognition of a broader range of forms of success (e.g., resilience, thriving, applied experience) than just academic performance in the university context would open opportunities for cultural membership to more students. In practice, this may involve lessening the weight placed on the grade point average, the primary determinant of academic accomplishment, in decisions made regarding student recognition. These are just a few of many possible ways to recognize the worth of a wider spectrum of campus members. Universities must take the necessary steps in determining which will work best in the context of their campus cultures.

Conclusion

Considering what we have learned from research about the ways the public makes sense of mental health and illness, it is past time for universities to develop new approaches for decreasing mental illness stigma on their campuses. To effectively address cultures of mental illness stigma in higher education, greater emphasis must be placed on locating stigma within everyday experiences in local campus contexts, fully engaging an equitable representation of campus stakeholders throughout the process, and actively deconstructing and replacing harmful cultural meanings with meanings that reaffirm the worth and belonging of campus members with mental illness. A whole university approach to mental health and illness should encourage a collective sense of responsibility for support and inclusion among community members while also holding powerful institutional actors accountable for ensuring prevention, risk, and regulation related to mental illness and its related stigmas are incorporated into all aspects of university life (Orygen, 2020).

Appendix 2.1 Public Stigma Dimensions

Social Distance—The reluctance to interact with members of devalued groups. Six items: (1) How willing are you to move next door to a person with a mental illness? (2) How willing are you to make friends with a person with a mental illness? (3) How willing are you to spend an evening socializing with a person with a mental illness? (4) How willing are you to start working closely on the job with a person with a mental illness? (5) How willing are you to have a group home for people with mental illness opened in your neighborhood? (6) How willing are you to have a person with a mental illness marry into your family? Response categories: definitely willing (1), probably willing (2), probably unwilling (3), and definitely unwilling (4).

Traditional Prejudice—Adherence to the belief that all members of the "marked" group are categorically inferior to others. Four items: (1) People with mental illness are just as intelligent as anyone else. (2) People with mental illness are just as productive as anyone else. (3) People with mental illness are just as trustworthy as anyone else. (4) People with mental illness are more creative than most other people. Response categories: strongly disagree (1), disagree (2), agree (3), and strongly agree (4). Items 1, 2, and 3 are reverse coded.

Exclusionary Sentiments—The willingness to reject persons with mental illness from the full benefits of citizenship. 5 items: (1) People with mental illness should not be allowed to hold public office. (2) People with mental illness should not be allowed to have children. (3) If a person with mental illness is qualified for a job, they should be hired like any other person. (4) People with mental illness should not be allowed to supervise others at work. (5) People with mental illness should not be allowed to teach children. Response categories: Response categories: strongly disagree (1), disagree (2), agree (3), and strongly agree (4). Item 3 is reverse coded.

Negative Affect—Popular public views that people with mental illness are difficult to interact with. 4 items: (1) Being around a person with mental illness would make me uncomfortable. (2) People with mental illness are unpredictable. (3) People with mental illness are hard to talk to. (4) Being around a person with mental illness would make me feel nervous. Response categories: Response categories: strongly disagree (1), disagree (2), agree (3), and strongly agree (4).

Disclosure Spillover—Negative consequences of revealing mental illness. 4 items: (1) People with mental illness should feel embarrassed about their situation. (2) People with mental illness have little or no hope of ever being accepted as a member of their community. (3) People with mental illness should feel afraid to tell others about their situation. (4) Family members of people with mental illness would be better off if their mental illness situation was kept secret. Response categories: Response categories: strongly disagree (1), disagree (2), agree (3), and strongly agree (4).

Treatment Carryover —Assessments that being known to have received mental health care carries long-lasting consequences. 3 items: (1) Getting mental illness treatment would make one an outsider in their community. (2) If other people knew one was getting mental illness treatment, they would lose some of their friends. (3) No matter how much one achieves, their opportunities would still be limited if people knew they had received mental illness treatment. Response categories: Response categories: strongly disagree (1), disagree (2), agree (3), and strongly agree (4).

Perception of Dangerousness—Fear that persons with mental illness represent a threat for violence to self and others. 2 items: (1) How likely is it that a person with mental illness would do something violent or harmful toward themselves? (2) How likely it is that a person with mental illness would do something violent or harmful toward other people? Response categories: not at all likely (1), not very likely (2), somewhat likely (3), very likely (4).

References

Abassi, B., Fekih-Romdhane, F., Maktouf, H., & Moalla, I. (2021). The relationship between stigma and help-seeking intentions in college students. *European Psychiatry, 13*(64), S393. https://doi.org/10.1192/j.eurpsy.2021.1052

Abelson, S., Ketchen Lipson, S., & Eisenberg, D. (2023). What works for improving mental health in higher education? American Council on Education. https://www.acenet.edu/Documents/What-Works-Mental-Health.pdf.

Abrica, E. J., Hatch-Tocaimaza, D., & Rios-Aguilar, C. (2023). On the impossibilities of advancing racial justice in higher education: Research through reliance on the campus climate heuristic. *Journal of Diversity in Higher Education, 16*(2), 144–156. https://doi.org/10.1037/dhe0000323

American Psychiatric Association. (2013). *Diagnostic and statistical manual of mental disorders (5th ed.).* https://doi.org/10.1176/appi.books.9780890425596

Amenta, E., & Polletta, F. (2019). The cultural impacts of social movements. *The Annual Review of Sociology, 45*, 279–299. https://doi.org/10.1146/annurev-soc-073018-022342

Baik, C., Larcombeb, W., & Brooker, A. (2018). How universities can enhance student mental wellbeing: The student perspective. *Higher Education Research & Development, 38*(4), 674–687. https://doi.org/10.1080/07294360.2019.1576596

Baklola, M., Terra, M., Taha, A., Elnemr, M., Yaseen, M., Maher, A., Buzaid, A. H., Alenazi, R., Mohamed, S. A. O., Abdelhady, D., & El-Gilany, A.-H. (2024). Mental health literacy and help-seeking behaviour among Egyptian undergraduates: A cross-sectional national study. *BMC Psychiatry, 24*, 202. https://doi.org/10.1186/s12888-024-05620-7

Best, R. K., & Arseniev-Koehler, A. (2023). The stigma of diseases: Unequal burden, uneven decline. *American Sociological Review, 88*(5), 938–969. https://doi.org/10.1177/00031224231197436

Billings, K. R. (2021). Stigma in class: Mental illness, social status, and tokenism in elite college culture. *Sociological Perspectives, 64*(2), 238–257. https://doi.org/10.1177/0731121420921878

Brennan, K. M., & Gorman, K. S. (2022). Altering the landscape of mental illness stigma on university campuses. *Stigma and Health, 7*(3), 358–369. https://doi.org/10.1037/sah0000398

Brewster, L., & Cox, A. M. (2022). Taking a 'whole-university' approach to student mental health: The contribution of academic libraries. *Higher Education Research & Development, 42*(1), 33–47. https://doi.org/10.1080/07294360.2022.2043249

Burns, S., Tapsell, A., Perlman, D., Patterson, C., & Moxham, L. (2022). Stigma in the media: Investigating journalism students' attitudes towards mental illness. *International Journal of Mental Health Nursing, 31*, 104–110. https://doi.org/10.1111/inm.12941

Campbell, F., Blank, L., Cantrell, A., Baxter, S., Blackmore, C., Dixon, J., & Goyder, E. (2022). Factors that influence mental health of university and college students in the UK: A systematic review. *BMC Public Health, 22*, 1778. https://doi.org/10.1186/s12889-022-13943-x

Chen, J., Romero, G. D., & Karver, M. S. (2016). The relationship of perceived campus culture to mental health help-seeking intentions. *Journal of Counseling Psychology, 63*, 677–684. https://doi.org/10.1037/cou0000095

Cialdini, R. B. (2007). Descriptive social norms as underappreciated sources of social control. *Psychometrika, 72*(2), 263–268. https://doi.org/10.1007/s11336-006-1560-6

Clair, M., Daniel, C., & Lamont, L. (2016). Destigmatization and health: Cultural constructions and the long-term reduction of stigma. *Social Science & Medicine, 165*, 223–232. https://doi.org/10.1016/j.socscimed.2016.03.021

Clement, S., Schauman, O., Graham, T., Maggioni, F., Evans-Lacko, S., Bezborodovs, N., Morgan, C., Rüsch, N., Brown, J. S. L., & Thornicroft, G. (2015). What is the impact of mental health-related stigma on help-seeking? A systematic review of quantitative and qualitative studies. *Psychological Medicine, 45*, 11–27. https://doi.org/10.1017/S0033291714000129

Corrigan, P. W., Kosyluk, K. A., Markowitz, F., Brown, R. L., Conlon, B., Rees, J., Rosenberg, J., Ellefson, S., & Al-Khouja, M. (2016). Mental illness stigma and disclosure in college students. *Journal of Mental Health, 25*(1), 224–230. https://doi.org/10.3109/09638237.2015.1101056

Dare, O., Jidong, D. E., & Premkumar, P. (2023). Conceptualising mental illness among university students of African, Caribbean and similar ethnic heritage in the United Kingdom. *Ethnicity & Health, 28*(4), 522–543. https://doi.org/10.1080/13557858.2022.2104817

Eisenberg, D., Golberstein, E., & Hunt, J. B. (2009). Mental health and academic success in college. *The B.E. Journal of Economic Analysis & Policy, 9*(1), 40. https://doi.org/10.2202/1935-1682.2191

Funkhouser, C. J., Zakriski, A. L., & Spoltore, J. D. (2017). Evaluating peer-peer depression outreach: College students helping peers approach and respond to students in crisis. *Psi Chi Journal of Psychological Research, 22*(1), 19–28. https://doi.org/10.24839/2325-7342.JN22.1.19

Gaddis, S. M., Ramirez, D., & Hernandez, E. L. (2018). Contextualizing public stigma: Endorsing mental health treatment stigma on college and university campuses. *Social Science & Medicine, 197*, 183–191. https://doi.org/10.1016/j.socscimed.2017.11.029

Gaddis, S. M., Ramirez, D., & Hernandez, E. L. (2020). Variations in endorsed and perceived mental health treatment stigma across U.S. higher education institutions. *Stigma and Health, 5*(3), 323–330. https://doi.org/10.1037/sah0000202

Gallego, J., Cangas, A. J., Aguilar, J. M., Trigueros, R., Navarro, N., Galván, B., Smyshnov, K., & Gregg, M. (2020). Education students' stigma toward mental health problems: A cross-cultural comparison. *Frontiers in Psychiatry, 11*, 587321. https://doi.org/10.3389/fpsyt.2020.587321

Gallup & Lumina Foundation. (2024). *The state of higher education 2024: A valuable, but obstructed path to great jobs and lives.* https://www.gallup.com/analytics/644939/state-of-higher-education.aspx

Gannon, K. R., Richardson, L. R., & Ritzert, T. R. (2024, January 25). The mental health climate and mental health-related academic help seeking on U.S. college campuses. *Stigma and Health.* Advance online publication. https://doi.org/10.1037/sah0000502

Gorman, K. S., & Brennan, K. M. (2023a). Mental illness public stigma and treatment seeking among university students. *Journal of College Student Psychotherapy, 37*(1), 52–70. https://doi.org/10.1080/87568225.2021.1891006

Gorman, K. S., & Brennan, K. M. (2023b). More sessions make a difference: University counseling centers and student retention. *Journal of Student Affairs Research and Practice, 61*(4), 475–487. https://doi.org/10.1080/19496591.2023.2201453

Gorman, K. S., & Brennan, K. M. (2024). The miseducation of mental health programming: The impact on stigma and beliefs about suicide. *Stigma and Health.* https://doi.org/10.1037/sah0000536

Gorman, K. S., Walden, D., Braun, L., & Hotaling, M. (2024). Navigating a path forward for mental health services in higher education. *Journal of College Student Mental Health, 38*, 1–19. https://doi.org/10.1080/28367138.2023.2298647

Hatzenbuehler, M. L., Phelan, J. C., & Link, B. G. (2013). Stigma as a fundamental cause of population health inequalities. *Journal of American Public Health, 103*(5), 813–821. https://doi.org/10.2105/AJPH.2012.301069

Healthy Minds Network. (2020, August). College student mental health action toolkit on mental health data and statistics. https://healthymindsnetwork.org/wp-content/uploads/2020/09/CollegeStudentMentalHealthActionToolkit.pdf

JED Foundation. (2022). Faculty guide to supporting student mental health. https://jedfoundation.org/wp-content/uploads/2022/04/JED-Higher-Education-Faculty-Guide-1.pdf

Julius, B., Putteeraj, M., & Somanah, J. (2024). A systematic review of university students' mental health in sub-Saharan Africa. *Transformation in Higher Education, 9*, a316. https://doi.org/10.4102/the.v9i0.316

Kim, C. H., & Choi, Y. B. (2017). How meritocracy is defined today: Contemporary aspects of meritocracy. *Economics and Sociology, 10*(1), 112–121. https://doi.org/10.14254/2071-789X.2017/10-1/8

Lamont, M. (2018). Addressing recognition gaps: Destigmatization and the reduction of inequality. *American Sociological Review, 83*(3), 419–444. https://doi.org/10.1177/0003122418773775

Li, X.-H., Wong, Y.-L. I., Wu, Q., Ran, M.-S., & Zhang, T.-M. (2024). Chinese college students' stigmatization towards people with mental illness: Familiarity, perceived dangerousness, fear, and social distance. *Healthcare, 12*, 1715. https://doi.org/10.3390/healthcare12171715

Link, B. G., & Phelan, J. C. (2001). Conceptualizing stigma. *Annual Review of Sociology, 27*, 363–385. https://doi.org/10.1146/annurev.soc.27.1.363

Loong, Y. Q., Tan, S. T., Yeoh, S. W., Poh, C. S. K., Yeop, A., Goh, Q. R., & Ho, M. C. (2024). The impact of social stigma and loss of face on mental health help-seeking behavior among university students in Malaysia: Examining mediating relationships. *International Journal of Education, Psychology and Counseling, 9*(56), 01–23. https://doi.org/10.35631/IJEPC.956001

Orygen. (2020). Australian university mental health framework report. https://www.orygen.org.au/Orygen-Institute/University-Mental-Health-Framework/Framework/University-Mental-Health-Framework-full-report

Parsons, T. (1951). *The social system*. The Free Press.

Parsons, T. (1958). Definitions of health and illness in the light of American values and social structure. In E. G. Jaco (Ed.), *Patients, physicians, and illness: Sourcebook in behavioral science and medicine* (pp. 165–187). Free Press.

Pescosolido, B. A., Halpern-Manners, A., Luo, L., & Perry, B. (2021). Trends in public stigma of mental illness in the U.S., 1996–2018. *JAMA Network Open, 4*(12), e2140202. https://doi.org/10.1001/jamanetworkopen.2021.40202

Pescosolido, B. A., & Martin, J. K. (2015). The stigma complex. *Annual Review of Sociology, 41*, 87–116. https://doi.org/10.1146/annurev-soc-071312-145702

Pescosolido, B. A., Martin, J. K., Lang, A., & Olafsdottir, S. (2008). Rethinking theoretical approaches to stigma: A framework integrating normative influences on stigma (FINIS). *Social Science & Medicine, 67*(3), 431–440. https://doi.org/10.1016/j.socscimed.2008.03.018

Pescosolido, B. A., Martin, J. K., Long, S., Medina, T. R., Phelan, J. C., & Link, B. G. (2010). 'A disease like any other'? A decade of change in public reactions to schizophrenia, depression, and alcohol dependence. *American Journal of Psychiatry, 167*(11), 1321–1330. https://doi.org/10.1176/appi.ajp.2010.09121743

Pescosolido, B. A., Medina, T. R., Martin, J. K., & Long, J. S. (2013). The 'backbone' of stigma: Identifying the global core of public prejudice associated with mental illness. *American Journal of Public Health, 103*(5), 853–860. https://doi.org/10.2105/AJPH.2012.301147

Reddy, I. R., Ukrani, J., Indla, V., & Ukrani, V. (2018). Creativity and psychopathology: Two sides of the same coin? *Indian Journal of Psychiatry, 60*(2), 168–174. https://doi.org/10.4103/psychiatry.IndianJPsychiatry_129_18

Rhydderch, D., Krooupa, A.-M., Shefer, G., Goulden, R., Williams, P., Thornicroft, A., Rose, D., Thornicroft, G., & Henderson, C. (2016). Changes in newspaper coverage of mental illness from 2008 to 2014 in England. *Acta Psychiatrica Scandinavica, 134*, 45–52. https://doi.org/10.1111/acps.12606

Sallee, M. W. (2016). Ideal for whom? A cultural analysis of ideal worker norms in higher education and student affairs graduate programs. *New Directions for Higher Education, 176*, 53–67. https://doi.org/10.1002/he.20209

Schnittker, J. (2008). An uncertain revolution: Why the rise of a genetic model of mental illness has not increased tolerance. *Social Science & Medicine, 67*(9), 1370–1381. https://doi.org/10.1016/j.socscimed.2008.07.007

Schomerus, G., & Angermeyer, M. C. (2021). Blind spots in stigma research? Broadening our perspective on mental illness stigma by exploring 'what matters most' in modern Western societies. *Epidemiology and Psychiatric Sciences, 30*(e26), 1–6. https://doi.org/10.1017/S2045796021000111

Schomerus, G., Schwahn, C., Holzinger, A., Corrigan, P. W., Grabe, H. J., Carta, M. G., & Angermeyer, M. C. (2012). Evolution of public attitudes about mental illness: A systematic review and meta-analysis. *Acta Psychiatrica Scandinavica, 125*(6), 440–452. https://doi.org/10.1111/j.1600-0447.2012.01826.x

Schueth, A. (2022). Reducing the stigma of academic mental health can save lives. *Nature Reviews Urology, 19*, 129–130. https://doi.org/10.1038/s41585-021-00549-y

Sontag-Padilla, L., Dunbar, M. S., Ye, F., Kase, C., Fein, R., Abelson, S., Seelam, R., & Stein, B. D. (2018). Strengthening college students' mental health knowledge, awareness, and helping behaviors: The impact of active minds, a peer mental health organization. *Journal of the American Academy of Child & Adolescent Psychiatry, 57*(7), 500–507. https://doi.org/10.1016/j.jaac.2018.03.019

Storrie, K., Ahern, K., & Tuckett, A. (2010). A systematic review: Students with mental health problems—A growing problem. *International Journal of Nursing Practice, 16*(1), 1–6. https://doi.org/10.1111/j.1440-172X.2009.01813.x

Stuart, H., Sartorius, N., Liinamaa, T., & The Images Study Group. (2015). Images of psychiatry and psychiatrists. *Acta Psychiatrica Scandanavica, 131*, 21–28. https://doi.org/10.1111/acps.12368

Tilli, N., & Villar, M. E. (2024). Universities and student mental health at the intersection of communication, representations, and stigma. An international comparative study. *Zer, 29*(56), 203–222. https://doi.org/10.1387/zer.24873

Turosak, A., & Siwierka, J. (2021). Mental health and stigma on campus: Insights from students' lived experience. *Journal of Prevention & Intervention in the Community, 49*(3), 266–281. https://doi.org/10.1080/10852352.2019.1654264

Wada, M., Suto, M. J., Lee, M., Sanders, D., Sun, C., Le, T. N., Goldman-Hasbun, J., & Chauhan, S. (2019). University students' perspectives on mental illness stigma. *Mental Health & Prevention, 14*, 200159. https://doi.org/10.1016/j.mph.2019.200159

Walsh, D. A. B., & Foster, J. L. H. (2021). A call to action: A critical review of mental health related anti-stigma campaigns. *Frontiers in Public Health, 8.*, Art 569539, 1–15. https://doi.org/10.3389/fpubh.2020.569539

Walsh, D. A. B., & Foster, J. L. H. (2022). Charting an alternative course for mental health-related anti-stigma social and behaviour change programmes. *International Journal of Environmental Research and Public Health, 19*, 10618. https://doi.org/10.3390/ijerph191710618

World Health Organization. (2021). *International statistical classification of diseases and related health problems (11th ed.).* https://icd.who.int/

Yang, L. H., Kleinman, A., Link, B. G., Phelan, J. C., Lee, S., & Good, B. (2007). Culture and stigma: Adding moral experience to stigma theory. *Social Science & Medicine, 64*(7), 1524–1535. https://doi.org/10.1016/j.socscimed.2006.11.013

Kathleen M. Brennan, Ph.D., is Professor of Sociology and Director of the Sociology Program at Western Carolina University, USA. For more than a decade, she has used quantitative methodologies to collaboratively examine mental illness stigma in the context of higher education. She has co-presented these research findings to professional audiences and co-authored papers in higher education, health, and other disciplinary publications. Additionally, she regularly teaches about and provides consultation on the sociology of mental health and illness on campus and in the regional community.

Kimberly S. Gorman, Ph.D., is Associate Vice Chancellor for Health & Wellness in the Student Affairs Division at Western Carolina University, USA. Dr. Gorman's primary research interests are related to collegiate mental health and mental illness stigma in the college population. She has co-authored several papers about the impacts of mental illness and its related stigma in college students. She is a licensed psychologist who has worked in the higher education setting for more than two decades. She has served on the governing board of the Association for University and College Counseling Center Directors and on the advisory board for the Center for Collegiate Mental Health.

Chapter 3
A Comprehensive Exploration of Mental Illness Stigma on Campuses Using the Model of Stigma Communication

Shawna L. Dias and Romy RW

Abstract This chapter addresses the pervasive issue of mental illness stigma that negatively impacts millions of students on college campuses. It examines the Model of Stigma Communication (MSC) as a framework for understanding and combatting stigmatizing messages. By exploring MSC's application in health communication research, the chapter proposes strategies for destigmatizing communication, including mental health education campaigns, prosocial messaging in classrooms, and fostering open discourse about mental illness. The responsibility for implementing these strategies falls on faculty and staff, who may require support from university administrators. Suggestions include forming committees, providing resources, incentivizing participation, and ensuring equitable access to mental health services. However, there's a lack of recent case studies on college mental health communication campaigns, and existing research predominantly focuses on undergraduate students, overlooking the experiences of graduate students and faculty. The chapter calls for research to fill these gaps, emphasizing the need to examine the effects of discourse and mental illness disclosure on stigma across various social networks. Additionally, scholars are encouraged to develop instruments for measuring these effects and explore strategies for reducing self-stigma and increasing help-seeking behaviors among college populations.

Keywords Mental illness · Stigma · Health communication · Higher education

The authors have no conflicts of interest to declare that are relevant to the content of this chapter.

S. L. Dias (✉)
Hanover Research, Arlington, VA, USA
e-mail: SDias@HanoverResearch.com

R. RW
Communication Studies, Loyola Marymount University, Los Angeles, CA, USA

© The Author(s), under exclusive license to Springer Nature Switzerland AG 2025

K. M. Brennan, K. S. Gorman (eds.), *A University-Wide Approach to Changing Campus Cultures of Mental Illness Stigma*, Knowledge Studies in Higher Education 18, https://doi.org/10.1007/978-3-031-86496-4_3

The problem of mental illness stigma on college campuses has long been an issue of concern for scholars, educators, and mental health practitioners (Rittel & Webber, 1973; Rudick & Dannels, 2018). Stigma is a leading cause of help-seeking avoidance, which can result in the worsening of symptoms and the development of serious mental illness over time (Corrigan, 2004; Schnyder et al., 2017). In the United States, recent survey research revealed roughly 59 million adults experience mental illness (Substance Abuse and Mental Health Services Administration [SAMHSA], 2023a), and a notable number of adults with moderate or serious mental illness will go on to develop substance use disorders (SAMHSA, 2023a, 2023b). Survey research from the American College Health Association (2023) revealed the majority of U.S. students experienced moderate or serious psychological distress during their college years, and students with higher distress were more likely to withdraw (Center for Collegiate Mental Health [CCMH], 2023; Gallup & Lumina Foundation, 2023). Students are far less likely to withdraw from college when mental illness stigma is addressed in the classroom and when instructors are willing to make accommodations to support students who experience mental illness (Rudick & Dannels, 2018). Although college instructors are generally unqualified to counsel students about their mental health, they have an ethical obligation to ensure classrooms are safe and welcoming spaces for all students; doing so often means establishing clear standards of communication and behavior for all students and ensuring course content and delivery are free of stigmatizing messages. Additionally, while a substantial body of research on mental illness stigma in college environments delves into the experiences and attitudes of undergraduate students, there is a notable gap in the exploration and differentiation of these experiences among graduate students and faculty members. Individuals in the latter groups are likely to encounter elevated stress and more severe forms of mental illness (Dias & Wang, 2023).

In this chapter, we explore the model of stigma communication (MSC) as a universal framework for understanding how stigmatizing messages are created and perpetuated. We also offer examples of MSC's application in health communication research and propose a framework for the design of destigmatizing messages based on the variables present in MSC. We offer recommendations for campus communication utilizing the outlined attributes, including (1) developing mental health education and intervention campaigns, (2) implementing prosocial norms and messaging in the classroom and course syllabi, (3) welcoming discourse and disclosure relative to students' mental health in the classroom, and (4) introducing students to self-regulation and metacognition exercises. We conclude this chapter with pathways for future research on the topic of mental illness stigma communication.

The Model of Stigma Communication

A person may speak positively about mental health conditions and express an understanding of the behaviors associated with them but still treat the individuals experiencing said conditions poorly. This stigma is perpetuated via the creation and spread of overt and covert messages, which may take written, oral, or behavioral forms.[1] According to Smith (2007), stigma communication is defined as "messages spread through communities to teach their members to recognize the disgraced (i.e., recognizing stigmata) and to react accordingly" (p. 464). Stigmatizing messages contribute to the breakdown of societies by encouraging their members to adopt "us against them" mentalities and prejudiced behaviors. Smith (2007) framed this messaging process in the model of stigma communication (MSC), depicted in Fig. 3.1, which is commonly used in the communication and public relations disciplines to examine communicative behaviors and effects associated with stigma-related interventions.

The MSC denotes four main features of stigma communication: marks, labels, responsibility/etiology, and peril (Smith, 2007; Smith et al., 2019). Theoretically, messages must have one or more of the following attributes to be stigmatizing: (1) contain attention-grabbing content, (2) endorse stereotyping or othering, and/or (3) rationalize negative emotional responses or discriminatory acts toward individuals with specific characteristics or experiences as a means of "protecting" the public majority. Marks and labels serve to draw attention to an individual and stereotype them. Messages that suggest or emphasize peril aim to trigger negative emotional responses, and attributions of responsibility toward a stereotyped person encourage discriminatory behaviors. In mental illness stigmatizing messages, individuals with mental illness are marked and characterized based on their health statuses, assigned labels to further distance them from those who do not have mental illness (e.g., calling someone who experiences schizophrenia disorder "a schizophrenic"), attributed responsibility and blame for their place in the marked group and its perceived public threat, and may be targeted for danger or identified as "dangerous" to the public (Smith, 2012, 2014).

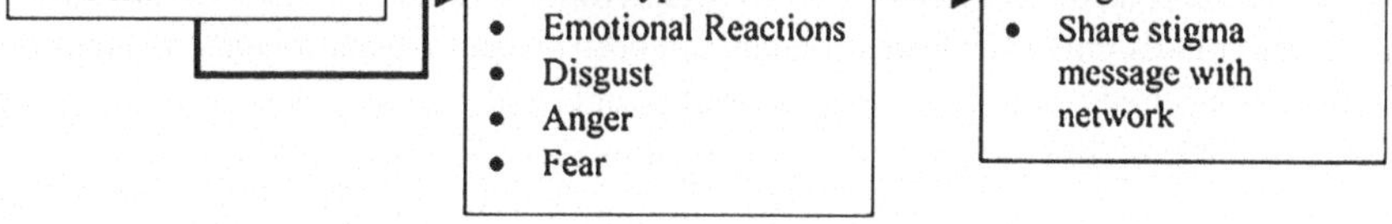

Fig. 3.1 The model of stigma communication (*Smith,* 2007).

[1] See Chap. 1 in this volume for a list of basic terms and definitions related to stigma.

Processing of stigmatizing messages happens in a linear fashion following one of two pathways; either the messages directly produce effects, or they produce preliminary reactions that influence the effects. The former occurs when message receivers behave without giving much thought to the message, such as sharing the message with others or avoiding a stigmatized person simply because the message sender suggested it. The latter pathway for processing stigmatizing messages involves cognitive processing of the message by the receivers, which often triggers affective responses (e.g., disgust, anger, fear, danger appraisal, shock, common ground) and antisocial behavioral effects (i.e., isolation and removal of the target) (Smith et al., 2019).

Applications of the Model of Stigma Communication

The model of stigma communication has been utilized globally by health communication scholars to understand how stigmatization occurs through messaging associated with health risks, conditions, and behaviors. Herein, we describe two novel studies that applied the model to the examination of stigma responses among U.S. college students. These studies can serve as exemplars to assist colleges in conducting similar research to better understand how their unique campus communities might respond to health-related issues that may be stigmatized, as well as campaign message designs aimed at reducing stigma.

Ledford et al. (2022) applied the model in experimental survey research on opioid use disorder (OUD) stigma messages, in which participants were exposed to fictional news articles about a person with OUD. The authors conducted two studies, the first analyzed survey responses from 231 college students at a mid-Atlantic university, and the second study's final sample included 245 responses from Amazon Mechanical Turk workers. In both studies, participants were assigned to one of four experimental conditions that assessed classification variables (markers and labels) against enactment variables (attributions of responsibility and peril/danger). Both studies found the use of markers or labels to identify or "other" people with OUD directly influenced public perceptions of and decision-making regarding people with OUD, and stigmatization increased when messages combine markers with labels. In the second study, respondents exposed to messages featuring stigmatizing classifications had an increased want for behavioral regulation and social distancing from individuals with OUD. Respondents in both studies who were exposed to messages with high attributions of responsibility and peril also had increased desire for behavioral regulation and distancing, as well as increased perceptions of being personally at risk of danger by individuals with OUD; however, study two respondents who were exposed to high enactment variables were less supportive of policies focused on behavioral rehabilitation.

Smith (2012) conducted an experiment using a hypothetical infectious disease alert to test stigma communication using the MSC. Participants were randomly presented with one of sixteen possible messages and their perceptions of perceived responsibility, dangerousness, group entitativity, affective states, intervention support, dissemination likelihood, stigma beliefs, and cynical worldview were assessed. The findings showed participants' reactions and outcomes were influenced by marks, labels, type of transmission vector, and peril. Marks that described visible symptoms of an infected person were more likely to be shared than messages that did not include these marks. Smith compared stigma messages to rumors and explained they "are more likely to be shared if they include content that elicits consistent emotional reactions, such as disgust. Although exposure to visible symptoms did not show a significant main effect for disgust, anger, or fear (analyzed separately or as the composite variable, negative affect), it may still provide a quality that makes it more viable to share with others" (p. 535). The author also explained the presence of visible symptoms may induce othering attitudes and social distancing toward infected persons and the proclivity to share such messages derives from a desire for social bonding with the majority, being non-infected persons. The type of vector mentioned in the messages, either mouse excrement or possible human-to-human contact, strongly impacted participants' attributions of blame and the perceived dangerousness of the infected persons. Infected persons were attributed more blame and less danger when the message indicated disease transmission was only mouse related. Participants who were exposed to high-peril messages had higher perceptions of dangerousness, increased group entitativity, more negative affective responses, stronger beliefs about the infected, and showed more support for intervention support than those who were exposed to low-peril messages.

These studies highlight the importance of addressing mental illness stigma. Their findings underscore the need for tailored interventions to combat stigmatizing messages, promoting a more inclusive and supportive environment within the higher education community. Smith's (2012) research offers valuable insights into how individuals perceive and respond to stigmatizing messages. Applying these findings to university communities in and outside of the United States can enhance collective efforts to address mental illness stigma, promoting empathy, understanding, and effective communication to create a more compassionate and stigma-free environment for all.

This section showcased two examples of the utility of the Model of Stigma Communication in comprehending health-related stigmatization. The examination of OUD stigma messages indicates the pivotal impact of markers, labels, and responsibility attributions on public perceptions, underscoring the necessity for strategically crafted and targeted interventions to counter stigma. The literature highlights how marks have traditionally been used as attention-gaining mechanisms that generate strong emotional responses, which increases sharing. Stigmatizing messages that combine marks and labels increase stigma, social avoidance, and discriminatory behaviors. Expanding upon this groundwork, the subsequent section delves into reverse engineering stigmatizing messages and manipulating their attributes to motivate stigma reduction responses.

Countering Stigmatizing Messages in Higher Education

The MSC outlines stigmatizing message characteristics, but the larger question of how to counter stigma through messaging remains. There is no consensus in current health and communications literature about what formula of attributes makes messages effectively destigmatizing; however, we reviewed health stigma reduction campaign messages and identified several attributes in them that contrasted with attributes common in stigmatizing messages. For example, messages from the Timiskaming Health Unit aim to reduce stigma toward individuals with drug addiction and use bolded text to emphasize positive labels, like "coach," "friend," "cousin," and "trans person," which humanize people who use drugs. Unlike stigmatizing messages that attribute responsibility and promote discrimination, the Timiskaming messages direct viewers to "stop the shame" and "stop the blame" (Timiskaming, 2020). The 1-in-5 Support Not Stigma campaign messages aim to reduce mental illness stigma by educating the public about the ubiquitousness of mental health conditions, rather than "other" people who experience them, and urge viewers to support people with mental health conditions and help stop stigma (1-in-5, 2024). The Stamping Out Stigma Campaign, organized by Oxfordshire and Buckinghamshire Mental Health, confronts labels commonly used to stigmatize people with mental health conditions. The campaign uses purposeful language like, "I'm dealing with depression" in place of "I am depressed" to demonstrate mental health conditions do not define the people who have them. It also advises viewers to "get a positive attitude" and consider how their thoughtless words regarding mental illness may affect others (Nelson, 2024).

Our assessments of these anti-stigma health messages informed the hypothesis that reverse engineering of stigmatizing messages could help scholars and communicators devise more effective stigma intervention messaging to encourage social support and help-seeking, considering the unique needs and experience of students as well as faculty members, who may also be vulnerable to the impacts of mental illness stigma. Although we have not yet tested a reverse-engineered framework combining all variables outlined herein, we propose that destigmatizing messages should have the following attributes: (1) contain attention-grabbing content, (2) endorse acceptance of differences and dissimilarities, (3) confront negative labels, (4) encourage information-seeking, self-reflection, and help-seeking, and (5) present negative emotional responses and discriminatory acts as irrational and dangerous.

Messages should contain attention-grabbing features so audiences may become aware of stigma as an important social issue and become emotionally vested in its resolution. Ledford et al. (2022) explain that emotional responses to stigmatizing messages increase sharing of messages; thus, we posit that emotional responses to destigmatizing messages will also result in increased sharing. Message creators can use positive marks, recognizable and/or relatable imagery that serve as mental health cues, telegraphic titles, shocking phrases, moral appeals, and narrative stories to draw attention to messages (Hall et al., 2010). Endorsing acceptance of differences and encouraging positive behaviors, like information-seeking, may help audiences respond with more empathy toward those who experience certain mental health conditions. Confronting negative labels, avoidance, and discriminatory responses toward people with stigmatized health conditions can trigger cognitive dissonance, which has proven efficacy as a stigma intervention tool, and generate more positive social consensus (Ciao & Latner, 2011; Meaney & Rieger, 2021).

Combating mental illness stigma in higher education requires a multi-pronged approach, incorporating destigmatizing messages across the curricula and instructor-to-student and peer-to-peer interactions. In the following sections, we outline proven avenues for disseminating destigmatizing messages utilizing one or more of the attributes outlined in our proposed framework.

Mental Health Education and Intervention Campaigns

Stigma communication campaigns not only help to reduce stigma through education but open the door for social discourse, which ultimately plays a larger role in the development of supportive social networks, mental health distress mitigation, and inspiring help-seeking. There is a scarcity of published research that has examined the outcomes of mental illness stigma reduction campaigns on higher education campuses, but here we outline a few.

Giroux and Geiss (2019) conducted survey research on the effects of a week-long mental health awareness campaign which featured messaging about mental health disorders and access to resources at their campus. The student-run campaign was organized by two prominent student organizations—Psi Chi, the international honor society in psychology, and the Black Student Union—and was heavily promoted by faculty members. The involvement of these groups served to draw attention to the initiative and demonstrated peer acceptance and support for community members who experience mental illness. The campaign confronted marks through open-mic nights where students talked about their personal experiences with mental illness and promoted information and help-seeking via informational slideshows, handout sheets, and open lectures given by faculty from the psychology department. Giveaways of stress balls and mental health awareness ribbons also helped to increase community awareness and message sharing. The authors hypothesized participants in the study would report decreased internalized stigma (or self-stigma) and public stigma toward mental illness and people who experience it after exposure to the week-long campaign. Results showed mental illness and help-seeking stigma was effectively reduced across the sample, and participants who became emotionally vested in the initiative and immersed themselves in the intervention campaign's activities experienced the greatest amount of stigma reduction.

Shahwan et al. (2020) conducted similar pre-posttest survey research on Singapore-based university students using a self-created stigma intervention campaign. All participants experienced the same intervention content, which included a professional lecture about mental health and depression, causes of mental illness, treatment options and their efficacy, avenues for help-seeking, and guidance on how to communicate with friends who may be experiencing mental health distress. As part of the intervention, students were also shown a video produced by the World Health Organization (WHO), in which the narrator describes his personal experience with and recovering from depression, as well as a live discussion with a female presenter who described her journey with mental illness and recovery. Lastly, campaign participants partook in a Q&A session with a consultant psychiatrist and a senior mental health researcher. Results indicated participants' attitudes toward help-seeking were positively changed by the intervention. The study's findings underscore the impact of encouraging help-seeking by imparting comprehensive information to students about mental health treatment options, leading to favorable shifts in their attitudes toward embracing mental health recovery solutions. The authors posit that the provision of a platform for students to directly engage with a psychiatrist and a mental health researcher may have played a pivotal role in demystifying misconceptions, alleviating concerns, and addressing specific issues not covered by standardized interventions, such as fears about medication addictiveness, potential side effects, associated costs, and confidentiality concerns.

Kirschner et al. (2022) examined the impact of an online interactive intervention campaign aimed at reducing self- and public stigma relative to mental health help-seeking. The intervention used kognito.com, a digital learning platform that aims to improve mental health in classrooms through role-play simulations and virtual conversations. On the platform, students were paired with virtual avatars that provided information about mental health conditions and advised students on how to respond helpfully to peers who showed signs of mental health distress. Using drop-down response options, participants responded to the avatars' portrayals of students experiencing mental health crises. The intervention tool had previously been designed and used to train college students and leaders on how to identify and approach students who may need a referral to supportive services, but it had not previously been tested for stigma intervention. As part of this test, participants were randomly assigned to participate in an intervention-oriented discussion or a control condition whereby they acted as store clerks interacting with avatar customers who intended to buy tobacco. Participants who completed the intervention simulation reported decreased concerns about public stigma related to mental health help-seeking and viewed help-seeking more positively. Perceptions about self-stigma for help-seeking remained unchanged in the intervention group and worsened for participants in the control group. The study suggests the use of novel approaches and technologies may help draw positive attention toward mental illness and offers some empirical evidence that the promotion of prosocial attitudes toward help-seeking reduces perceived public stigma; however, it may not directly affect self-stigma and could make it worse.

Establishing Prosocial Classroom Norms

One way to counter stigmatizing messages is by changing the narrative around mental illness (Goldman, 2018). Changing the narrative should begin in higher education classrooms, where faculty can establish norms of behavior and expectations for communication regarding mental health. The course syllabus, which all students are required to read, is a useful tool for drawing students' attention toward mental health, relaying expectations for reflexivity and peer acceptance, and influencing in-classroom discussions about mental health (Thompson, 2007). On the first day of a new course, instructors usually spend time going over the syllabus to acquaint their students with the curriculum and address things that may help or hinder their success, such as study habits, attendance, and participation. Because mental illness can greatly impact students' ability to focus, complete coursework, or be fully present in their classes, instructors must address mental health in the syllabi, provide resources for help-seeking, and outline protocols for students to follow when mental illness impacts their performance. Furthermore, instructors should engage their students in discussions about how to publicly talk about and respond to mental illness when it becomes a focal point or topic for in-class discussion. Establishing class norms that confront labeling and stereotyping is an important step toward reducing mental illness stigma in the classroom (Goldman, 2018; Horan et al., 2011). The process for establishing class norms about labels and stereotyping should involve open discourse about which marks and labels students associate with mental illness and how they respond to them. Instructors should work with students to establish communication norms by introducing activities, like the creation of positive and negative word clouds, in which students indicate the types of terms they consider acceptable and unacceptable when discussing mental health. Class discussions can also enlighten students about why stigma and the use of unacceptable terms are irrational and dangerous to individual and collective health and success.

Prosocial classroom norms of acceptance and support toward mental illness can be reinforced through consistent encouragement of information-seeking and the introduction of related educational materials in the classroom. Information about on-campus resources and helplines should be included in the course syllabus as an immediate resource for those who may be experiencing mental health crises, but instructors should regularly share additional resources, such as notifications about pertinent school-sponsored events and new research publications that align mental health with the course material. Materials should be circulated in the classroom and made available on the course's online learning platform. Goldman (2018) explains, "Instructors, whose opinions are highly valued by students, can be instrumental in recalibrating norms and stigmas related to help-seeking and may ultimately influence students to use the resources on campus to address their mental health" (p. 401).

Welcoming Discourse and Disclosure in the College Classroom

Spagnolo et al. (2008) proposed mental illness stigma could be significantly reduced by introducing adolescents to people who experience mental illness and allowing them to learn more about how those individuals live with and experience their conditions. Engaging with stigmatized individuals on a personal level through discourse helps others to see past negative stereotypes and labels and, in some cases, leads to increased attention toward personal mental health needs and more social acceptance of differences (Dias & Wang, 2023; Zhang et al., 2024). Stelling and West (2021) examined the effects of faculty disclosure of mental health conditions, including depression, on students and resident physicians who attended a 2016 medical conference. The objective of their research was to determine if disclosure could reduce mental illness stigma among medical trainees and increase help-seeking. Three faculty members spoke publicly about their mental illness experiences at the conference, after which students completed anonymous surveys that assessed their knowledge, attitudes, and behaviors involving mental illness during their training. All survey respondents (n = 39) reported they enjoyed the conference, 89.7% indicated an increased knowledge of medical resources after their attendance, and 84.6% revealed they intended to seek more mental health resources. All except one participant experienced reduced self-stigma and increased self-reflection after hearing faculty members disclose their mental health issues. The survey respondents in this study are more likely than the average student to experience mental health distress and burnout, due to the pressure and long hours of work and study involved with medical training. For those same reasons, medical trainees are also more likely to postpone or avoid help-seeking for mental distress. The results of Stelling and West's (2021) research offer evidence to support disclosure as an approach to mental illness stigma as a catalyst for stereotype avoidance and increased help-seeking for graduate-level students and professional trainees.

Buizza et al. (2017) conducted survey research with faculty, researchers, and administrative staff to gain a better understanding of knowledge, beliefs, and attitudes about mental health within the academy. The authors found having a higher level of education and experience with teaching was positively correlated with increased knowledge about and accepting attitudes toward persons with mental health disorders. Furthermore, the more educated participants were more likely to agree people experiencing mental health disorders are not personally responsible for the development of their disorders. Respondents who personally experienced mental illness were also more knowledgeable about mental health, broadly. This and other research (see Manago & Krendl, 2023) emphasize the importance of label confrontation, information sharing, and the development of prosocial cultural norms around mental illness and show the power of transparency and discourse surrounding mental health in higher education, particularly among graduate students, faculty, and academic professional staff. Oftentimes, people struggle with mental illness in silence because they fear speaking about it will increase their likelihood of experiencing stigma from the public and their social networks. However, this research provides evidence mental illness disclosure is more likely than not to be met with acceptance in higher education, particularly among academic elites, which further suggests open discourse and destigmatizing messages about mental illness at institutions of higher education will lead to a reduction in internalized/self-stigma and public stigma, and in some situations, a reduction in close social network stigma.

Teaching Students the Art of Self-Regulation and Metacognition

College instructors can further guide students in becoming more aware of their mental health struggles and internalized stigmas by embedding reflexive self-regulation and metacognition tasks and activities into their course plans, which often lead to information-seeking. Vohs and Baumeister (2004) define self-regulation as "the exercise of control over oneself, especially concerning bringing the self into line with preferred (thus, regular) standards" (p. 2). Essentially, self-regulation is the practice of being in control *by* and *of* oneself. Self-regulation is an approach to self-discipline, which happens when humans set goals that require resistance toward internalized responses, like resisting unhealthy food cravings when trying to improve personal fitness. Metacognition is the practice of thinking about thinking, whereby individuals commit to self-observation and learning, set goals, and reflect on their performance concerning those goals before devising plans to move forward (Goldman, 2018; Zimmerman & Schunk, 2011). Instructors can support students' self-regulation and metacognition in several ways, including asking reflective questions during class discussions that challenge their thinking and reactions toward mental illness and its associated public stigma. Journaling is also a useful approach for building metacognition in students, and many scholars found journaling also helps students manage their stress and recognize signs of mental health conditions they may be experiencing (Houghton et al., 2012; Khanna & Singh, 2021). Assigning graded journaling activities also helps course instructors be more reflexive and aware of escalating mental health concerns among their students, which may call for future intervention or indicate a need for lesson plan modifications. During our doctoral studies, a colleague assigned weekly journaling in her public speaking course for participation points and tasked her students with responding to three prompts each week, the latter of which always asked students to reflect on how they were feeling and invited them to share issues of concern regarding course content, delivery, and classroom communication. Our colleague shared that the activity helped her to better understand when course content was not being delivered effectively or if it was done so in a way that made students feel overwhelmed, and it also helped her to understand which discussion topics triggered mental health concerns or stigma, and how to better navigate those discussions.

Conclusion and Pathways for Future Research

Improving the way students and faculty communicate is the most direct approach toward resolving mental illness stigma on college campuses. Communication is not bound by words spoken or written; it can also occur through our expressions, behaviors, and the messages we choose to share, attend, or ignore. The MSC outlines how stigmatizing messages are perpetuated through the labels that we apply to people with specific experiences or attributes that society deems "undesirable," "unsafe," or "unacceptable." Stigmatization also occurs through our decisions to include or exclude people, ostracize them, pass along negative messages about them, or develop fear toward them because of their differences. Destigmatizing communication requires intentionality and reflexivity; we must be conscientious of how our words and actions affect and reflect on others. Most scholars, particularly those with qualitative experience, develop a habit of reflexivity in their work and often assess their performance to identify and correct unconscious biases. However, college students are often less equipped or less adept at doing so and require more guidance from their instructors. In this chapter, we offered some ways course instructors can aid students in developing behaviors that will aid in the reduction of internalized and public stigma, such as establishing norms of acceptance, metacognition exercises, and open discourse. Most of these approaches toward communication emphasize confrontation of marks and labels, endorsement of social acceptance toward differences, and encouragement of information-seeking and reflexivity. We find these attributes to be the most powerful and effective for stigma reduction, particularly when they are used consistently in various forms of messaging in and out of the university classroom. We also proposed college campuses be more proactive about organizing (or, ideally, inspiring students to organize) mental health education and intervention campaigns, and we provided some examples of research on campaigns that were deemed successful in reducing mental illness stigma and increasing students' help-seeking.

Implementation of our framework and suggestions for mental illness stigma reduction in university environments place a significant amount of responsibility on faculty and staff members to create, maintain, and assess the performance of messages. Faculty, who may otherwise support the proposed initiatives, could perceive there is little incentive to take on the extra workload. Thus, we propose university administrators take the following steps to support faculty in this endeavor: (1) form a compensated committee tasked with the development of strategic mental health initiatives, identification of drivers, creation of university-wide materials (e.g., syllabi templates, resource information sheets, lecture materials, discussion-based activities, etc.), development of performance assessment protocols, performance evaluation, and performance reporting; (2) task the marketing and communication team with the creation of stigma reduction message materials for social media and on-campus display; (3) develop and maintain a resource hub on the university's learning management system where faculty and staff can share mental health-related messages, news, and learning activities; (4) incentivize faculty participation in stigma reduction initiatives through awards and recognition programs; (5) encourage tenure review committees to consider faculty members' contributions toward stigma reduction as part of the service requirements for tenure; and (6) ensure students, faculty, and staff have equitable access to mental health counseling and other supportive services. Our sixth suggestion to administrators is particularly important because stigma reduction work often involves significant emotional labor that could cause or worsen mental health conditions in those who undertake it. Additionally, department administrators should consider creating internal committees to encourage collective anti-stigma work and fairly disperse tasks across faculty in the program or department. It is best practice for administrators to consult with peers at institutions who have developed similar initiatives to gain an understanding of which processes, drivers, and resources have proven successful.

Because there is a dearth of recent case studies on college mental health communication campaigns, we recommend scholars examine this topic further and conduct experimental research using the attributes we proposed for designing destigmatizing messages. Furthermore, the body of literature that examines mental illness stigma campaigns predominantly does so with a focus on reducing self-stigma and increasing help-seeking and overlooks public and close social network stigma. Most of the research on mental illness stigma in college environments examines the experiences and attitudes of undergraduate students but does not examine or differentiate those of graduate students and faculty members who likely experience higher levels of stress and more severe forms of mental illness. A handful of scholars have established a foundation for research in this area, but there are still significant gaps for scholars to fill (Dias & Wang, 2023; Janouskova et al., 2017; Stelling & West, 2021; Watson et al., 2017). Lastly, we recommend scholars try to better understand the effects of discourse and mental illness disclosure on public, close social network, and self or internalized stigma. Quantitative scholars might also consider developing instruments to assist researchers in measuring these effects.

References

1-in-5. (2024, March 3). #Supportnotstigma Campaign [Campaign Graphic]. https://www.1in5.info/1in5-antistigma-campaign

American College Health Association. (2023, October 14). American College Health Association-National College Health Assessment III: Reference group executive summary spring 2023. https://www.acha.org/documents/ncha/NCHA-III_SPRING_2023_REFERENCE_GROUP_EXECUTIVE_SUMMARY.pdf

Buizza, C., Ghilardi, A., & Ferrari, C. (2017). Beliefs and prejudices versus knowledge and awareness: How to cope stigma against mental illness. A college staff e-survey. *Community Mental Health Journal, 53*, 589–597. https://doi.org/10.1007/s10597-017-0116-9

Center for Collegiate Mental Health. (2023, January). 2022 Annual Report (Publication No. STA 23–168). https://ccmh.psu.edu/assets/docs/2022%20Annual%20Report.pdf?

Ciao, A. C., & Latner, J. D. (2011). Reducing obesity stigma: The effectiveness of cognitive dissonance and social consensus interventions. *Obesity, 19*(9), 1768–1774. https://doi.org/10.1038/oby.2011.106

Corrigan, P. (2004). How stigma interferes with mental health care. *American Psychology, 59*(7), 614624. https://doi.org/10.1037/0003-066X.59.7.614

Dias, S., & Wang, X. (2023). Exploring participants' experiences of mental health and stigma in American colleges. *Journal of American College Health, 71*, 1–11. https://doi.org/10.1080/07448481.2021.1954652

Gallup & Lumina Foundation. (2023). *Stressed out and stopping out: The mental health crisis in higher education.* https://www.luminafoundation.org/wp-content/uploads/2023/03/Stressed-Out-and-Stopping-Out.pdf

Giroux, D., & Geiss, E. (2019). Evaluating a student-led mental health awareness campaign. *Psi Chi Journal of Psychological Research, 24*(1), 61–66. https://doi.org/10.24839/2325-7342.JN24.1.61

Goldman, Z. W. (2018). Responding to mental health issues in the college classroom. *Communication Education, 67*(3), 399–404. https://doi.org/10.1080/03634523.2018.1465191

Hall, T. E., Ham, S. H., & Lackey, B. K. (2010). Comparative evaluation of the attention capture and holding power of novel signs aimed at park visitors. *Journal of Interpretation Research, 15*(1), 15–36. https://doi.org/10.1177/109258721001500103

Horan, S. M., Houser, M. L., Goodboy, A. K., & Frymier, A. B. (2011). Students' early impressions of instructors: Understanding the role of relational skills and messages. *Communication Research Reports, 28*, 74–85. https://doi.org/10.1080/08824096.2011.541362

Houghton, J. D., Wu, J., Godwin, J. L., Neck, C. P., & Manz, C. C. (2012). Effective stress management: A model of emotional intelligence, self-leadership, and student stress coping. *Journal of Management Education, 36*(2), 220–238. https://doi.org/10.1177/105256291143020

Janoušková, M., Weissová, A., Formánek, T., Pasz, J., & Bankovská Motlová, L. (2017). Mental illness stigma among medical students and teachers. *International Journal of Social Psychiatry, 63*(8), 744–751. https://doi.org/10.1177/002076401773534

Khanna, P., & Singh, K. (2021). Stress management training and gratitude journaling in the classroom: An initial investigation in Indian context. *Current Psychology, 40*(11), 1–12. https://doi.org/10.1007/s12144-020-01242-w

Kirschner, B., Goetzl, M., & Curtin, L. (2022). Mental health stigma among college students: Test of an interactive online intervention. *Journal of American College Health, 70*(6), 1831–1838. https://doi.org/10.1080/07448481.2020.1826492

Ledford, V., Lim, J. R., Namkoong, K., Chen, J., & Qin, Y. (2022). The influence of stigmatizing messages on danger appraisal: examining the model of stigma communication for opioid-related stigma, policy support, and related outcomes. *Health Communication, 37*(14), 1765–1777. https://doi.org/10.1080/10410236.2021.1920710

Manago, B., & Krendl, A. C. (2023). Cultivating contact: How social norms can reduce mental illness stigma in college populations. *Stigma and Health, 8*(1), 61–71. https://doi.org/10.1037/sah0000363

Meaney, T., & Rieger, E. (2021). Integrating cognitive dissonance and social consensus to reduce weight stigma. *Body Image, 37*, 117–126. https://doi.org/10.1016/j.bodyim.2021.02.003

Nelson, K. (2024). Stamping Out Stigma Campaign [Campaign Graphic]. Nelson Digital Media. https://knelsondigitalmedia.blogs.lincoln.ac.uk/2016/02/26/stamp-out-stigma/

Rittel, H. W. J., & Webber, M. M. (1973). Dilemmas in a general theory of planning. *Policy Sciences, 4*, 155–169. https://doi.org/10.1007/BF01405730

Rudick, C. K., & Dannel, D. P. (2018). Yes, and…: Continuing the scholarly conversation about mental health stigma in higher education. *Communication Education, 67*(3), 404–408. https://doi.org/10.1080/03634523.2018.1467563

Schnyder, N., Panczak, R., Groth, N., & Schultze-Lutter, F. (2017). Association between mental health-related stigma and active help-seeking: Systematic review and meta-analysis. *British Journal of Psychiatry, 210*(4), 261–268. https://doi.org/10.1192/bjp.bp.116.189464

Shahwan, S., Lau, J. H., Goh, C. M. J., Ong, W. J., Tan, G. T. H., Kwok, K. W., Samari, E., Lee, Y. Y., Teh, W. L., Seet, V., Chang, S., Chong, S. A., & Subramaniam, M. (2020). The potential impact of an anti-stigma intervention on mental health help-seeking attitudes among university students. *BMC Psychiatry, 20*(1), 1–14. https://doi.org/10.1186/s12888-020-02960-y

Smith, R. A. (2007). Language of the lost: An explication of stigma communication. *Communication Theory, 17*(4), 462–485. https://doi.org/10.1111/j.1468-2885.2007.00307.x

Smith, R. A. (2012). An experimental test of stigma communication content with a hypothetical infectious disease alert. *Communication Monographs, 79*(4), 522–538. https://doi-org.proxy-um.researchport.umd.edu/10.1080/03637751.2012.723811

Smith, R. A. (2014). Testing the model of stigma communication with a factorial experiment in an interpersonal context. *Communication Studies, 65*(2), 154–173. https://doi-org.proxy-um.researchport.umd.edu/10.1080/10510974.2013.851095

Smith, R. A., Zhu, X., & Fink, E. L. (2019). Understanding the effects of stigma messages: Danger appraisal and message judgments. *Health Communication, 34*(4), 424–436. https://doi-org.proxy-um.researchport.umd.edu/10.1080/10410236.2017.1405487

Spagnolo, A. B., Murphy, A. A., & Librera, L. A. (2008). Reducing stigma by meeting and learning from people with mental illness. *Psychiatric Rehabilitation Journal, 31*(3), 186–193. https://doi.org/10.2975/31.3.2008.186.193

Stelling, B. E. V., & West, C. P. (2021). Faculty disclosure of personal mental health history and resident physician perceptions of stigma surrounding mental illness. *Academic Medicine, 96*(5), 682–685. https://doi.org/10.1097/ACM.0000000000003941

Substance Abuse and Mental Health Services Administration. (2023a). Key substance use and mental health indicators in the United States: Results from the 2022 National Survey on Drug Use and Health (HHS Publication No. PEP23-07-01-006, NSDUH Series H-58). https://www.samhsa.gov/data/report/2022-nsduh-annual-national-report

Substance Abuse and Mental Health Services Administration. (2023b, October 14). Prevention of substance use and mental disorders. http://www.samhsa.gov/prevention

Thompson, B. (2007). The syllabus as a communication document: Constructing and presenting the syllabus. *Communication Education, 56*(1), 54–71. https://doi.org/10.1080/03634520601011575

Timiskaming Health Unit. (2020). #Stopthestigma Campaign [Campaign Graphic]. New Liskeard, Ontario, Canada. https://timiskaminghu.com/90509/anti-stigma-campaign-and-resources

Vohs, K. D., & Baumeister, R. F. (2004). Understanding self-regulation: An Introduction. In R. F. Baumeister & K. D. Vohs (Eds.), *Handbook of self-regulation: Research, theory, and applications* (pp. 1–9). Guildford Press.

Watson, A. C., Fulambarker, A., Kondrat, D. C., Holley, L. C., Kranke, D., Wilkins, B. T., Stromwall, L. K., & Eack, S. M. (2017). Social work faculty and mental illness stigma. *Journal of Social Work Education, 53*(2), 174–186. https://doi.org/10.1080/10437797.2016.1260506

Zhang, Z., Morgan, A., Armstrong, G., Campbell, A., & Reavley, N. (2024). Public mental illness disclosure on social media and the effects on stigma toward people with mental illness: A systematic review. *Stigma and Health*. Advance online publication. https://doi.org/10.1037/sah0000531

Zimmerman, B. J., & Schunk, D. H. (2011). *Handbook of self-regulation of learning and performance*. Routledge.

Shawna L. Dias, Ph.D., is presently a senior researcher at Hanover Research Council, where she leads projects and provides clients with critical intelligence and strategic direction for mitigating risks and gaining new business. She graduated from the University of Maryland, College Park, where she specialized in public relations, emphasizing behavioral health intervention, DEIB, and organizational crisis communication. Her published research examines the role of reputation management during compounding health crises, leadership development in public relations practice, student perceptions of inclusivity and mental health in higher education, and the influences of specific message frames and social support groups on intervention campaign outcomes.

Romy RW, Ph.D., is an assistant professor at Loyola Marymount University. She earned her Ph.D. in communication from the University of Maryland, College Park. Dr. RW's research focuses on the interrelationships among intercultural communication, mental health, and mediated technologies. She specifically addresses using communication strategies to promote college students' mental health. Additionally, she examines the power dynamics, stereotyping, and prejudice prevalent in intercultural communication that contribute to poorer health outcomes for marginalized and underserved populations.

Chapter 4
Addressing Intersectionality: Challenging Standard Approaches to Addressing Mental Illness Stigma in Higher Education

Jada M. Copeland-Hayes and Jessica D. Remedios

Abstract Mental illness stigma persists in higher education and has negative effects on student help-seeking behaviors, self-esteem, and sense of belonging on campus. Although mental illness stigma is an important issue to address on college campuses, progress cannot be achieved without considering how students from minoritized backgrounds are impacted by intersectional stigma. In this chapter, we consider how students experience mental illness stigma in the context of their various identities and unique lived experiences. We do so by describing the types of stigma and stereotyping students face, institutional ignorance of students' lived experiences, the impact of the institutional past and present on minoritized students, and inadequate and culturally ignorant practices on college campuses. To address intersectional mental illness stigma, we recommend that institutions recognize the needs of the entire student body and not only individuals from various privileged groups. This can be achieved through the active collaboration of multiple departments across campus and addressing policies and procedures that further stigmatize minoritized students. Further, we provide an example of an institution making progress toward incorporating intersectionality theory to address concerns around mental illness stigma on campus.

Keywords Intersectionality · Mental illness · Stigma · Higher education

Historically, higher education in the United States has marginalized individuals from minoritized populations, including faculty, staff, students, and the broader community it serves. Although some would argue substantial progress has been made, especially in the post-Civil Rights Movement era, it is clear there are

---

The authors have no conflicts of interest to declare that are relevant to the content of this chapter.

J. M. Copeland-Hayes (✉) · J. D. Remedios
Department of Psychology, Tufts University, Medford, MA, USA
e-mail: Jada.Copeland@tufts.edu

© The Author(s), under exclusive license to Springer Nature Switzerland AG 2025

K. M. Brennan, K. S. Gorman (eds.), *A University-Wide Approach to Changing Campus Cultures of Mental Illness Stigma*, Knowledge Studies in Higher Education 18, https://doi.org/10.1007/978-3-031-86496-4_4

intentional efforts to maintain the cis-heteronormative, White, patriarchal environment in which higher education was originally created (Academic Leadership Institute, 2021; Carnevale et al., 2018). Impactful events, especially post-2020, have made it clear that minoritized students' experiences and safety, whether physical or psychological, are not priorities for many leaders on and off campus. Some of the many events to which we refer include police brutality toward Black communities, discrimination toward Asian Americans, especially during the COVID-19 pandemic, the Israel-Palestine conflict, frequent hate crimes and mass shootings, and the overturning of affirmative action. This is especially concerning considering higher education has also seen the elimination of diversity, equity, and inclusion (DEI) efforts and spaces coinciding with political and discriminatory agendas to sustain persistent systemic and institutional discrimination in higher education (Chronicle Staff, 2024; Taylor, 2024a).

Indeed, misleading legislation seeks to further disenfranchise minoritized populations (Taylor, 2024a). Several states across the United States have already considered and some already enforced anti-DEI legislation, disproportionally affecting universities in midwestern and southern states (Chronicle Staff, 2024). These efforts have a multitude of consequences, including the prohibition of diversity statements and training, the erasure of resources designated for minoritized populations (e.g., identity-based resource centers), and the teaching of inaccurate histories of discrimination in the United States. Thus, it is imperative to consider how students from minoritized backgrounds, and the resources created for them, are being targeted and how this ultimately is impacting student mental health. This is especially true considering before these occurrences, minoritized students' mental health had already been a concern. Historically, campuses have shown their unwavering commitment to students of privileged backgrounds while only slowly devising efforts, many ineffective and unsustainable, to consider minoritized students. In this chapter, we emphasize the importance of considering the experiences of all students and how their experiences are uniquely shaped by the multiple intersecting identities they possess to address mental health concerns and stigma on campus.

This chapter aims to assess mental illness stigma with an emphasis on intersectional stigma. As such, we focus on services meant to support student mental health that, if ineffective and culturally ignorant, may actually *contribute* to additional stigmatization of minoritized students, sending the signal these services are not designed for their specific needs. We assert adding more resources, programs, and departmental collaboration for students and other members of the campus community, especially faculty and staff, is imperative. Such investments will not be effective at curbing mental health issues if universities are not willing to acknowledge and dismantle institutional and systemic barriers seeking to oppress, exclude, and further stigmatize students from minoritized backgrounds. We acknowledge this chapter does not cover every intersectional experience and encourage universities to use our ideas as a guide to assist with learning about their student body and the histories of the students on their campus. Such education is critical when considering the changes institutions may need to make to consider intersectionality in serving their campus community.

Intersectionality and Mental Illness Stigma

Countless individuals across the United States coping with mental health conditions are unable to acquire necessary treatments and go without care due to fear of judgment from others around them. Research shows people with mental health conditions fail to seek care because they feel at risk of both public and self-stigma (Waqas et al., 2020).[1] College students who view others as holding discriminatory attitudes toward mental illness exhibit low help and treatment seeking behaviors (e.g., medication use, seeking counseling) (Dias & Wang, 2023; Gaddis et al., 2018). They report they cannot disclose mental health concerns to family members holding dismissive beliefs (Dias & Wang, 2023) or to health providers who imply mental illness recovery is not possible (Arboleda-Flórez & Stuart, 2012). Likewise, students who hold discriminatory attitudes toward themselves due to mental illness struggle with low levels of self-esteem and an inability to believe in themselves, resulting in detrimental consequences not only on their productivity but, holistically, to their well-being (Dias & Wang, 2023; Rüsch et al., 2014). These findings are especially concerning for students from minoritized backgrounds given they are also navigating *stereotype threat*, or concerns others are evaluating them using identity-based stereotypes (Aronson et al., 2005).

Importantly, the historical context of mental illness has influenced the stigma present today. From the Middle Ages (500 AD to 1500) through the Enlightenment (1685–1815), society globally perceived individuals dealing with mental illness as being punished by God, leading to their imprisonment and/or execution (Rössler, 2016). Discourse specifically associated Blackness with mental illness to maintain power structures to categorize enslaved African Americans as violent and racially inferior compared to White individuals (Jarman, 2011; Schalk, 2022). Although over time, enslaved peoples were freed, those dealing with mental illness were still targeted and killed, with the scale and scope of such campaigns peaking at various points in history, especially during the atrocities of the Holocaust (Rössler, 2016).

The disenfranchisement of those with mental illness has been exacerbated by negative media portrayal of individuals with mental illnesses and the use of inaccurate, misleading, and often violent, representations rooted in stereotypes (Rössler, 2016). Individuals navigating mental illness are often stereotyped as unpredictable, dangerous, and unreliable (Arboleda-Flórez & Stuart, 2012; Martin, 2010; Rössler, 2016). Simultaneously, Black, Middle Eastern, and Latine individuals navigate stereotypes labeling groups members as dangerous and/or violent (Ghavami & Peplau, 2013). Given the interconnectedness between the stereotyping of individuals with mental illnesses and identity-based stereotypes (e.g., racial, ethnic, religious), it is imperative to focus on the experiences of those with mental illness facing simultaneous forms of oppression.

Intersecting forms of discrimination and exclusion (e.g., racism, sexism, mental illness stigma) create unique experiences and challenges for individuals

[1] Chapter 1 provides a list of these terms and their definitions.

transitioning to college, such as concerns about social exclusion and isolation within a predominately privileged environment (Walton & Cohen, 2011). Individuals who face multiple forms of exclusion are particularly at risk of experiencing struggles with their mental health (Smith & Applegate, 2018). Intersectionality theory seeks to understand unique experiences of marginalization by accounting for the interlocking nature of systems of oppression. In other words, intersectionality calls attention to the qualitatively different experiences faced by individuals with multiple stigmatized identities versus individuals with one or no stigmatized identities (Cole, 2009; Crenshaw, 1989). Only with an intersectional approach will universities be able to provide the most effective and informed mental health services for students while acknowledging students' unique experiences of mental illness stigma. This is crucial considering many students facing the detrimental outcomes of mental illness stigma are also facing various forms of intersectional stigma.

Intersectional Invisibility

Intersectionality theory enables us to understand the complexity and uniqueness of lived experiences and the oppression of individuals who possess multiple stigmatized identities (e.g., marginalization due to religion, race, disability). Intersectionality theory serves not only as a framework within which we can comprehend unique experiences but also to understand how institutions have failed to consider such experiences. The lack of a frame—both psychological and structural—for understanding intersectional experiences leads to *intersectional invisibility* (Coles & Pasek, 2020). Intersectional invisibility demonstrates the ways in which the intersecting ideologies of *androcentrism* (tendency to establish a typical individual as male), *ethnocentrism* (tendency to establish a typical individual within the dominant ethnic group), and *heterocentrism* (tendency to establish a typical individual as heterosexual) deems dominant group members experiences as most important and the societal standard (Purdie-Vaughns & Eibach, 2008). In the context of the United States, these ideologies construct a narrative where White, male, heterosexual experiences are the default human experience resulting in the formation of group-based hierarchies disproportionately allocating resources to dominant groups while stigmatizing and marginalizing subordinate groups (Purdie-Vaughns & Eibach, 2008). Higher education is not exempt from this, as predominately White institutions (PWI) receive more resources (e.g., financial) compared to minority serving institutions. Even when minoritized students attend PWIs, the resources are disproportionally allocated to privileged students in comparison to minoritized students (Carnevale et al., 2018; Estrada et al., 2016).

Purdie-Vaughns and Eibach (2008) emphasized how individuals possessing multiple stigmatized identities (e.g., Black women, trans women of color) experience intersectional invisibility, such that their experiences are ignored and minimized. For example, several studies have demonstrated Black women's faces and contributions to social justice movements (e.g., #MeToo movement) have been ignored in addition to their experiences of discrimination being downplayed in social justice initiatives (e.g., Black Lives Matter) (Biernat & Sesko, 2013; Onwuachi-Willig, 2018; Sesko & Biernat, 2010). Research has identified additional consequences of intersectional invisibility, including the misrepresentation and disempowerment of affected individuals (Purdie-Vaughns & Eibach, 2008; Remedios & Snyder, 2018). For example, historically in the United States, the contributions to social movements (e.g., civil rights movement) by women of color and gay men of color have not been represented in historical texts (Purdie-Vaughns & Eibach, 2008). Additionally, individuals possessing multiple stigmatized identities are burdened with heightened concerns of facing stereotyping and discrimination (Purdie-Vaughns & Eibach, 2008; Remedios & Snyder, 2018). Remedios and Snyder (2018) showed college students possessing multiple stigmatized identities were more likely to feel invisible and at risk for experiencing discrimination and stereotyping in comparison to students possessing single or no stigmatized identities. Higher education is not immune to perpetuating intersectional invisibility because it has an influence on representation, the impact of discrimination, and the allocation of resources on campus. In the subsequent sections, we examine why and how higher education has failed to consider the experiences and mental health concerns of students who possess multiple stigmatized identities.

Impact of Institutional Past and Present on Minoritized Students

Examining the history of discrimination within higher education and the experiences of individuals on and off campus is necessary for understanding mental illness stigma toward minoritized students. Recognizing the influence of the institutional past on the present highlights how systems of oppression, such as racism, sexism, heterosexism, ableism, and other exclusionary practices and ideologies, structure institutions of higher education.

History of Higher Education

Higher education was created to serve a very specific population among citizens in the United States. Most U.S. universities were established on stolen Indigenous land, rooted in Christian practices and beliefs, and catered exclusively to White, able-bodied, cisgender, heterosexual, Christian men (Academic Leadership Institute, 2021). Federal and state legislature legally permitted the discrimination of college applicants from minoritized backgrounds until the Civil Rights Act of 1964, when institutions adopted efforts (such as implementing affirmative action-like policies) to increase equity and diversity among students (FindLaw, 2016; Cleeton,

2012). However, these efforts were then, and are today, almost always met with pushback from legislators, members of the institution's administration, and faculty/staff. The recent (at the time of writing this chapter in March 2024) overturn of affirmative action represents a prominent example of such pushback, as do numerous examples of passed anti-DEI legislation and anti-DEI legislation that will be up for vote soon (Taylor, 2024a). The mistreatment and oppression of individuals from minoritized groups impacts not only present group members, but also future generations (Sotero, 2006; Vines et al., 2017). It is important to acknowledge historical trauma experienced by minoritized individuals in higher education, as well as the accumulation of pain across generations.

Historical trauma has a long-standing impact on students from minoritized backgrounds. For example, research indicates how historical forms of colonialization, such as religious persecution of Muslim and other non-Christian practicing individuals, disenfranchisement of Indigenous populations through land loss, enslavement of Black individuals, and residential segregation of Black and Latine communities, has led to psychological distress among current generations (Sotero, 2006; Vines et al., 2017). This is especially important to consider given there are students who possess multiple stigmatized identities (e.g., stigmatization due to race, ethnicity, socioeconomic status (SES), sexual orientation, ability status) who are simultaneously facing these historical traumas while also facing present day discrimination and exclusion. Ultimately, university leadership must remember these historically inhumane events took place on the same land and in the same states occupied by universities in which current generations of minoritized students face intersecting forms of oppression today.

Discrimination and Mental Health

Minoritized students, especially those facing intersecting forms of oppression, navigate feelings of invisibility in addition to fear of discrimination on campus (Davis, 2008; Remedios & Snyder, 2018). Martin (2010) conducted a survey among Australian college students revealing students navigating mental illness have concerns about stereotyping and prejudice. Considering substantial evidence of maladaptive health outcomes caused by discrimination, the mental health of students possessing multiple stigmatized identities should be a pressing concern on college campuses (Grinshteyn et al., 2022; Massie, 2020; Moody et al., 2023; Seng et al., 2012; Shelton & Lester, 2022; Vines et al., 2017). Grinshteyn et al. (2022) found racially minoritized individuals, women, LGBT, and gender nonconforming students demonstrated a positive correlation between fear of discriminatory violence and poor mental health outcomes (e.g., depression and anxiety). It is imperative for universities to prioritize resources for minoritized student needs by considering identity and other forms of stigma embedded in current mental health support. In the following sections, we discuss these embedded structural barriers including the lack of diverse representation on multiple social identity dimensions, the lack of cultural competency in resource development on campus, and institutional ignorance of students' lived experiences.

Current University Mental Health Services

Mental health services in higher education date back to 1910, when Princeton University offered students emotional support to ease their "academic suffering" (Kraft, 2011). Since then, universities have developed new and more effective ways to support student mental health; however, these mechanisms must specifically target attitudes and concerns held by students of minoritized backgrounds, especially those navigating multiple forms of oppression (Eisenberg et al., 2009). This is essential considering individuals from minoritized backgrounds—especially first-generation students, students of color, immigrant students, undocumented students, and lower SES students—are more at risk of experiencing mistreatment and abuse from mental health providers engaging in harmful and oppressive conduct compared to students of privileged backgrounds (Eisenberg et al., 2009; Mizock & Russinova, 2015; Schalk, 2022). Intersectional invisibility is deeply embedded within university mental health services, creating barriers to accessing conventional avenues of mental health care, such as seeking therapy and counseling. In the following section, we will discuss how current mental health services stigmatize minoritized students.

Lack of Diversity in Staff Representation and Training

Diversity among staff who work in mental health services is an important indicator of whether on-campus services are accessible to minoritized students. The vast majority of the psychiatry physician workforce in the United States, as of 2016, is comprised of White individuals (67.2%) and a nearly even split within the gender binary (50.5% female and 49.5% male) (Wyse et al., 2020). College mental health services tend to lack diversity (on multiple social identity dimensions, including race, ethnicity, sexual orientation, and religion) among staff who are also not trained in areas of identity, diversity, and inclusion to work with minoritized populations (Dias & Wang, 2023; Kraft, 2011). This lack of representation and training has negative effects on students' perceptions of on-campus mental health services, as it indicates these services are not intended for their use and were not designed with students from diverse backgrounds in mind. Students often report feeling disempowered after having negative experiences of being stigmatized by mental health providers (Martin, 2010). Jackson et al. (2022) interviewed first-generation women of color in college who expressed discomfort when seeking counseling and mental health support due to the absence of racial diversity among staff. Consequently, this further limits accessibility, forcing students to suffer in silence or seek outside resources to make up for this lack of support, often with the inaccurate assumption that students have the necessary financial and other forms of support to feasibly access these resources (Martin, 2010).

Inadequate and Culturally Ignorant Campus Resources

Research indicates students are concerned about the lack of education surrounding mental illness and mental illness stigma, the lack of culturally competent mental health training for faculty and staff, and the lack of consideration surrounding culture differences in perceptions of mental health and how it relates to stigma (Moody et al., 2023; Vidourek & Burbage, 2019). Moody et al. (2023) found offering stigma reduction education for students and group therapy services in which minoritized students could dialogue about shared experiences reduced students' self-blame and overall experiences of stigma in relation to their single and intersectional identities. Mental health providers and educators tend not to be properly trained to address intersectional stigma, making conventional avenues of seeking help (e.g., therapy and counseling) not as resourceful (Dias & Wang, 2023). Historically, this has resulted in inaccurate and/or culturally inappropriate mental health diagnoses and differential patient treatment and will often cause on-campus providers to recommend off-campus resources even though students may not have the financial resources to access these services (Dias & Wang, 2023; Massie, 2020). This is especially concerning if the student prefers mental health support from someone who is knowledgeable about working with individuals from their social groups and/or shares identities similar to themselves or if the student does not have financial support, access to health insurance, an accessible means of getting to off-campus services, or lives in certain areas that, by legislation, do not prioritize the needs of minoritized groups (Bradley, 2000; Martin, 2010; Vidourek & Burbage, 2019). These experiences are exacerbated for students living where anti-DEI legislation has already began hindering opportunities for staff and campus leadership to engage in culturally competent training, including counseling center staff (Chronicle Staff, 2024).

Ignorance of Students' Lived Experiences

Students in higher education are often treated as students first, and as human beings second. Students are constantly impacted by distressing and anxiety provoking local and global events (e.g., hate speech on campus, police brutality, international conflicts) that may not even be discussed on mainstream media causing faculty and university leadership to be ignorant to these ongoing issues and fail to empathize with students (Conley et al., 2013; Dias & Wang, 2023). Even more concerning, university leadership and faculty rarely acknowledge these stressors even when they are aware of such events, leaving students to face these challenges while university business proceeds as if nothing has happened (Huston & DiPietro, 2007; Linsenmeyer & Lucas, 2017). Higher education's willingness to neglect these students and failure to recognize the profound impact of on- and off-campus events, especially concerning intersecting forms of identity-based discrimination in which students identify with the victims, results in a severe case of intersectional invisibility and causes students to feel their experiences and mental health are not a priority (Huston & DiPietro, 2007). In some cases, university leadership and faculty do nothing, and in other cases they make statements that inadequately address the specific occurrences. Neither response empowers students and reflect faculty and university leaders' unwillingness to directly address these issues; this results in detrimental mental health outcomes for impacted students such as diminished sense of belonging resulting from insufficient institutional support (McKenzie, 2020). Research has shown the importance of faculty and university leaders' recognition of students' lived experiences on and off campus, considering students are looking to them for support whether by simply acknowledging these issues or through more structured support in the classroom (e.g., more flexibility, discussions of the event in the course material) (Huston & DiPietro, 2007; Linsenmeyer & Lucas, 2017).

Practices in Mental Illness Stigma Reduction

Research on mental illness stigma reduction has shown several ways to approach stigma reduction on campus, especially through educational initiatives aimed to combat misinformation and contact-based education (Arboleda-Flórez & Stuart, 2012; Rössler, 2016; Smith & Applegate, 2018; Waqas et al., 2020). Conley (2013) conducted an evaluative review assessing the effectiveness of 83 intervention strategies conducted in higher education focusing on mental health promotion and prevention showcasing the importance of collaboration among multiple departments (e.g., student affairs, counseling centers, advising) to achieve maximum outreach to the student population. Many of these methods have included ineffective anti-stigma campaigns, especially on social media, originally intended to inform students of resources or mitigate stigma felt by students given some students are unaware of the services offered at their institution (Hyun et al., 2006). Even when several different methods (e.g., social media campaign, information sessions, changing/updating websites) are used to combat mental illness stigma on campus, students have indicated receiving information on mental health resources is more beneficial and accessible when it comes directly from the students' academic department (Dias & Wang, 2023). Future use of institutional and departmental education-based programming for faculty, staff, and students should emphasize intersectional experiences to reach students facing very unique challenges of intersectional invisibility within existing mental illness stigma reduction practices (Oexle & Corrigan, 2018). The next section of this chapter includes examples of practical approaches used at one university to address some of these concerns.

Tufts University as a Practical Approach

Given the current issues (e.g., failing to consider intersectionality) in mental illness services and stigma in higher education, it is imperative for departments to collaborate across the university to maximize accessibility to mental health support. Critically, accessibility looks different for every student, and this chapter seeks to provide a concrete example of a university, Tufts University, making strides in departmental collaboration across campus to address students' needs holistically. We highlight some (but not all) departments and resources at Tufts reflecting efforts to prioritize students' needs surrounding the intersection of mental illness and identity-based stigma.

Tufts University, a private, prestigious university with a substantial endowment, was founded in 1852 in the state of Massachusetts on stolen land from the following Indigenous tribes: the Massachusett Tribe and Mashpee Wampanoag Tribe. Tufts was initially founded as a Christian institution but no longer identifies as such. Although the institution has seen increasing diversity among faculty, students, and staff, Tufts remains as a predominantly White institution with more progress to be achieved ("History of Tufts University," n.d.). The student, faculty, and staff populations are primarily composed of women—the majority of whom identify as White—and most students are from the United States (Office of the Vice Provost for Institutional Inclusive Excellence, n.d.). We acknowledge and recognize Tufts University has also encountered the issues highlighted earlier in this chapter (e.g., discrimination in its institutional history, understaffed resources, difference in communication regarding resources for undergraduate and graduate/professional students). We also understand there is certain state legislation in Massachusetts (e.g., expansion of the protected class) making it possible for Tufts to have certain identity-based services and spaces, programming, and resources for students that schools in other states may not be able to employ. Although Tufts has more progress to make regarding addressing intersectional mental illness stigma, university-wide collaborative efforts have enabled departments to be more intentional about recognizing student experiences regarding different identities they may possess through creating multiple spaces of seeking care beyond standard routes.

We encourage other universities to initiate dialogue between campus-wide departments, especially counseling services and identity-centered spaces, to discuss programming and structural approaches tailored to community needs. Importantly, we emphasize adding resources and programs will not address the deeper systemic and structural inequities embedded within an institution but can provide students with valuable support while navigating these challenges. The next sections of this chapter will include information about various departments at Tufts implementing intersectional mental illness stigma reduction resources on campus. Department staff were contacted for clarification of offered services and resources to provide an accurate representation of department efforts.

Identity Centers

The identity centers fall under the Tufts University Division of Student Diversity and Inclusion (Division of Student Diversity and Inclusion, n.d.). Their purpose is to prioritize students' needs by providing safe spaces for students possessing various social identities who may not feel represented in other spaces across campus. Identity-based spaces are essential as they provide community and space for minoritized experiences with research underscoring the importance for students to have identity-based spaces as they may serve as more reliable and empowering support in comparison to mental health services for some minoritized students (Taylor, 2024b; Zhang et al., 2022). There are eight Identity Centers at Tufts: the Africana Center, Asian American Center, Center for STEM Diversity, FIRST (First Resource) Center, Indigenous Center, Latinx Center, LGBT Center, and Women's Center. These centers often collaborate and communicate with one another to consider the intersectional needs of students and consult with Counseling and Mental Health Services (CMHS). Two of the main goals of the centers is to (1) help Tufts shift away from traditional ways of thinking about mental health services and stigma and (2) make progress toward diversity in representation among the employed staff. Additionally, the centers evaluate whether resources, including funding and staff members, are equitably distributed across the centers. Below, we highlight four of these centers to provide examples of how these identity-based spaces address students' intersecting needs through programming, resources, and other forms of support.

Asian American Center

The Asian American Center (AAC) supports Asian and Asian American students through identity development (e.g., considering immigrant status, being multiracial, and adoptee experiences), processing historical trauma related to the treatment of Asian communities in the United States, and navigating institutional systems in higher education (Asian American Center, n.d.). The center holds space for discussing experiences surrounding being an international student and the difficulties international students have while navigating marginalization and isolation (Bradley, 2000). Specifically, the center hosts programming to support community building among and within diverse ethnicities and cultures in the Asian community (Asian American Center Resources, n.d.). Notably, the AAC holds a peer leadership program for first-year and transfer students by providing space for mentorship and holding workshops to learn more about Asian American identity and on-campus resources. Through this, supporting student organizations in the *Pan Asian Council*, and other collaboratively created resources mentioned below (e.g., CMHS liaison and Chaplaincy liaison), the center can provide students with support that considers multiple aspects of their identity.

FIRST Resource Center

The FIRST Resource Center serves students who self-identify as first-generation, low-income, undocumented, and any combination of these identities (FIRST Resource Center, n.d.). The center provides a safe space recognizing each student faces a unique struggle. Some of this support may include access codes alleviating course costs, summer bridge programs to build community before arriving at Tufts, and financial support for study abroad opportunities. The center makes it clear that concerns surrounding lack of finances, knowledge about resources, and documentation causes unfair disparities between privileged and minoritized students in professional and academic opportunities which may contribute to unfair burdens, including poor mental health outcomes, for the students who make use of their resources. Importantly, we recognize the active efforts of the center to protect students such that they refrain from publicizing all aspects of their work and programming to avoid exploiting students and instead, directly contact students who possess these various identities.

LGBT Center

The LGBT (lesbian, gay, bisexual, transgender) Center seeks to provide a safe and celebratory space for queer students and allies on campus while also providing education on gender, sexuality, and intersections of these and other identities (LGBT Center, n.d.). The center also provides support to students who are transitioning in their gender identity and sexuality given students may experience these changes during their time on campus. Staff members pay careful attention to programming, resources, and diversity of their staff to provide an inclusive space given queer communities may also experience marginalization by others in the queer community due to other identities (e.g., race, gender, socioeconomic status) they possess. Specifically, the center supports several student groups that focus on LGBT issues, such as the *Queer Desis* and *Disability Queers* (LGBTQIA+ Student Groups, n.d.). Queer Desis is a student group, supported by the LGBT Center, the Women's Center, and the Asian American Center, designated as a space for queer South Asian students to discuss their experiences and build community. Disability queers is a peer-led group that centers the experiences of students who identify as queer and disabled to build community in exploring intersecting forms of oppression routed in heterosexism and ableism. Through student groups such as these, in addition to other provided resources (e.g., online materials and training for faculty/staff and students), the center provides students with community and support using an intersectional lens.

Women's Center

The Women's Center is unlike many traditional women's centers on college campuses because it focuses on the social construct of gender and how it is shaped by oppression (Women's Center, n.d.). The staff prioritizes having diversity among its employees and openly does not act within a White feminist framework that prioritizes cisgender heterosexual women from privileged socioeconomic and religious backgrounds (Borah et al., 2023; Jonsson, 2016). Instead, the Women's Center welcomes students from all gender identities who want to discuss and dismantle patriarchal systems and provides safe spaces for conversations about gender that deconstruct the binary of men and women. The center also supports students by prioritizing important conversations surrounding gender and current events (e.g., social movements, international conflicts) that students are navigating to consider the overall wellness of the students. The center makes it clear there are multiple effective ways to provide mental health support to students (e.g., providing mentorship and noticing changing behaviors among students, such as physical health, lack of engagement, and social withdrawal) to ensure that minoritized students are being reached.

Center for Awareness, Resources, and Education

The Center for Awareness, Resources, and Education (CARE) is a confidential resource that functions to fulfill two main goals: (1) responding to and (2) preventing sexual misconduct across the university (CARE: Sexual Misconduct Resources and Prevention, n.d.). They also prioritize messages of inclusion of queer communities through their use of cues, including the LGBTQIA+ flag in the center logo and a LGBTQ+ resource page (LGBTQ+, n.d.), and promote feelings of safety for queer individuals and other minoritized students through collaboration efforts with the identity centers to make sure students are not being neglected. The center also provides numerous online identity-based resources, such as the *National Queer and Trans Therapist of Color Network*, for students who have experienced intersecting forms of violence and for students seeking counseling from practitioners with similar identities who center these intersectional experiences. Through providing resources such as these and bringing in a diversity, equity, inclusion, and well-being specialist focusing on violence, the center has been able to recognize their privilege and create strategic plans toward ensuring maximum outreach and implementing diversity, equity, inclusion, and justice practices.

Chaplaincy

The University Chaplaincy provides confidential support for the Tufts community considering the role of religion, spirituality, ethics, and culture throughout a student's lifespan (University Chaplaincy, n.d.). The Chaplaincy serves as a space for students to bring concerns surrounding mental health and conflict in navigating conversations about mental illness, especially concerns of how conversations about mental illness may be stigmatized in various religious and cultural contexts. Upon entering this environment, students might already be grappling with both public and self-stigma. They require thoughtful support, especially if they have encountered dismissive attitudes in prior discussions on mental health, particularly from individuals whose religious beliefs link mental illness to spirituality rather than recognizing it as a genuine concern (Massie, 2020). The Chaplaincy has developed protocols for helping community members with mental health needs and collaborates with other departments at Tufts on diverse approaches for offering students daily support while considering the uniqueness and complexity of their experiences. For example, the Chaplaincy collaborates with the LGBT Center through an initiative called *True Colors* to provide space for queer (LGBTQ community) students to discuss the intersections of their queer and religious experiences with other queer students (LGBTQIA+ Student Groups, n.d.). Initiatives such as this ensure the creation of a collaborative community of care that does not make assumptions about students' mental health needs but prioritizes students' needs without limiting students' access to mental health support based on their own religious or spiritual practice.

Counseling and Mental Health Services

Tufts' Counseling and Mental Health Services (CMHS) provides students with comprehensive mental health support and education while prioritizing prevention and outreach (Counseling and Mental Health Service, n.d.). Prevention and outreach methods include an annual wellness fair that showcases other resources on campus (e.g., identity centers) and continuing education for staff on best practices. CMHS considers representation of language in addition to identities among staff to increase the options for students who may need identity-based support. In addition, CMHS holds *Let's Talk* in the identity centers to provide a space for low commitment conversations with a CMHS counselor for students facing multiple forms of stigma and mental health concerns (Let's Talk, n.d.). They have also appointed liaisons to the identity centers to promote conversations with students surrounding life as a student, mental health concerns, and make referrals where appropriate based on student needs. This sensitivity to intersectional needs empowers CMHS to provide informed resources for specific student needs based on their various identities, such as a portal for students seeking providers of a specific identity (e.g., Latine therapist) and identity-based counseling groups and workshops (Counseling Groups and Workshops, n.d.; Identity Based Resources, n.d.). This has allowed CMHS to reach students who may be more prone to encountering mental illness stigma and other forms of stigma while equipping them to help themselves and seek support on campus outside of CMHS.

Conclusion

Although efforts to mitigate the effects of mental illness stigma have been implemented in institutions of higher education, such efforts tend to center around students whose identities are privileged. Effective and sustainable initiatives addressing mental illness stigma on campus must involve efforts from university leadership to further their understanding of the multifaceted experiences of students. Cultural competency and willingness to diversify staff are essential in mental illness services and stigma reduction given the efforts to remove identity considerations, especially from an intersectional lens. Universities must understand there is no standard way to approach mental health or stigma reduction as so-called "standards" stigmatize students whose mental health support may involve connecting with identity-based services and resources rather than conventional avenues of seeking help (e.g., therapy and counseling). Relying on these inadequate and culturally ignorant mental health services and stigma reduction methods will continue to perpetuate exclusion of overlooked and unheard students, especially those navigating multiple forms of oppression simultaneously.

References

Academic Leadership Institute. (2021). The history of diversity in higher education | ALI series part I. https://sites.lsa.umich.edu/leadership-institute/2021/06/25/the-history-of-diversity-in-higher-education-ali-series-part-i/.

Arboleda-Flórez, J., & Stuart, H. (2012). From sin to science: Fighting the stigmatization of mental illnesses. *The Canadian Journal of Psychiatry, 57*(8), 457–463. https://doi.org/10.1177/070674371205700803

Aronson, E., Wilson, T. D., & Sommers, S. R. (2005). *Social psychology*. Pearson Education India.

Asian American Center. (n.d.). Arts and sciences, engineering, SMFA at Tufts. https://students.tufts.edu/division-student-diversity-and-inclusion/communities/asian-american-center

Asian American Center Resources. (n.d.). Arts and sciences, engineering, SMFA at Tufts. https://students.tufts.edu/division-student-diversity-and-inclusion/communities/asian-american-center/asian-american-center-resources

Biernat, M., & Sesko, A. K. (2013). Evaluating the contributions of members of mixed-sex work teams: Race and gender matter. *Journal of Experimental Social Psychology, 49*(3), 471–476. https://doi.org/10.1016/j.jesp.2013.01.008

Borah, P., Ghosh, S., Suk, J., Mini, D. S., & Sun, L. (2023). Feminism not for all? The discourse around white feminism across five social media platforms. *Social Media+ Society, 9*(3), 20563051231186862. https://doi.org/10.1177/20563051231186862

Bradley, G. (2000). Responding effectively to the mental health needs of international students. *Higher Education, 39*(4), 417–433. https://doi.org/10.1023/A:1003938714191

CARE: Sexual Misconduct Resources and Prevention. (n.d.). Tufts University. https://care.tufts.edu/

Carnevale, A. P., Van Der Werf, M., Quinn, M. C., Strohl, J., & Repnikov, D. (2018). Our separate & unequal public colleges: How public colleges reinforce white racial privilege and marginalize Black and Latino students. Georgetown University Center on Education and the Workforce. https://cew.georgetown.edu/wp-content/uploads/SAUStates_FR.pdf

ChronicleStaff.(2024)DEIlegislationtracker.TheChronicalofHigherEducation.https://www.chronicle.com/article/here-are-the-states-where-lawmakers-are-seeking-to-ban-colleges-dei-efforts.

Cleeton, C. (2012). Access to higher education: A national and Princeton timeline. Princeton University Archives. https://universityarchives.princeton.edu/2012/10/access-to-higher-education-a-national-and-princeton-timeline/

Cole, E. R. (2009). Intersectionality and research in psychology. *American Psychologist, 64*(3), 170–180. https://doi.org/10.1037/a0014564

Coles, S. M., & Pasek, J. (2020). Intersectional invisibility revisited: How group prototypes lead to the erasure and exclusion of Black women. *Translational Issues in Psychological Science, 6*(4), 314–324. https://doi.org/10.1037/tps0000256

Conley, C. S., Durlak, J. A., & Dickson, D. A. (2013). An evaluative review of outcome research on universal mental health promotion and prevention programs for higher education students. *Journal of American College Health, 61*(5), 286–301. https://doi.org/10.1080/07448481.2013.802237

Counseling and Mental Health Service. (n.d.). Arts and sciences, engineering, SMFA at Tufts. https://students.tufts.edu/health-wellness/mental-health/counseling-and-mental-health-service

Counseling Groups and Workshops. (n.d.). Arts and sciences, engineering, SMFA at Tufts. https://students.tufts.edu/health-wellness/counseling-and-mental-health-service/our-services/counseling-groups-and-workshops

Crenshaw, K. (1989). Demarginalizing the intersection of race and sex: A Black feminist critique of antidiscrimination doctrine, feminist theory, and antiracist politics. *University of Chicago Legal Forum, 1*(8), 139–167. https://chicagounbound.uchicago.edu/uclf/vol1989/iss1/8/

Davis, K. (2008). Intersectionality as buzzword: A sociology of science perspective on what makes a feminist theory successful. *Feminist Theory, 9*(1), 67–85. https://doi.org/10.1177/1464700108086364

Dias, S., & Wang, X. (2023). Exploring participants' experiences of mental health and stigma in American colleges. *Journal of American College Health, 71*(7), 2074–2084. https://doi.org/10.1080/07448481.2021.1954652

Division of Student Diversity and Inclusion. (n.d.). Arts and sciences, engineering, SMFA at Tufts. https://students.tufts.edu/division-student-diversity-and-inclusion-dsdi

Eisenberg, D., Downs, M. F., Golberstein, E., & Zivin, K. (2009). Stigma and help seeking for mental health among college students. *Medical Care Research and Review, 66*(5), 522–541. https://doi.org/10.1177/1077558709335173

Estrada, M., Burnett, M., Campbell, A. G., Campbell, P. B., Denetclaw, W. F., Gutiérrez, C. G., Hurtado, S., John, G. H., Matsui, J., McGee, R., Okpodu, C. M., Robinson, T. J., Summers, M. F., Werner-Washburne, M., & Zavala, M. (2016). Improving underrepresented minority student persistence in STEM. *CBE—Life Sciences Education, 15*(3), es5. https://doi.org/10.1187/cbe.16-01-0038

FindLaw. (2016, September 9). Affirmative action and college admissions. https://www.findlaw.com/education/higher-education/affirmative-action-and-college-admissions.html

FIRST Resource Center. (n.d.). Arts and sciences, engineering, SMFA at Tufts. https://students.tufts.edu/division-student-diversity-and-inclusion/communities/first-resource-center

Gaddis, S. M., Ramirez, D., & Hernandez, E. L. (2018). Contextualizing public stigma: Endorsed mental health treatment stigma on college and university campuses. *Social Science & Medicine, 197*, 183–191. https://doi.org/10.1016/j.socscimed.2017.11.029
Ghavami, N., & Peplau, L. A. (2013). An intersectional analysis of gender and ethnic stereotypes: Testing three hypotheses. *Psychology of Women Quarterly, 37*(1), 113–127. https://doi.org/10.1177/0361684312464203
Grinshteyn, E., Whaley, R., & Couture, M. C. (2022). High fear of discriminatory violence among racial, gender, and sexual minority college students and its association with anxiety and depression. *International Journal of Environmental Research and Public Health, 19*(4), 2117. https://doi.org/10.3390/ijerph19042117
History of Tufts University. (n.d.). Tufts university undergraduate admissions. https://admissions.tufts.edu/discover-tufts/tufts-history/
Huston, T. A., & DiPietro, M. (2007). 13: In the eye of the storm: Students' perceptions of helpful faculty actions following a collective tragedy. *To Improve the Academy, 25*(1), 207–224. https://doi.org/10.1002/j.2334-4822.2007.tb00483.x
Hyun, J. K., Quinn, B. C., Madon, T., & Lustig, S. (2006). Graduate student mental health: Needs assessment and utilization of counseling services. *Journal of College Student Development, 47*(3), 247–266. https://doi.org/10.1353/csd.2006.0030
Identity Based Resources. (n.d.). Arts and sciences, engineering, SMFA at Tufts. https://students.tufts.edu/health-wellness/counseling-and-mental-health-service/identity-based-resources
Jackson, A., Colson-Fearon, B., & Versey, H. S. (2022). Managing intersectional invisibility and hypervisibility during the transition to college among first-generation women of color. *Psychology of Women Quarterly, 46*(3), 354–371. https://doi.org/10.1177/03616843221106087
Jarman, M. (2011). Coming up from underground: Uneasy dialogues at the intersections of race, mental illness, and disability studies. In C. M. Bell (Ed.), *Blackness and disability: Critical examinations and cultural interventions* (pp. 9–30). Michigan State University Press.
Jonsson, T. (2016). The narrative reproduction of white feminist racism. *Feminist Review, 113*(1), 50–67. https://doi.org/10.1057/fr.2016.2
Kraft, D. P. (2011). One hundred years of college mental health. *Journal of American College Health, 59*(6), 477–481. https://doi.org/10.1080/07448481.2011.569964
Let's Talk. (n.d.). Arts and sciences, engineering, SMFA at Tufts. https://students.tufts.edu/health-wellness/counseling-and-mental-health-service/our-services/lets-talk
LGBT Center. (n.d.). Arts and sciences, engineering, SMFA at Tufts. https://students.tufts.edu/division-student-diversity-and-inclusion/communities/lgbt-center
LGBTQIA+ Student Groups. (n.d.). Arts and sciences, engineering, SMFA at Tufts. https://students.tufts.edu/division-student-diversity-and-inclusion/communities/lgbt-center/lgbt-student-groups-and-centers
Linsenmeyer, W., & Lucas, T. (2017). Student perceptions of the faculty response during the civil unrest in Ferguson, Missouri. *International Journal of Teaching and Learning in Higher Education, 29*(3), 524–533. https://files.eric.ed.gov/fulltext/EJ1150795.pdf
Martin, J. M. (2010). Stigma and student mental health in higher education. *Higher Education Research & Development, 29*(3), 259–274. https://doi.org/10.1080/07294360903470969
Massie, M. (2020). A facilitators guide: Intersectional approaches to mental health education. The University of British Columbia. https://wellbeing.ubc.ca/sites/wellbeing.ubc.ca/files/u9/Facilitator%20Guide%20-%20Intersectionality%20and%20Mental%20Health.pdf.
McKenzie, L. (2020). Words matter for college presidents, but so will actions. Inside Higher Ed. https://insidehighered.com/news/2020/06/08/searching-meaningful-response-college-leaders-killing-george-floyd.
Mizock, L., & Russinova, Z. (2015). Intersectional stigma and the acceptance process of women with mental illness. *Women & Therapy, 38*(1–2), 14–30. https://doi.org/10.1080/02703149.2014.978211
Moody, A. T., Lewis, J. A., & Owens, G. P. (2023). Gendered racism, coping, and traumatic stress among Black women: The moderating roles of the strong Black woman schema

and womanist attitudes. *Psychology of Women Quarterly, 47*(2), 197–212. https://doi.org/10.1177/03616843221143752

Oexle, N., & Corrigan, P. W. (2018). Understanding mental illness stigma toward persons with multiple stigmatized conditions: Implications of intersectionality theory. *Psychiatric Services, 69*(5), 587–589. https://doi.org/10.1176/appi.ps.201700312

Office of the Vice Provost for Institutional Inclusive Excellence. (n.d.). Diversity overview. https://diversity.tufts.edu/diversity-overview/

Onwuachi-Willig, A. (2018). What about #UsToo?: The invisibility of race in the #MeToo movement. *The Yale Law Journal, 128*, 105. https://www.yalelawjournal.org/forum/what-about-ustoo

Purdie-Vaughns, V., & Eibach, R. P. (2008). Intersectional invisibility: The distinctive advantages and disadvantages of multiple subordinate-group identities. *Sex Roles, 59*(5), 377–391. https://doi.org/10.1007/s11199-008-9424-4

Remedios, J. D., & Snyder, S. H. (2018). Intersectional oppression: Multiple stigmatized identities and perceptions of invisibility, discrimination, and stereotyping. *Journal of Social Issues, 74*(2), 265–281. https://doi.org/10.1111/josi.12268

Rössler, W. (2016). The stigma of mental disorders: A millennia-long history of social exclusion and prejudices. *EMBO Reports, 17*(9), 1250–1253. https://doi.org/10.15252/embr.201643041

Rüsch, N., Corrigan, P. W., Heekeren, K., Theodoridou, A., Dvorsky, D., Metzler, S., Müller, M., Walitza, S., & Rössler, W. (2014). Well-being among persons at risk of psychosis: The role of self-labeling, shame, and stigma stress. *Psychiatric Services, 65*(4), 483–489. https://doi.org/10.1176/appi.ps.201300169

Schalk, S. (2022). *Black disability politics*. Duke University Press.

Seng, J. S., Lopez, W. D., Sperlich, M., Hamama, L., & Reed Meldrum, C. D. (2012). Marginalized identities, discrimination burden, and mental health: Empirical exploration of an interpersonal-level approach to modeling intersectionality. *Social Science & Medicine, 75*(12), 2437–2445. https://doi.org/10.1016/j.socscimed.2012.09.023

Sesko, A. K., & Biernat, M. (2010). Prototypes of race and gender: The invisibility of Black women. *Journal of Experimental Social Psychology, 46*(2), 356–360. https://doi.org/10.1016/j.jesp.2009.10.016

Shelton, S. A., & Lester, A. O. S. (2022). A narrative exploration of the importance of intersectionality in a Black trans woman's mental health experiences. *International Journal of Transgender Health, 23*(1–2), 108–121. https://doi.org/10.1080/26895269.2020.1838393

Smith, R. A., & Applegate, A. (2018). Mental health stigma and communication and their intersections with education. *Communication Education, 67*(3), 382–393. https://doi.org/10.1080/03634523.2018.1465988

Sotero, M. (2006). A conceptual model of historical trauma: Implications for public health practice and research. *Journal of Health Disparities Research and Practice, 1*(1), 93–108. https://ssrn.com/abstract=1350062

Taylor, A. (2024a, January 18). 3 ways that anti-DEI efforts are changing how colleges operate. *The Chronical of Higher Education*. https://www.chronicle.com/article/3-ways-that-anti-dei-efforts-are-changing-how-colleges-operate

Taylor, A. (2024b, January 26). Colleges need to understand the link between discrimination and student mental health, report says. *The Chronical of Higher Education*. https://www.chronicle.com/article/colleges-need-to-understand-the-link-between-discrimination-and-student-mental-health-report-says

University Chaplaincy. (n.d.). Tufts University. https://chaplaincy.tufts.edu/

Vidourek, R. A., & Burbage, M. (2019). Positive mental health and mental health stigma: A qualitative study assessing student attitudes. *Mental Health & Prevention, 13*, 1–6. https://doi.org/10.1016/j.mhp.2018.11.006

Vines, A. I., Ward, J. B., Cordoba, E., & Black, K. Z. (2017). Perceived racial/ethnic discrimination and mental health: A review and future directions for social epidemiology. *Current Epidemiology Reports, 4*, 156–165. https://doi.org/10.1007/s40471-017-0106-z

Walton, G. M., & Cohen, G. L. (2011). A brief social-belonging intervention improves academic and health outcomes of minority students. *Science, 331*(6023), 1447–1451. https://doi.org/10.1126/science.1198364

Waqas, A., Malik, S., Fida, A., Abbas, N., Mian, N., Miryala, S., Amray, A. N., Shah, Z., & Naveed, S. (2020). Interventions to reduce stigma related to mental illnesses in educational institutes: A systematic review. *Psychiatric Quarterly, 91*(3), 887–903. https://doi.org/10.1007/s11126-020-09751-4

Women's Center. (n.d.). Arts and sciences, engineering, SMFA at Tufts. https://students.tufts.edu/division-student-diversity-and-inclusion/communities/womens-center

Wyse, R., Hwang, W. T., Ahmed, A. A., Richards, E., & Deville, C. (2020). Diversity by race, ethnicity, and sex within the US psychiatry physician workforce. *Academic Psychiatry, 44*(5), 523–530. https://doi.org/10.1007/s40596-020-01276-z

Zhang, X., Wong, G. T. F., Liu, C. H., Hahm, H. C., & Chen, J. A. (2022). International student stressors and mental health during the COVID-19 pandemic: A qualitative study. *Journal of American College Health, 72*(4), 1027–1033. https://doi.org/10.1080/07448481.2022.2068015

Jada M. Copeland-Hayes, M.S. is a doctoral candidate at Tufts University, studying social psychology in the Social Identity and Stigma Lab (SIS) led by Dr. Jessica Remedios. Her research focuses on the sociocontexual factors that influence identity-based experiences of discrimination in institutions (e.g., higher education and workplace) at the interpersonal and systemic level. Particularly, her work considers the role of intersectionality in lived experiences of discrimination faced by minoritized communities.

Jessica D. Remedios, Ph.D., is an associate professor of psychology at Tufts University and PI of the Social Identity and Stigma Lab. Her research examines how people experience their social identities and cope with stigma caused by prejudice and discrimination. Her research draws on theories of intergroup relations and social cognition to understand the psychological effects of stigma. Because stigmas (caused by, for example, systems of racism and sexism) are experienced simultaneously, she aims to take an intersectional approach in her research.

Chapter 5
Risks and Rewards: A Black Scholar's Efforts to Fight Stigma Through Disclosure

Daniel J. Blake

Abstract In this chapter, I reflect on the effects of my decision to publicly disclose that I have bipolar disorder. As an early career, Black scholar in the United States, this decision had risks related both to the precarity of my position in academia and the racialized stigma of mental illness facing Black communities. I contextualize my experiences by briefly reviewing research that sheds light on how mental illness diagnoses have been weaponized against Black communities, resulting in a unique form of stigma. I reflect on some of the personal tolls of sharing that I have bipolar disorder, which have manifested at various stages of my disclosure. Subsequently, I discuss how my disclosure has led to a range of positive outcomes, some of which I hoped for at the time I made the decision to disclose, and others which have been unexpected. I conclude by pointing to ways in which various stakeholders can more critically examine barriers facing people of color with mental illnesses in higher education and advance more inclusive campus environments.

Keywords Mental illness · Disability · Stigma · Intersectionality · Black faculty

> I posit the importance of disclosure exactly because we do occupy high-status positions, positions that we were able to achieve in spite of having a severe mental illness…. Having succeeded despite suffering from bipolar disorder, I see myself as someone who students might look up to…. [W]e cannot be models of success, we cannot shift the ways in which we have been portrayed by mainstream society, if we do not reveal ourselves to be who we truly are. (Skogen, 2012, p. 493)

I am a Black man with bipolar disorder who is a tenure-track assistant professor of higher education in the United States. The journey to writing those words has been one of highs and lows, doubts and anxieties, and affirmation and joy.

The author has no conflicts of interest to declare that are relevant to the content of this chapter.

D. J. Blake (✉)
Department of Education Policy Studies, Georgia State University, Atlanta, GA, USA
e-mail: dblake11@gsu.edu

© The Author(s), under exclusive license to Springer Nature Switzerland AG 2025

K. M. Brennan, K. S. Gorman (eds.), *A University-Wide Approach to Changing Campus Cultures of Mental Illness Stigma*, Knowledge Studies in Higher Education 18, https://doi.org/10.1007/978-3-031-86496-4_5

I first experienced symptoms of bipolar disorder at the age of 22, when I was a master's student studying Arabic. My mental health spiraled after Trayvon Martin was killed and while in crisis I was arrested and taken to jail. In jail, I was brutalized by correctional officers. I was resistant to my diagnosis for years but eventually accepted it and began to receive care for it.

When I was 26, I began my PhD program. I completed my coursework and dissertation on time without accommodation. Had I needed accommodations, I doubt I would have sought them due to my resistance to the idea of disclosing that I have bipolar disorder. I probably would have left the program rather than share my diagnosis. I did not disclose to anyone—new friends I made in my graduate program and field, professors, or collaborators—due to risks my disclosure would alienate me and jeopardize my career. My numerous experiences hearing others in academia speak disparagingly about people with mental illnesses and hurl "bipolar" as an insult confirmed these risks were very real.

I completed my PhD program in 2020, during the beginning of the COVID-19 pandemic, and began a postdoctoral fellowship. The racial justice protests and continued brutality of Black people by police led me to write an op-ed in *Diverse Issues in Higher Education* in which I shared my personal experience with police brutality and discussed having bipolar disorder (Blake, 2020a). This was my first act of public disclosure and the first time many people I know—in and out of academia—learned about my experiences and this aspect of my identity.

In this chapter, I reflect on the effects of my decision to publicly disclose that I have bipolar disorder. I contextualize my experiences by briefly reviewing research on the relationship between mental illness and Black communities as well as literature about mental illness stigma in academia. I also reflect on the personal tolls of my disclosure before discussing the ways in which my disclosure has been rewarding. I conclude by pointing to ways in which various stakeholders can more critically examine barriers facing people of color with mental illnesses in higher education and advance more inclusive campus environments.

Risks of Disclosure

In this section I first contextualize the risks of my disclosure through sketching the unique historical stigma of mental illness in Black communities, which is rooted in how mental illness has been weaponized to oppress us. Second, I discuss mental illness stigma in academia and further situate my disclosure by discussing risks related to my career stage and academic field. Subsequently, I discuss risks as I personally experienced them during my disclosure.

Weaponization of Mental Illness against Black Communities

Skepticism about mental illness diagnoses is common in Black communities and is a logical response to how mental illness has been weaponized to subjugate Black people in the United States. This history has led many Black people to disidentify from mental illness and avoid discussing it (Bailey & Mobley, 2019). Mental illness was used as a rationale to enslave Africans (Baynton, 2017). Supporters of slavery pathologized Black people's behaviors when they undermined the institution of slavery. The desire for freedom and attempt to escape captivity was classified as "drapetomania," for which whipping was both a preventative measure and cure (Baynton, 2017). "Dysaesthesia aechiopis" was purportedly a mental illness that caused mischief and laziness (Baynton, 2017).

The weaponization of mental illness as a rationale for oppressing Black people has persisted beyond the abolishment of slavery. During the civil rights movement, psychiatrists introduced "protest psychosis" as a symptom of schizophrenia (Metzl, 2010). These psychiatrists asserted that Black people's participation in protest was a result of their psychotic breaks from reality, as opposed to a rational response to systemic racism and the denial of their civil and human rights (Metzl, 2010). Protest psychosis was thus leveraged to detain Black protestors in psychiatric institutions (Metzl, 2010).

Contemporary research sheds light on persistent ways in which mental illness is weaponized against Black communities. Black children are overrepresented in the foster care system and mental illness diagnoses are among the rationale used to remove children from their families (Roberts, 2022). These family separations are often done expeditiously rather than as a last resort, and with lack of consideration of existing supports and potential forms of assistance (Roberts, 2022). Studies also suggest Black people with mental illnesses are disproportionately criminalized and incarcerated (Appel et al., 2020), which is another mechanism through which Black families are separated.

Further, mental illness is used as a justification for police violence against Black people (Perry & Carter-Long, 2016). Black people with mental illnesses are over-represented among victims of police brutality (Perry & Carter-Long, 2016). These realities are what motivated me to write publicly about having bipolar disorder and my experience of police brutality, as I sought to act in solidarity and push for changes in responses to people who are experiencing mental health crises. However, the historical stigma of mental illness in Black communities meant that one risk of my disclosure was alienation within my community for embracing and being open about having bipolar disorder (Campbell, 2021; Hines-Martin et al., 2003; Jones et al., 2015). While mental illness stigma permeates U.S. society and public disclosure broadly increases my vulnerability to bias, the prospect of my disclosure uniquely alienating me within my own cultural community was unsettling. The paradox of taking a risk to help my community that would potentially ostracize me within my community was something I wrestled with, but it was ultimately a risk I pursued.

Mental Illness Stigma in Academia

Higher education, as a microcosm of broader society, is also a context in which mental illness stigma is pervasive. Scholars with mental illnesses often do not disclose because of the "culture of fear and stigma" surrounding mental illness in academia (Price & Kerschbaum, 2017, p. 6). Stereotypes such as that people with mental illnesses are violent, incapable, and unstable contribute to making colleges and universities exclusive and hostile toward people with mental illnesses (Kruse & Oswal, 2018). Concurrently, cultural associations between genius and insanity provide a layer of protection for some academics as their eccentricities are viewed as "a function of their genius" (Pickens, 2019, p. 243). Yet, tropes of "quirky" or "weird" professors who are brilliant and non-threatening are primarily associated with straight White men. For others, such leeway toward their eccentricities is not granted and they are more likely to be penalized and excluded in academia for eccentricities and deviations from "normal" ways of being (Pickens, 2019).

As a scholar of higher education, I have also perceived how the stigma of mental illness is implicitly perpetuated via its neglect as a topic of scholarly inquiry in my disciplinary field. Research about students with mental illnesses is limited in higher education literature (Kimball & Thoma, 2019), despite increasing attention and public discourse regarding the prevalence of mental health issues among college students (Center for Collegiate Mental Health, 2024; Flannery, 2023). Research about faculty with mental illnesses is even more sparse (Friedensen et al., 2021). The intersecting factors of the broad fear of disclosure among academics and the lack of scholarly engagement within the field of higher education left me feeling that my disclosure might also alienate me within my scholarly community. Moreover, I had a lack of role models—faculty who were public about having a mental illness—and therefore lacked mentors with lived experience of mental illness who could help guide me after my disclosure. As an early career scholar in a limited-term postdoctoral fellowship, this lack of mentorship was particularly salient given the precarity of my position in academia. Amid an increasingly competitive academic job market my disclosure made me vulnerable to discriminatory evaluation of my candidacy that would penalize me for having a mental illness (Hipes et al., 2016).

Personal Tolls of My Disclosure

The various stages of my public disclosure that I have bipolar disorder have all had personal tolls that have been challenging to navigate. Disability Studies[1] scholars have nuanced and deconstructed the notion that disclosure is a singular event (Price et al., 2017):

> Instead of being a single occurrence that leads to subsequent understanding, disability disclosure is better understood as an ongoing rhetorical process in which faculty members repeatedly need to address their disability for various audiences, across many different contexts (Kerschbaum et al., 2013). Moreover, disability disclosure is inevitably entangled with other identity markers, including race, gender, academic rank, and so forth. (p. 6)

At my career juncture, as a postdoc and not a tenured faculty member, disclosing placed serious risks to my career aspirations due to the prevalence of mental illness stigma in academia. Moreover, my disclosure was unique in that it included vivid description of my mental health crisis and experience of police brutality. In addition to dealing with the general stigma connected to "bipolar disorder" as a label, my intimate retelling of my story makes me vulnerable to judgment based on the details of my story. Racist beliefs about Black men also exacerbate the stigma as racial stereotypes intersect with and amplify stereotypes about mental illness, such as being dangerous to others. Going forward with publishing my op-ed was a decision I made after careful consideration of these risks, and the process of thinking through these risks was a stressful one.

Writing about my journey with bipolar disorder was both cathartic and re-traumatizing. While I had accepted my diagnosis and received mental health care at the point of writing my op-ed, bipolar disorder was still not an aspect of my identity I identified closely with. It was certainly not a source of pride for me, but rather one of shame. Mentally, I distanced myself from it, and while I was vigilant in taking care of myself, I buried my painful experiences with bipolar disorder deeply within myself. Through reflecting and writing about my experiences I did find pride in thinking about all I have overcome. However, thinking and writing about being brutalized, and the parallels between my experiences with those who were brutalized and did not survive, was and continues to be deeply upsetting.

Beyond employment-specific considerations, disclosing entailed risk in how people would perceive and interact with me both within and outside of the academy. I have navigated anxiety around the unknown of how people now think about me due to knowing my diagnosis and story. The process of making peace with that unknown has been a long one. Ultimately, I cannot control others' biased views, I can only rest assured knowing I am doing my best each day and prioritizing my health and wellbeing. Having my diagnosis and story in the public sphere also

---

[1] Mental illnesses are considered disabilities in legal and policy contexts (ADA National Network, n.d.). Disability Studies is an interdisciplinary academic field exploring various topics related to disability, such as its meanings in society, disability cultures, and "the personal experiences of disability in all its variations" (Ferguson & Nusbaum, 2012, p. 70).

means I cannot control how and when it is shared. For example, someone once introduced me to someone else at a conference reception saying I had "written about being a bipolar man." This was frustrating not only because they did not have my permission to disclose on my behalf, but also because I use person-first language to refer to myself (e.g., "I have bipolar disorder"). Through taking ownership of my story and sharing it with others I have simultaneously ceded control over how and with whom I share that I have bipolar disorder.

In line with how Disability Studies scholars have theorized disclosure as an "ongoing rhetorical process" (Price et al., 2017, p. 6), I have disclosed to various audiences, via circulation of my police brutality op-ed (Blake, 2020a) and a subsequent op-ed about academia's role in fighting mental illness stigma (Blake, 2020b), social media engagement, public speaking opportunities, class sessions with my students, conversation, and now through this chapter. These experiences have been rewarding, and I discuss them in the subsequent section. At the same time, these various forms of disclosure, which are all inherently acts of vulnerability, consistently bring me stress. I wonder if others' awareness that I have bipolar disorder undermines my credibility, particularly with colleagues and students, and if it will negatively influence evaluations of my collegiality and teaching effectiveness. I question the extent to which my feeling of responsibility to disclose and share my story is actually a manifestation of survivor's guilt.[2] I find myself questioning whether drawing from my pain to educate others is something I should continue to do. Navigating these considerations and making choices I can find peace with will be an ongoing journey.

Rewards of Disclosure

In this section I discuss various positive outcomes I have experienced since disclosing I have bipolar disorder, some of which I hoped for at the time I made the decision to disclose, and others which have been unexpected.

Community

Publicly sharing my story has brought me into community with several disabled scholars, including scholars of color. I did not anticipate the extent to which disclosing would cultivate these connections, nor the depth of these new relationships. People have reached out to me, both publicly and privately, to share their

[2] Survivor guilt was included in the fourth edition of the Diagnostic and Statistical Manual of Mental Disorders (it is not included in the fifth edition) and defined as "guilt about surviving when others have not" (American Psychiatric Association, 1994). In this instance, I am speculating about underlying guilt I may be carrying about surviving police brutality when many others have not.

appreciation for my vulnerability and visibility as a scholar with a mental illness. These have included students and scholars who navigate academia without disclosing they have a disability. I appreciate the risk they take in reaching out to me, and it makes me feel less alone in my experiences.

Meeting a handful of scholars of color who are public about having a mental illness has also been inspiring and opened my eyes to different ways of existing in the academy. For example, a Latinx scholar who shares a diagnosis of bipolar disorder with me has disclosed at each juncture of his graduate school trajectory, despite the risk that disclosing could lead to his applications getting rejected. Yet, he has been accepted to top programs in the field and is thriving in his doctoral program. We are now able to support one another and are pursuing a research collaboration in which we explore our divergent experiences in higher education.

I have also pursued a range of other collaborations with disabled scholars. Examples include planning and co-editing a special issue on race and disability in a higher education disability journal, developing and presenting an interactive symposium titled "Fighting Stigma and Holding Institutions Accountable: Mental Disability Disclosure and Racial Identity in Higher Education" at the Association for the Study of Higher Education (ASHE) conference, and taking on leadership positions to advance disability justice within ASHE. These efforts have truly revealed to me the meaning of strength in numbers, and I am proud of the progress we have made thus far.

Impact

In addition to bringing me into community with other scholars, I have seen various ways in which my disclosure and public writing about mental illness have made an impact. My disclosure led to me having conversations with administrators at the University of Pennsylvania (my doctoral and postdoc institution) about how to be more supportive of students, staff, and faculty with mental illnesses. We discussed ideas such as educating the campus community about mental illness and how to recognize signs that someone may be struggling, implementing flexible mental health leave of absence policies, and supporting programming that humanizes people with mental illnesses through sharing their voices and perspectives. My op-ed on mental illness stigma was shared via social media by Penn Graduate School of Education's platforms and incorporated in a recommended reading list by Rutgers University's central diversity, equity, and inclusion office (Rutgers University Equity and Inclusion Office, n.d.). It was also circulated by ASHE, which is the leading scholarly association in my field. Moreover, the outlet through which these op-eds were published, *Diverse Issues in Higher Education*, is the leading news outlet focusing on diversity, equity, and inclusion at U.S. colleges and universities. While writing publicly about my experiences was inherently meaningful and important for me, these various forms of institutional validation have advanced the impact

I hoped to make in terms of educating the public and sparking critical discussion about mental illness, racial justice, and disability inclusion.

Institutional validation and the positive reactions I have received have also had unique personal impacts for me. To write about my diagnosis and experiences I have held shame about for years and be met with such a great level of support has been deeply moving. Disclosing has bolstered my sense of purpose and given me more confidence in myself as I now know that an aspect of myself I felt I had to hide for so long is bringing about positive change and inspiring others.

New Professional Directions

Among the foremost rewards of disclosure that I did not anticipate was how it would lead me to expand my research agenda to grapple with disability and ableism. My research centers faculty experiences and had focused primarily on axes of race and gender. After disclosing, I began to dive deeply into research on disability in higher education and found that empirical research on faculty with disabilities was limited and rarely considers the intersections of disability with other marginalized identities. As a scholar of color who aspired to become a faculty member, part of my motivation in exploring this literature was to seek understanding of other disabled scholars of color's hiring experiences and how they navigated the academy. When I realized there was a dearth of research in this area, I was motivated to launch my own study, and it became the primary focus of my postdoc.

In 2022 I launched the largest qualitative study on the experiences of Black faculty with disabilities to date. While the study is inclusive of various forms of disability and does not exclusively focus on scholars with mental illnesses, I have so far conducted interviews with 11 Black faculty who have been diagnosed and/or self-identify as having a mental illness. Most of these scholars navigate their institutions without sharing with others that they have a mental illness. However, their confidential participation in the study is a form of disclosure that will surface the presence of Black scholars with mental illnesses in the academy and shed light both on barriers they face and strategies they use to persevere. My positionality as a Black scholar with a mental illness enhances my ability to be perceptive and sensitive during the research process, and participants have expressed gratitude for having the opportunity to share their stories and help inform equitable policy and practice in higher education. Research is a key avenue through which the perspectives and lived experiences of people with mental illnesses can be documented, and I look forward to advancing this work in publications focused on the study.

My disclosure and shift in my research agenda also had implications for my job applications. The 2022–2023 application cycle was the first time I applied for faculty positions since I was a doctoral student, and I reframed how I discussed my identity and research. I decided to not directly name that I have bipolar disorder or a mental illness in my cover letters because I thought that doing so would too directly connect me to stereotypes and stigmatize me during initial review of my application. However, I did mention that I live with a disability and included my op-eds on my curriculum vitae. Ultimately, I do not know if bias played a role in job searches in which my candidacy did not advance. The outcome of the application cycle was that I attained a tenure-track assistant professor of higher education position at Georgia State University, where the community expressed great enthusiasm about my research talk and plans and seems genuinely invested in my success. Students have expressed their appreciation of my openness about living with a mental illness, which is particularly meaningful for me as I am now the role model I wish I had had after my diagnosis and disclosure. I am excited about my journey at Georgia State University, especially because of the impact I can make as a Black disabled faculty member at a leading predominantly Black institution in the cultural milieu of Atlanta.

Concluding Thoughts and Suggestions

Institutions, researchers, and practitioners must recognize that disability is intersectional and that experiences of mental illness stigma vary by the other privileged and marginalized identities people hold. As I described in the Weaponization of Mental Illness Against Black Communities section, the use of mental illness to marginalize Black people throughout U.S. history has exacerbated mental illness stigma within Black communities. Further, racist stereotypes that Black people are angry and violent are inherently linked to mental illness stigma as they are rooted in the idea that Black people are irrational and mentally unsound. The shortcomings in acknowledging how mental illness stigma is racialized are symptomatic of a broader lack of engagement with the intersections of race and disability.

Bell (2006) satirically proposed "White Disability Studies" to critique the hegemony of Whiteness in disability literature and higher education research and practice are also characterized by a centering of Whiteness (Stapleton & James, 2020). In my op-ed about academia's role in fighting mental illness stigma, I referred to how many racially minoritized victims of police brutality have disabilities, but their disability is rarely surfaced in media coverage (Perry & Carter-Long, 2016) and argued that higher education overlooks intersections between disability and racial marginalization in similar ways (Blake, 2020b). Campus climate research focuses on race but rarely considers intersections of racism and ableism. One example of such an intersection is how disabled students of color report facing greater opposition than their White disabled peers when they attempt to access accommodations from instructors and disability services offices (Karpicz, 2020; Mireles, 2022). Such realities have implications for students of color's sense of inclusion and for their ability to achieve in their coursework, but treating race and disability as siloed phenomena precludes stakeholders from identifying and addressing these kinds of intersectional inequities.

While some campus climate studies highlight racism as a psychosocial stressor that disadvantages students of color, these studies often fail to link racism to broader conversations about barriers for students with mental illnesses (Clark & Mitchell, 2018), and the racialized ways mental illness stigma obstructs students of color from accessing accommodations. Disabled people of color navigate higher education with awareness of, and vulnerability to, racist stereotypes that people of color are less hardworking, less intelligent, and untrustworthy (Mireles, 2022; Petersen, 2009; Steele, 2011). Beyond a cultural disassociation from disability due to historical oppression, disabled people of color who may indeed accept diagnoses and embrace disability identity still must consider how to navigate racialized institutional contexts (Berry, 2023; Koren & Evans-El, 2020; Stephens, 2022). For people of color who are neurodiverse and/or have mental illnesses, which are less apparent or "hidden" to others, racist stereotypes intersect with stigma to pose unique obstacles to their pursuit of accommodations. Disabled students of color grapple with concerns about seemingly confirming stereotypes and/or being perceived as, and reprimanded for, trying to cheat accommodation systems (Mireles, 2022; Petersen, 2009).

Disability services offices must be vigilant in ensuring equitable accommodation processes for disabled students of color and human resources offices must do the same for staff and faculty. Inclusion for staff and faculty with mental illnesses is interconnected with that of students (Rodríguez Lemus, 2021) and institutions should investigate intersections of racism and ableism for students, staff, and faculty in internal assessments of campus climate. Ways to approach this could include conducting voluntary (and preferably compensated) focus groups with students, staff, and faculty of color around these issues, and including open-ended questions on surveys that prompt participants to share their perceptions, experiences, and suggestions. These assessments can help to identify context-specific sources of inequity, which can serve as a basis for developing and reforming policies and practices to address them. More effective support of staff and faculty might also lead them to be more open about their mental illnesses with students, which can reduce stigma and allow them to serve as role models for students with mental illnesses (Skogen, 2012). Another area where representation is particularly salient is in disability services offices, where diverse racial, gender, and disability representation of staff can make offices less intimidating for a range of students.

Institutions should also consider how to actualize principles of disability justice (Sins Invalid, 2019) and cultivate environments that promote "interdependence, access, and collaboration rather than a strict reliance on individual processes of disclosure and accommodation" (Council on Ethnic Participation Accessibility and Equity/Inclusion Sub-Committee, 2023). One way such environments can be advanced is through raising awareness of the lived experiences of people with disabilities. Learning about lived experiences can help community members be more self-aware and supportive, such as by not using stigmatizing language about mental illness and educating others when they hear them using such language (Blake, 2020b). Framing disability as an intersectional and valued aspect of diversity rather than from a deficit perspective, such as through campus programming that highlights the agency and efforts of Black people with disabilities (Schalk, 2022), might also mitigate stigma and enhance feelings of belonging and safety, which could lead to increased use of supports.

In this chapter, I shared a perspective that is rarely heard, as a Black man and scholar who has publicly disclosed living with a mental illness. I hope readers acknowledge it is just one perspective on a multidimensional topic and that they are inspired to read and discuss other literature at the nexus of race and disability, such as the many works cited in this chapter. Further, I hope readers do not view my suggestions for practice as a checklist with an end, but rather that they serve as an impetus for exploration and reflection on ways in which they can fight stigma as individuals and within their roles as campus stakeholders. One useful resource I have come across is Price and Kerschbaum's (2017) "Promoting Supportive Academic Environments for Faculty with Mental Illnesses" report, which offers several recommendations for practice that have broad implications for institutional culture and climate. Addressing mental illness stigma should be viewed as crucial to racial equity and as critical as addressing other intersecting forms of marginalization such as those based on gender, socioeconomic status, and sexuality. It is incumbent upon individuals to recognize the ways in which they can work to mitigate mental illness stigma in their daily lives and for colleges and universities to take leadership in combatting mental illness stigma and bringing about a more just society.

References

ADA National Network. (n.d.). *Mental health conditions in the workplace and the ADA*. ADA National Network. https://adata.org/factsheet/health

American Psychiatric Association. (1994). *Diagnostic and statistical manual of mental disorders* (4th ed.).

Appel, O., Stephens, D., Shadravan, S. M., Key, J., & Ochoa, K. (2020). Differential incarceration by race-ethnicity and mental health service status in the Los Angeles County jail system. *Psychiatric Services, 71*(8), 843–846. https://doi.org/10.1176/appi.ps.201900429

Bailey, M., & Mobley, I. A. (2019). Work in the intersections: A black feminist disability framework. *Gender & Society, 33*(1), 19–40. https://doi.org/10.1177/0891243218801523

Baynton, D. C. (2017). Disability and the justification of inequality in American history. In L. J. Davis (Ed.), *The disability studies reader* (pp. 27–39). Taylor & Francis.

Bell, C. (2006). Introducing white disability studies: A modest proposal. In L. J. Davis (Ed.), *The disability studies reader* (pp. 275–282). Routledge.

Berry, C. (2023). Between blackness and disability. In A. D. Tomlin & S. Cupid (Eds.), *Voices of the field: DEIA champions in higher education* (pp. 125–132). Information Age Publishing.

Blake, D. (2020a, September 11). I, too, experienced police brutality. *Diverse Issues in Higher Education*. https://www.diverseeducation.com/demographics/african-american/article/15107736/i-too-experienced-police-brutality

Blake, D. (2020b, December 11). Academia's role in fighting mental illness stigma. *Diverse Issues in Higher Education*. https://www.diverseeducation.com/campus-climate/article/15108343/academias-role-in-fighting-mental-illness-stigma

Campbell, A. D. (2021). Clergy perceptions of mental illness and confronting stigma in congregations. *Religions, 12*(12), 1110. https://doi.org/10.3390/rel12121110

Center for Collegiate Mental Health. (2024). 2023 annual report. Penn State University Center for Collegiate Mental Health. https://ccmh.psu.edu/assets/docs/2023_Annual%20Report.pdf

Clark, I., & Mitchell, D. (2018). Exploring the relationship between campus climate and minority stress in African American college students. *Journal Committed to Social Change on Race and Ethnicity (JCSCORE), 4*(1), 67–95. https://doi.org/10.15763/issn.2642-2387.2018.4.1.66-95

Council on Ethnic Participation Accessibility and Equity/Inclusion Sub-Committee. (2023). Accessibility (un)statement. Association for the Study of Higher Education. https://www.ashe.ws/disabilityjustice.

Ferguson, P. M., & Nusbaum, E. (2012). Disability studies: What is it and what difference does it make? *Research and Practice for Persons with Severe Disabilities, 37*(2), 70–80. https://doi.org/10.1177/154079691203700202

Flannery, M. E. (2023). The mental health crisis on college campuses. National Education Association. https://www.nea.org/nea-today/all-news-articles/mental-health-crisis-college-campuses

Friedensen, R. E., Horii, C. V., Kimball, E., Lisi, B., Miller, R. A., Siddiqui, S., Thoma, H., Weaver, J. E., & Woodman, A. (2021). A systematic review of research on faculty with disabilities. *Journal of the Professoriate, 12*(2), 1–25. https://caarpweb.org/wp-content/uploads/2022/01/research_on_faculty_with_disabilities_friedensen_et_al._12_2_1.pdf

Hines-Martin, V., Malone, M., Kim, S., & Brown-Piper, A. (2003). Barriers to mental health care access in an African American population. *Issues in Mental Health Nursing, 24*(3), 237–256. https://doi.org/10.1080/01612840305281

Hipes, C., Lucas, J., Phelan, J. C., & White, R. C. (2016). The stigma of mental illness in the labor market. *Social Science Research, 56*, 16–25. https://doi.org/10.1016/j.ssresearch.2015.12.001

Jones, L. V., Hopson, L., Warner, L., Hardiman, E. R., & James, T. (2015). A qualitative study of Black women's experiences in drug abuse and mental health services. *Affilia: Journal of Women and Social Work, 30*(1), 68–82. https://doi.org/10.1177/0886109914531957

Karpicz, J. R. (2020). "Just my being here is self-advocacy": Exploring the self-advocacy experiences of disabled graduate students of color. *JCSCORE, 6*(1), 137–163. https://doi.org/10.15763/issn.2642-2387.2020.6.1.137-163

Kerschbaum, S. L., Garland-Thomson, R., Oswal, S. K., Vidali, A., Ghiaciuc, S., Price, M., Dolmage, J., Meyer, C. A., Brueggemann, B. J., & Samuels, E. (2013). Faculty members, accommodation, and access in higher education. Profession. http://profession.commons.mla.org/2013/12/09/faculty-members-accommodation-and-access-in-higher-education/

Kimball, E. W., & Thoma, H. S. (2019). College experiences for students with disabilities: An ecological synthesis of recent literature. *Journal of College Student Development, 60*(6), 674–693. https://doi.org/10.1353/csd.2019.0062

Koren, E. R., & Evans-El, S. X. (2020). Laissez-faire ableism in the academy: Contouring the map with graduate student perspectives. *Critical Education, 11*(14), 14–30. https://doi.org/10.14288/ce.v11i14.186519

Kruse, A. K., & Oswal, S. K. (2018). Barriers to higher education for students with bipolar disorder: A critical social model perspective. *Social Inclusion, 6*(4), 194–206. https://doi.org/10.17645/si.v6i4.1682

Metzl, J. M. (2010). *The protest psychosis: How schizophrenia became a black disease*. Beacon Press.

Mireles, D. (2022). Theorizing racist ableism in higher education. *Teachers College Record, 124*(7), 17–50. https://doi.org/10.1177/01614681221111428

Perry, D. M., & Carter-Long, L. (2016). The Ruderman white paper on media coverage of law enforcement use of force and disability. Ruderman Family Foundation. https://rudermanfoundation.org/wp-content/uploads/2017/08/MediaStudy-PoliceDisability_final-final.pdf.

Petersen, A. J. (2009). "Ain't nobody gonna get me down": An examination of the educational experiences of four African American women labeled with disabilities. *Equity & Excellence in Education, 42*(4), 428–442. https://doi.org/10.1080/10665680903245284

Pickens, T. A. (2019). *Black madness: Mad blackness*. Duke University Press.

Price, M., & Kerschbaum, S. L. (2017). Promoting supportive academic environments for faculty with mental illnesses: Resource guide and suggestions for practice. Temple University Collaborative on Community Inclusion of Individuals with Psychiatric Disabilities. https://tucollaborative.org/wp-content/uploads/2023/08/Promoting-Supportive-Academic-Environments-for-Faculty-with-Mental-Illnesses-Resource-Guide-and-Suggestions-for-Practice.pdf

Price, M., Salzer, M. S., O'Shea, A., & Kerschbaum, S. L. (2017). Disclosure of mental disability by college and university faculty: The negotiation of accommodations, supports, and barriers. *Disability Studies Quarterly, 37*(2) https://ojs.library.osu.edu/index.php/dsq/article/view/5487/4653

Roberts, D. (2022). *Torn apart: How the child welfare system destroys black families—And how abolition can build a safer world.* Basic Books.

Rodríguez Lemus Jr, G. (2021, October 14). The invisibility of mental illness in academe: The politics of mental health. *PsychoSocial.* https://psychosocial.media/2021/10/14/the-invisibility-of-mental-illness-in-academe-the-politics-of-mental-health/

Rutgers University Equity and Inclusion Office. (n.d.). Inclusive academy resource list. Rutgers, The State University of New Jersey. https://diversity.rutgers.edu/inclusive-academy-reading-list

Schalk, S. (2022). *Black disability politics.* Duke University Press.

Sins Invalid. (2019). *Skin, tooth, and bone: The basis of movement is our people (2nd ed.).* Sins Invalid.

Skogen, R. (2012). "Coming into presence" as mentally ill in academia: A new logic of emancipation. *Harvard Educational Review, 82*(4), 491–510. https://doi.org/10.17763/haer.82.4.u1m8g0052212pjh8

Stapleton, L., & James, L. (2020). Not another all white study: Challenging color-evasiveness ideology in disability scholarship (practice brief). *Journal of Postsecondary Education and Disability, 33*(3), 215–222. https://files.eric.ed.gov/fulltext/EJ1281055.pdf

Steele, C. M. (2011). *Whistling Vivaldi: How stereotypes affect us and what we can do.* W.W. Norton & Company.

Stephens, K. (2022). *The gendered, racialized, & dis/abled experiences of neurodivergent Black women graduate students across higher education.* [Doctoral dissertation, University of Massachusetts Amherst]. https://scholarworks.umass.edu/dissertations_2/2664/

Daniel J. Blake, Ph.D., is an assistant professor of higher education in the Department of Educational Policy Studies at Georgia State University. He earned his Ph.D. in higher education at the University of Pennsylvania Graduate School of Education. Blake's research focuses on organizational culture, policy, and practice in higher education, with particular attention to how race, gender, and disability shape career experiences in the academic workforce. His research has been published in outlets including *The Journal of Higher Education, Journal of Women and Gender in Higher Education, Journal of Diversity in Higher Education, Journal of Faculty Development, and Education Sciences.*

Chapter 6
Shining a Light on Mental Illness Stigma in Graduate Mental Health Programs

Kimberly S. Gorman

Abstract One important, yet neglected, area of focus of stigma within higher education is in the training of mental health professionals. In this chapter, I center my discussion on how stigma is introduced and reinforced by mental health graduate programs (counseling, psychology, and social work). I discuss the impact of this stigma on the development of skills and the use of language by students training to be a mental health professional, using programs within the United States as example. I propose ways to alter the development and delivery of the curriculum to challenge mental illness stigma.

Keywords Mental illness · Clinicians · Graduate programs · Stigma · Curriculum

Graduate programs in the mental health professions (counseling, psychology, and social work) are charged with preparing their students to provide ethical, effective, and quality mental health services. Graduate programs are designed to adhere to university curricular requirements as well as accreditation standards to help students obtain licensure after the successful completion of their training. These programs conferred more than 84,000 master's and doctoral degrees in the United States in 2020 (Council for Accreditation of Counseling and Related Educational Programs, 2022; Council on Social Work Education, 2021; National Center for Education Statistics, n.d.). Graduates become clinicians, researchers, and/or educators; the impact they have on clients' lives cannot be overstated.

Generally, we expect the graduates providing mental health services to be aware of the impact of mental illness stigma. Clinicians often hear from their clients that the reason for the delay in help seeking is the client's concern about how engaging

The author has no conflicts of interest to declare that are relevant to the content of this chapter.

K. S. Gorman (✉)
Division of Student Affairs, Western Carolina University, Cullowhee, NC, USA
e-mail: ksgorman@wcu.edu

© The Author(s), under exclusive license to Springer Nature Switzerland AG 2025

K. M. Brennan, K. S. Gorman (eds.), *A University-Wide Approach to Changing Campus Cultures of Mental Illness Stigma*, Knowledge Studies in Higher Education 18, https://doi.org/10.1007/978-3-031-86496-4_6

in therapy will impact them, especially if a boss, a partner, or a professor knows about their therapy (as suggested in Corrigan et al., 2014). Knowledge about the impact of stigma is important and clinicians have the opportunity to either reproduce stigma in their practice or to challenge and, ultimately, change it. Unfortunately, many counseling, psychology and social work graduates leave their programs without the skills to challenge stigma; accreditation and licensure boards do not mandate stigma as a content area and thus it is not a focus for many programs. This is unfortunate and concerning since the provider's stigma has been demonstrated to impact clients' recovery (Dell et al., 2021; Deng et al., 2022).

The concern moves beyond the mere absence of content and conversation in graduate programs about stigma and its impact on trainees and their future clients. This chapter focuses on a significant problem: the presence of stigma in counseling, social work, and psychology programs (hereafter called mental health graduate programs). I am calling attention to this problem since programs rarely, if ever, focus on their own perpetuation of stigmatized beliefs and practices. We cannot continue to ignore, or pretend, that graduate mental health programs are immune to perpetuating the stigma within higher education simply because their programs are centered in an understanding of the impact of mental illness on human beings. Rather, highlighting how programs continue stigmatization allows them to acknowledge, observe and work to change the stigma within their departments. These shifts will be beneficial both for the students in these programs as well as for their future clients.

Mental Health in Graduate School

One in five people in the United States (National Alliance on Mental Illness, n.d.) and one in eight people worldwide (World Health Organization [WHO], 2022) experience mental illness each year. Although the public may believe mental health clinicians have "figured it out" and do not experience mental health challenges, the reality is clinicians and educators in the field also have mental illnesses such as anxiety, depression, eating disorders, and bipolar illness. In fact, researchers have found the frequency of mental health problems among psychologists occur at a frequency that parallels the general public (Tay et al., 2018; Victor, et al., 2022).

Personal experience with mental illness is often cited as a reason why people choose to pursue graduate studies in mental health (Graves & Wright, 2007; Huynh & Rhodes, 2011). This personal experience might represent one's own mental health journey but it may also reflect the experience of being with a family member or a friend as they managed a mental illness diagnosis. Students may be inspired to become a counselor either because they (or a loved one) had a positive therapy experience, or, alternatively, had a terrible experience with a mental health provider. Researchers have determined this personal experience is very common, as a recent study found 67% of trainees reported they had lived experience with mental health challenges; anxiety and depression were the most common diagnoses cited (Grice et al., 2018). Additional research indicates this personal experience may impact the choice of a college major, as students in the behavioral and social sciences, social work, and arts and humanities disciplines are more likely to use substances and report mental health problems than engineering and business students (Allen et al., 2022).

Given the statistics about the prevalence of mental illness in this specific student population, we hope these students will be willing to use available treatment options, especially since they are considering going into a profession designed to treat the very illness they experience. However, researchers found less than one in four undergraduate psychology students stated they would seek treatment (Thomas et al., 2014). What prohibits someone from using services from a licensed professional, especially if that someone is studying to be a therapist? It may be students are concerned other students and/or faculty will discover their diagnosis and are concerned about the consequences of such discovery. Gorman and Brennan (2023) found students who hold exclusionary sentiments about individuals with mental illness, that is students who believed people with mental illness are likely to lose opportunities or to be excluded from them, are less likely to engage in treatment on campus. Stigma is likely impacting nearly everyone in graduate mental health programs, yet no one is talking about it. This silence is concerning.

The Silence of Stigma

It is a great irony that faculty reference the stigma reduction techniques suggested by researchers (Strassle, 2018), but have yet to consider, and thus may not realize, how they are engaging in stigmatizing practices. Stigmatizing attitudes toward individuals with mental illness are found in students enrolled in the range of health care focused programs (Masedo et al., 2021; Sandhu et al., 2019; Subu et al., 2024). These attitudes are also embedded in the way the curriculum is taught. For instance, Barenie et al. (2023) recently studied perceptions about substance use in academic programs. They found most faculty, staff, and students reported challenges, mainly communication problems, when interacting with a person with a substance use disorder (SUD). However, the study highlighted few faculty and students recalled hearing negative comments about people with a SUD from peers within their academic programs. The authors' conclusion suggested programs could consider how to implement more training on communicating with individuals with SUDs. However, just because no one remembers hearing negative comments within their program does not mean stigma is not present. The concern is that there is silence about the presence of stigma. In fact, we know stigma finds energy and growth in silence as there is nothing, and no one, to challenge it.

One example of the impact of the silence is when no one feels comfortable disclosing their experience with a mental health challenge. Students in Siegel and Keeler's (2020) study stated a primary reason they did not want professors to know about their experiences with depression was a fear of being stigmatized. The perception that the public stigma suggesting someone with mental illness is socially unacceptable (Parscesepe & Cabassa, 2013) is more prevalent than self-stigma, the internalized acceptance of public stigma (Pescosolido & Martin, 2015), creates concerns about negative consequences for a student's career (Tay et al., 2018). The silence, or the need to stay silent, is borne out of shame that is created and reinforced by stigma. And, unfortunately, this stigma impacts those students' attitudes toward help seeking (Digiuni et al., 2013).

Another important way silence is operative in graduate programs relates to the research focus on stigma. Most of the research has centered on stigma of those with substance use concerns as well as those with schizophrenia, as if these are the only two mental health concerns that are stigmatized. While it is true there are many misperceptions and judgments made about substance misuse and schizophrenia, singularly focusing on stigma about these issues is itself stigmatizing. Mood disorders and anxiety related disorders are far more common (Substance Abuse and Mental Health Service Administration [SAMHSA], 2022). However, we do not talk about the stigmatized views toward individuals with these diagnoses and we certainly do not talk about the stigmatized views about people in graduate school who experience mood and anxiety disorders. This silence only provides more opportunities for stigma to be reinforced.

Stigma and Faculty Members

We were unable to find any existing studies about stigmatized views of faculty in graduate mental health programs. This hole in the literature is yet another example of the way stigma is reflected in faculty members of graduate mental health programs. The closest research we have to understanding the stigma of faculty is by generalizing research findings about stigma in mental health professionals. Faculty in counseling, psychology, and social work must complete clinical rotations prior to graduating with their terminal degree, and thus have been providers at some point in their career. Some faculty are licensed and provide clinical care in addition to their academic responsibilities. Lauber et al. (2006) found no difference in stigma beliefs in the general population and in mental health professionals. In other words, they found professionals held similar negative beliefs about individuals with mental illness. Pescosolido et al. (2021) recently reported trends in stigma from 1996 through 2018; they found rates are still high with about one in six individuals desiring to maintain social distance from those with mental illness while at work as well as while socializing.

Faculty demonstrate their stigmatized beliefs in subtle but powerful ways; one primary way is through assumptions apparent during lectures. For example, when lecturing about substance misuse, rather than acknowledging that someone in the classroom may be in recovery, they assume this is not the case and allude to students maybe having a family member in recovery. This assumption might be related to additional maligned beliefs that recovery is a long process and would interfere with, or at least inhibit, studying and thus students in recovery cannot be successful in a graduate program. Faculty also make assumptions about students outside the stigma of substance misuse. For instance, I have had many clients initiate counseling at my university counseling center after their faculty made a suggestion to the graduate students in mental health programs that the students should engage in therapy so they can learn what it is like to be a client. This presumes students have not engaged or are not currently engaged in ongoing counseling.

Faculty rarely engage in self-disclosure about their own struggles, either as a person with a mental illness challenge or as someone living with or supporting another who has a mental illness challenge. This may explain the dearth of research on the use of self-disclosure as a teaching technique. The view of faculty self-disclosure may be connected to the view of self-disclosure in therapeutic practice; many therapists are cautious about using it as a therapeutic technique despite its many benefits to clients (Brown & Walker, 1990; de Vos et al., 2016; Kronner, 2013). However, the lack of self-disclosure must also be considered through the lens of stigma. Is the silence, the lack of disclosure of lived experience, an example of self-stigma instead? Are the faculty more worried about how they will be viewed? How their tenure and/or promotion process may be impacted?

Stigma in the Curriculum

Stigma is present in the curriculum of the program and in the licensure preparation process in various ways. The titles of classes are a key example of this. "Psychopathology" is one common title (usually shortened in everyday discussions about the class to "Psychopath"). "Addictions" is another class title commonly used. The problem with both titles is that they erase the individuals who should be centered in the diagnostic and treatment process. Often times in these classes, various labels are used as shorthand for identifying individuals with mental health challenges. Thus, conversations in classes center on "borderlines" (sic) or "anorexics" (sic); students learn to communicate about these issues and individuals struggling with them in this stigmatized way.

Throughout their time in the program, students in the United States are taught using the medical model derived from the use of the Diagnostic and Statistical Manual-5-TR (American Psychiatric Association, 2022) to learn how to assess, diagnose, and treat the person. Thus, there is a focus on teaching what is "normal" and what is "aberrant." These words suggest a person with a mental illness, whether that be someone with major depression, with post-traumatic stress disorder, or with schizophrenia are "not normal." Programs tend to prioritize teaching the process of assessment during the first year of the program. Once that is done, they then offer a separate class focusing on diversity. They usually do not offer a class on how to understand and work with people who have experienced trauma. Thus, the programs highlight how to evaluate someone with less focus on understanding them, their environment, and their circumstances. Narrowly focusing on symptoms that meet diagnostic criteria as a way to determine what a client needs from therapy is problematic in many ways (see Mullan, 2023). At the very least, this focus on what is 'wrong' with people is a form of stigma.

This stigma impacts students and their beliefs and, eventually, how they approach their work with clients. For instance, Covarrubias and Han (2011) found social work students who indicated they believe individuals with serious mental illness are likely to be dangerous wanted more social distance from these individuals. Deng et al. (2022) found healthcare providers working in psychiatric settings were concerned about how they were viewed by colleagues who work in other settings. Such beliefs and attitudes likely contribute to the existing global shortage of mental health care providers (Endale et al., 2020). Rather than reinforcing these beliefs, we may only imagine how things could be different for students and their clients if programs took responsibility for challenging stigma. How programs can do this is the focus of the next section.

Finally, stigma is embedded within the licensure process. Graduate mental health programs must provide a curriculum that is aligned with licensure requirements for that jurisdiction. Thus, many of the above noted stigma related concerns in the curriculum are also related to licensing boards. Additional stigmatized practices within the licensure process relate to the character references prospective licensees must provide. What is the character of someone with bipolar illness? With PTSD? With major depression? Of course, it should not matter, yet beliefs that individuals with mental illness are different and should not be afforded the same rights and benefits to which others have access (Pescosolido et al., 2013) may interrupt, delay, and/or prohibit a graduate from achieving licensure. This may be particularly true for students who have had a history of convictions related to previous substance misuse, as these convictions introduce additional barriers to licensure. This is an example of structural stigma, which focuses on the impact of institutional policies on stigmatized individuals (Corrigan et al., 2004).

Now that I have pointed out the many ways stigma is embedded within mental health graduate programs, I turn to suggestions for graduate mental health programs to begin to change their approach and to provide a welcoming, non-stigmatized, environment for all students and faculty.

Changing Stigma in Graduate Mental Health Programs

Naming and Acknowledging Stigma

One of the first steps graduate mental health programs can take is to acknowledge stigma exists within the program and within the individuals involved in it. By naming stigma, we take away the power it holds when it is allowed to operate in silence. This first step involves inviting conversations about stigma as a discussion point in each and every course offered by the department. When we assert stigma exists, it means we can all take responsibility to challenge it when it is operating. Thus, faculty should identify when and how they are challenging and/or addressing stigma in each course. Faculty should also name stigma when it shows up in discussions among students. This allows a natural laboratory for understanding how prevalent stigma is and how to challenge it as a community. Finally, faculty also need to be willing to be challenged when they express or behave in ways that reproduce stigma.

One example is to build a community that is willing to change language and to keep each other accountable for doing so (Kelly et al., 2016; National Institute on Drug Abuse, 2021). As a supervisor who served as a final signatory on clinical notes written by trainees, I reviewed documentation for any stigmatizing language. I would ask the trainee to correct the language while also giving the reason for my request for the change. I would often ask trainees to change language about substance misuse. For example, rather than saying a client's mother "is in "rehab" (sic), I asked the trainee to write that the client's mother sought inpatient treatment. Interestingly, there were times when these trainees indicated the client was the one who using the stigmatized word and so the trainee used the client's language in their note. Unfortunately, this was a missed opportunity for the trainee to challenge stigma in the client. This miss became another part of our conversation during our clinical supervision time. Another example of challenging stigma through language was when our clinic staff agreed to challenge each other to not use the word "normal' or "normalized" in language about clients. We believed eliminating this word was necessary to acknowledge there is no standard by which our clients should be measured; rather we wanted to consider the client's world and how it shaped the client's current situation. This was a part of our focus on using trauma informed care, an approach based on unraveling stigma (Menschner & Maul, 2016). Changing language about "normal" was a humbling experience. I realized how many times I had stigmatized clients with the clinical language I had used and how I had taught students in my classes to do the same. This was particularly true in teaching students how to use the mental status exam, a staple in graduate mental health programs (Sultzer, 1994). When using the mental status exam, the clinician can denote an aspect of functioning (e.g., mood, motor activity, or thought processes) is "within normal limits." Prior to my recognition of how stigmatizing this notation was, I had not invited students to challenge me when I was stigmatizing clients. I have since been very forthright about the need to correct me as needed.

Self-Disclosure

As referenced above, many individuals enter the mental health field because of their lived experience with mental illness. Research suggests that 70% of adults globally have experienced a traumatic event (WHO, 2024); this high prevalence of trauma has given rise to the saying "trauma is in the room" when we are with others; similarly, the prevalence of mental illness (WHO, 2022) suggests we should recognize lived experience of mental illness is also "in the room." Many times, this means there are faculty in the classroom with lived experience. Researchers have found a primary way of combating stigma is for those with some power to disclose their history with mental illness (Corrigan & Rao, 2012). There is research support for psychologists to do this as well (Victor et al., 2022). As a feminist trained psychologist, self-disclosure was an important deliberate intervention I used (Brown & Walker, 1990; Worell & Remer, 2003). Just as I appropriately disclosed with clients, I also appropriately disclosed my mental illness history and my history of treatment-seeking with my students and clinical supervisees. Inevitably, doing this invited conversations about my journey as a psychologist with this history, a journey I am proud to share.

The use of self-disclosure of mental illness has become more prevalent in the larger culture, and we have witnessed elite athletes who have discussed their history with mental illness challenges. In fact, several campaigns have launched around this initiative such as the "Kicking the Stigma" campaign by the Indianapolis Colts (https://www.colts.com/community/kicking-the-stigma/). Naomi Osaka (a professional tennis player) and Simone Biles (a professional gymnast) were very open about the need to withdraw from their sport activities because of mental illness struggles (Kallingal, 2021; Osaka, 2021). Such disclosures initiated many conversations about the importance of talking about mental health in different environments. Graduate mental programs should and could follow this lead.

Just as faculty should not suggest students engage in counseling to learn what it is like to be a client, they also should not compel students to talk about any counseling experience they or family members have had. And, they need not shy away when a student brings up the experience once it has been welcomed by the self-disclosure of others. In the university counseling centers I have worked and wherein we provided practicum experiences for master's level students and internship experiences for doctoral interns, we utilized a statement about self-disclosure that discussed the balance between learning and therapy. This statement highlighted the importance and expectation that the trainee will engage in self-exploration and self-reflection as part of the training program. The statement notes this might lead to disclosure about the trainee's history and cultural context as it relates to the interpersonal dynamics of the relationship with the client and with the supervisor. The statement concluded with a focus on the importance of safety, trust and respect in the supervisory relationship for such disclosure to work and an acknowledgment that trainees have the right to refuse to disclose such personal information. We discussed this expectation with our trainees at the beginning of their experience with us. Doing so was a declaration that we recognized the life experiences of the trainee are influential and important and invited an ongoing dialogue with the trainee, within a trusting relationship, that allowed for reflection on how their history of managing mental illness, and perhaps working with a therapist, impacts their work with clients. This achieved two simultaneous outcomes: Teaching trainees about ethical practice and destigmatizing mental illness.

Curricular Interventions

In addition to the aforementioned strategies, departments should consider how to incorporate intentional training about challenging stigma to both faculty members as well as to the students in the program. This training could focus on how to teach in such a way as to challenge stereotypes about individuals with mental illness. Research has found such intentionality is impactful to address stigma and helps trainees to improve their skills in managing the stigma in the clients they will serve (Rubio-Valera et al., 2018).

While researching this chapter, I found it noteworthy I could not find any existing program to teach stigma reduction for mental health professionals even though there are examples of such training to students in other health-related programs (e.g., Patel et al., 2024; Potts et al., 2022). This dearth of literature reinforces my argument regarding the assumption of the absence of stigma in mental health programs and their graduates. Either faculty are not comfortable teaching stigma reduction, do not know how to teach it, or are not aware they need to teach it.

Outcomes of stigma reduction trainings suggest they are effective for professionals (e.g., Cerully et al., 2016). Challenging stigma is an outcome of Mental Health First Aid (MHFA), a curriculum developed and administered by the National Council for Mental Wellbeing. Researchers have established the effectiveness of the program (e.g., Morgan et al., 2018). I became a MHFA trainer in 2016 to bring this important program to my campus. Although I had been a licensed psychologist for 16 years at the time of my MHFA training, it was the first time I had been reminded by a trainer/supervisor of the importance of talking about the impact of stigma on those with mental health challenges.

A broad training about mental health challenges is helpful and thus is an important component of graduate mental health programs. However, given the prominent and persistent stigma toward individuals who struggle with substance misuse (Pescosolido et al., 2021), departments should consider how they are providing training to students who will deliver substance use counseling. The persistence of the stigma indicates we have not figured out how to change the course of these beliefs. Graduate mental health programs could play an important part in altering this stigma. Firstly, programs could require students to enroll in at least one course about substance use. It is important that this course be taught from a neuroscience perspective; this would help begin to alter the stigmatized belief that substance misuse is a result of a moral failing.

Finally, faculty need to think about and challenge the titles used for their classes. As mentioned above, these courses are offered to meet state/jurisdictional licensure requirements. However, there is no requirement that the course have a specific name, only that the course must teach specific content. Changing a name of a course usually involves several bureaucratic steps, including having a curriculum committee approve a new name and the registrar changing the name in the university catalogue. While this usually takes time, faculty could, in the interim, provide a different, non-stigmatized name for their course. For instance, “Psychopathology” could be referred to as the "Diagnostic Method" class. Imagine opening a syllabus and seeing a different name than expected. Moreover, imagine reading the explanation for why there is a different name being used.

Conclusion

In this chapter, I discussed the various ways that graduate mental health programs have ignored, or at the very least been reluctant to consider, the way stigma is operating within its literal and figurative walls. Unfortunately, the resulting silence has provided a fertile ground for stigma to develop and strengthen. Since graduate mental health programs are focused on training the next generation of mental health professionals, they have an opportunity to join the call to alter the landscape of mental illness stigma (Pescosolido & Martin, 2015). They can do this by highlighting the persistence of stigma, by asserting its presence in the fabric of the program, by offering opportunities to challenge it in real time during classes and in training, and intentionally incorporating stigma reduction strategies into the curriculum. The hesitancy in doing this to date may be related to the worry of acknowledging stigma exists in the most unlikely place, that is, in the mental health field. Actually acknowledging it does exist in these programs could be the most important step in challenging it. Graduate mental health programs could become a leader on campus by demonstrating how to confront stigma directly by shining a light on it and building a pathway to changing it.

References

Allen, H. K., Lilly, F., Green, K. M., Zanjani, F., Vincent, K. B., & Arria, A. M. (2022). Substance use and mental health problems among graduate students: Individual and program-level correlates. *Journal of American College Health, 70*(1), 65–73. https://doi.org/10.1080/07448481.2020.1725020

American Psychiatric Association. (2022). *Diagnostic and statistical manual of mental disorders (5th ed., text rev.).* https://doi.org/10.1176/appi.books.9780890425787

Barenie, R. E., Cernasev, A., Heidel, R. E., Stewart, S., & Hohmeier, K. (2023). Faculty, staff, and student perceptions of substance use disorder stigma in health profession training programs: A quantitative study. *Substance Abuse Treatment, Prevention & Policy, 18*(1), 1–10. https://doi.org/10.1186/s13011-022-00509-8

Brown, L. S., & Walker, L. E. (1990). Feminist therapy perspectives on self-disclosure. In G. Stricker & M. Fisher (Eds.), *Self-disclosure in the therapeutic relationship* (pp. 135–154). Springer.

Cerully, J. L., Collins, R. L., Wong, E. C., Roth, E., Marks, J. S., & Yu, J. (2016). Effects of stigma and discrimination reduction trainings conducted under the California mental health services authority. *RAND Health Quarterly, 5*(3), 5. https://www.rand.org/pubs/periodicals/health-quarterly/issues/v5/n3/05.html

Corrigan, P. W., Druss, B. G., & Perlick, D. A. (2014). Impact of mental health stigma on seeking and participating in mental health care. *Psychological Science in the Public Interest, 15*, 37–70. https://doi.org/10.1177/1529100614531398

Corrigan, P. W., Markowitz, F. E., & Watson, A. C. (2004). Structural levels of mental illness stigma and discrimination. *Schizophrenia Bulletin, 30*(3), 481–491.

Corrigan, P. W., & Rao, D. (2012). On the self-stigma of mental illness: Stages, disclosure, and strategies for change. *Canadian Journal of Psychiatry, 57*(8), 464–469. https://doi.org/10.1177/070674371205700804

Council for Accreditation of Counseling and Related Educational Programs. (2022). CACREP vital statistics 2019: Results from a national survey of accredited programs. https://www.cacrep.org/wp-content/uploads/2023/01/Vital-Stats-Report-2020.pdf

Council on Social Work Education. (2021). 2020 statistics on social work education in the United States. https://www.cswe.org/getattachment/726b15ce-6e63-4dcd-abd1-35d2ea9d9d40/2020-Annual-Statistics-On-Social-Work-Education-in-the-United-States.pdf?lang=en-US

Covarrubias, I., & Han, M. (2011). Mental health stigma about serious mental illness among MSW students: Social contact and attitude. *Social Work, 56*(4), 317–325. https://doi.org/10.1093/sw/56.4.317

de Vos, J. A., Netten, C., & Norordenbos, G. (2016). Recovered eating disorder therapists using their experiential knowledge in therapy: A qualitative examination of the therapists' and the patients' view. *Eating Disorders, 24*(3), 207–223. https://doi.org/10.1080/10640266.2015.1090869

Dell, N. A., Vidovic, K. R., Vaughn, M. G., & Sasaki, N. (2021). Mental health provider stigma, expectations for recovery, and perceived quality of care provided to persons with mental illness. *Stigma and Health, 6*(2), 247–250. https://doi.org/10.1037/sah0000227

Deng, Y., Wang, A., Frasso, R., Ran, M., Zhang, T., Kong, D., & Wong, Y. I. (2022). Mental health-related stigma and attitudes toward patient care among providers of mental health services in a rural Chinese county. *International Journal of Social Psychiatry, 68*, 610–618. https://doi.org/10.1177/0020764021992807

Digiuni, M., Jones, F. W., & Camic, P. M. (2013). Perceived social stigma and attitudes towards seeking therapy in training: A cross-national study. *Psychotherapy, 50*(2), 213–223. https://doi.org/10.1037/a0028784

Endale, T., Qureshi, O., Ryan, G. K., Esponda, G. M., Verhey, R., Eaton, J., De Silva, M., & Murphy, J. (2020). Barriers and drivers to capacity-building in global mental health projects. *International Journal of Mental Health Systems, 14*, 89. https://doi.org/10.1186/s13033-020-00420-4

Gorman, K. S., & Brennan, K. M. (2023). Mental illness public stigma and treatment seeking among university students. *Journal of College Student Psychotherapy, 37*(1), 52–70. https://doi.org/10.1080/87568225.2021.1891006

Graves, S. L., & Wright, L. B. (2007). Comparison of individual factors in school psychology graduate students: Why do students pursue a degree in school psychology? *Psychology in the Schools, 44*, 865–872. https://doi.org/10.1002/pits.20271

Grice, T., Alcock, K., & Scior, K. (2018). Mental health disclosure amongst clinical psychologists in training: Perfectionism and pragmatism. *Clinical Psychology & Psychotherapy, 25*(5), 721–729. https://doi.org/10.1002/cpp.2192

Huynh, L., & Rhodes, P. (2011). Why do people choose to become psychologists? A narrative inquiry. *Psychology Teaching Review, 17*(2), 64–70. https://eric.ed.gov/?id=EJ959027

Kallingal, M. (2021, October 22). Simone Biles opens up about her mental health post-Olympics: 'I'm still scared to do gymnastics'. CNN. https://www.cnn.com/2021/10/22/sport/simone-biles-gymnastics-spt/index.html

Kelly, J. F., Saitz, R., & Wakeman, S. (2016). Language, substance use disorders, and policy: The need to reach consensus on an "addiction-ary". *Alcohol Treatment Quarterly, 34*(1), 116–123. https://doi.org/10.1080/07347324.2016.1113103

Kronner, H. W. (2013). Use of self-disclosure for the gay male therapist: The impact on gay males in therapy. *Journal of Social Service Research, 39*(1), 78–94. https://doi.org/10.1080/01488376.2012.686732

Lauber, C., Nordt, C., Braunschweig, C., & Rössler, W. (2006). Do mental health professionals stigmatize their patients? *Acta Psychiatrica Scandinavica Supplementum, 429*, 51–59. https://doi.org/10.1111/j.1600-0447.2005.00718.x

Masedo, A., Grandón, P., Saldivia, S., Vielma-Aguilera, A., Castro-Alzate, E. S., Bustos, C., Romero-López-Alberca, C., Pena-Andreu, J. M., Xavier, M., & Moreno-Küstner, B. (2021). A multicentric study on stigma towards people with mental illness in health sciences students. *BMC Medical Education, 21*(1), 324. https://doi.org/10.1186/s12909-021-02695-8

Menschner, C., & Maul, A. (2016, April). Key ingredients for successful trauma-informed care implementation. SAMHSA. https://www.samhsa.gov/sites/default/files/programs_campaigns/childrens_mental_health/atc-whitepaper-040616.pdf

Morgan, A. J., Ross, A., & Reavley, N. J. (2018). Systematic review and meta-analysis of mental health first aid training: Effects on knowledge, stigma, and helping behaviour. *PLoS One, 13*(5), e0197102. https://doi.org/10.1371/journal.pone.0197102

Mullan, J. (2023). *Decolonizing therapy: Oppression, historical trauma, and politicizing your practice*. Norton.

National Alliance on Mental Illness. (n.d.). Mental health by the numbers. https://nami.org/mhstats?gclid=CjwKCAjwue6hBhBVEiwA9YTx8IQZcA-mHaZBqcqBoannVppXcJf3OgPuMkMs0TG4FjUiQSjvyk98-xoC0wYQAvD_BwE

National Center for Education Statistics. (n.d.). IPEDS data explorer. *U.S. Department of Education, Institute of Education Sciences*. https://nces.ed.gov/ipeds/Search?query=graduate%20psychology%20programs&query2=graduate%20psychology%20programs&resultType=all&page=1&sortBy=relevance&overlayDigestTableId=202296

National Institute on Drug Abuse. (2021, November 29). Words matter: Terms to use and avoid when talking about addiction. https://nida.nih.gov/nidamed-medical-health-professionals/health-professions-education/words-matter-terms-to-use-avoid-when-talking-about-addiction

Osaka, N. (2021, July 8). It's o.k. not to be okay. Time. https://time.com/6077128/naomi-osaka-essay-tokyo-olympics/

Parscesepe, A. M., & Cabassa, L. J. (2013). Public stigma of mental illness in the United States: A systematic literature review. *Administration and Policy in Mental Health, 40*(1), 1–22. https://doi.org/10.1007/s10488-012-0430-z

Patel, A. D., Sharma, M. P., Pal, A., Verma, U. K., Tiwari, P., & Alam, Z. (2024). Perceived stigma among undergraduate medical students towards people with psychiatric illness: A cross sectional study. *Journal of Family Medicine and Primary Care, 13*, 4910–4915. https://doi.org/10.4103/jfmpc.jfmpc_442_24

Pescosolido, B. A., Halpern-Manners, A., Luo, L., & Perry, B. (2021). Trends in public stigma of mental illness in the U.S., 1996–2018. *JAMA Network Open, 4*(12), e2140202. https://doi.org/10.1001/jamanetworkopen.2021.40202

Pescosolido, B. A., & Martin, J. K. (2015). The stigma complex. *Annual Review of Sociology, 41*(1), 87–116. https://doi.org/10.1146/annurev-soc-071312-145702

Pescosolido, B. A., Medina, T. R., Martin, J. K., & Long, J. S. (2013). The 'backbone' of stigma: Identifying the global core of public prejudice associated with mental illness. *American Journal of Public Health, 103*(5), 853–860. https://doi.org/10.2105/AJPH.2012.301147

Potts, L. C., Bakolis, I., Deb, T., Lempp, H., Vince, T., Benbow, Y., Waugh, W., Kim, S., Raza, S., Henderson, C., & The INDIGO READ Study Group. (2022). Anti-stigma training and positive changes in mental illness stigma outcomes in medical students in ten countries: A mediation analysis on pathways via empathy development and anxiety reduction. *Social Psychiatry and Psychiatric Epidemiology, 57*, 1861–1873. https://doi.org/10.1007/s00127-022-02284-0

Rubio-Valera, M., Aznar-Lou, I., Vives-Collet, M., Fernández, A., Gil-Girbau, M., & Serrano-Blanco, A. (2018). Reducing the mental health-related stigma of social work students: A cluster RCT. *Research on Social Work Practice, 28*(2), 164–172. https://doi.org/10.1177/1049731516641

Sandhu, H. S., Arora, A., Brasch, J., & Streiner, D. L. (2019). Mental health stigma: Explicit and implicit attitudes of Canadian undergraduate students, medical school students, and psychiatrists. *Canadian Journal of Psychiatry, 64*, 209–217. https://doi.org/10.1177/0706743718792193

Siegel, J. T., & Keeler, A. (2020). Storm, stress, silence: A focus group examination of mental health culture and challenges among graduate students currently or previously experiencing depression. *Journal of College Counseling, 23*(3), 207–220. https://doi.org/10.1002/jocc.12166

Strassle, C. G. (2018). Reducing mental illness stigma in the classroom. *Teaching of Psychology, 45*(4), 351–357. https://doi.org/10.1177/0098628318796922

Substance Use and Mental Health Service Administration. (2022). *Key substance use and mental health indicators in the United States: Results from the 2021 National Survey on Drug Use and Health.* (HHS publication no: PEP22-07-01-005). https://www.samhsa.gov/data/sites/default/files/reports/rpt39443/2021NSDUHFFRRev010323.pdf

Subu, M. A., Dias, J. M., Mottershead, R., Ahmed, F. R., Narulita, S., Maryuni, M., et al. (2024). Exploring mental health stigma among Indonesian healthcare students towards individuals with mental illnesses: A qualitative study. *International Journal of Qualitative Studies on Health and Well-Being, 19*(1), 2327103. https://doi.org/10.1080/17482631.2024.2327103

Sultzer, D. L. (1994). Mental status examination. In C. E. Coffey, J. L. Cummings, M. R. Lovell, & G. D. Pearlson (Eds.), *The American psychiatric press textbook of geriatric neuropsychiatry* (pp. 111–127). American Psychiatric Association.

Tay, S., Alcock, K., & Scior, K. (2018). Mental health problems among psychologists: Stigma and its impact on disclosure and help-seeking. *Journal of Clinical Psychology, 74*(9), 1545–1555. https://doi.org/10.1002/jclp.22614

Thomas, S., Caputi, P., & Wilson, C. (2014). Specific attitudes which predict psychology students' intentions to seek help for psychological distress. *Journal of Clinical Psychology, 70*(3), 273–282. https://doi.org/10.1002/jclp.22022

Victor, S. E., Schledier, J. L., Ammerman, B. A., Bradford, D. E., Devendorf, A. R., Gruber, J., Gunaydin, L. A., Hallion, L. S., Kaufman, E. A., Lewis, S. P., & Stage, D. L. (2022). Leveraging the strengths of psychologists with lived experience of psychopathology. *Perspectives on Psychological Science, 17*(6), 1624–1632. https://doi.org/10.1177/17456916211072826

Worell, J., & Remer, P. (2003). *Feminist perspectives in therapy: Empowering diverse women* (2nd ed.). John Wiley & Sons Inc.

World Health Organization. (2022, June 8). *Mental disorders.* https://www.who.int/news-room/fact-sheets/detail/mental-disorders

World Health Organization. (2024, May 27). Post-traumatic stress disorder. https://www.who.int/news-room/fact-sheets/detail/post-traumatic-stress-disorder#:~:text=Around%2070%25%20of%20people%20globally,in%20their%20lives%20(2).

Kimberly S. Gorman, Ph.D., is Associate Vice Chancellor for Health & Wellness in the Student Affairs Division at Western Carolina University, USA. Dr. Gorman's primary research interests are related to collegiate mental health and mental illness stigma in the college population. She has co-authored several papers about the impacts of mental illness and its related stigma in college students. She is a licensed psychologist who has worked in the higher education setting for more than two decades. She has served on the governing board of the Association for University and College Counseling Center Directors and on the advisory board for the Center for Collegiate Mental Health.

Chapter 7
U Bring Change to Mind: A High-Touch, Peer-to-Peer, Empowerment Approach to Addressing Mental Health Challenges on College Campuses

Bernice A. Pescosolido

Abstract College has changed—changed in operation, student population, and sense of responsibility for the whole student. In higher education's embrace of mental health, one critical issue becomes how to address well-being beyond clinical services. This paper introduces an evidence-based model, U Bring Change to Mind, a "high-touch" student empowerment program designed to make campuses "safe and stigma-free zones." The contemporary challenge, rationale, scientific foundations, evaluation results, and examples of student-developed activities provide an initial introduction.

Keywords Stigma · Social networks · Empowerment · Evidence-based

The Changing College Campus

Anyone interested in college students and their eventual impact on society is aware of the relatively new "facts" that challenge current undergraduate cohorts. Suicide rates among youth have risen, mental health issues are identified earlier and better than in the past, and a "triple bind" now faces young women in particular (Hinshaw & Kranz, 2009). These challenges have only been compounded by the aftereffects of COVID-19 pandemic's lockdown isolation and pre-existing health disparities for college students from diverse cultures and socioeconomic backgrounds. Mental health issues have now come to the fore in higher education (Blanco et al., 2008;

The author has no conflicts of interest to declare that are relevant to the content of this chapter.

B. A. Pescosolido (✉)
Irsay Institute for Sociomedical Sciences, Indiana University, Bloomington, IN, USA
e-mail: pescosol@iu.edu

© The Author(s), under exclusive license to Springer Nature Switzerland AG 2025

K. M. Brennan, K. S. Gorman (eds.), *A University-Wide Approach to Changing Campus Cultures of Mental Illness Stigma*, Knowledge Studies in Higher Education 18, https://doi.org/10.1007/978-3-031-86496-4_7

Busby et al., 2020; Harvey, 2021, Kadison & DiGeronimo, 2004; Zhou & Eisenberg, 2022). Even with a narrower focus on addressing student mental health to maintain and improve retention, the neglect and lost potential and productivity of past generations will be heightened by the approaching "demographic cliff."

Together these forces intensify changes college students have always faced—new living arrangements, new expectations about independent living and academic work, the loss of old social ties, the challenge of creating new ones—and create multiple cross-pressures for emerging adults (Hurst et al., 2013; Kadison & DiGeronimo, 2004). The once common notion that students with mental health problems are "not here" or, even worse, "should not be here" is now untenable. College years bracket the major years (ages 15–24) of onset of most mental illnesses (de Girolamo et al., 2019). The Project Healthy Minds data reveal nearly one in three college students in the United States reports struggling with anxiety and depression alone, while more than 1,000 contemporary college students die by suicide each year (Eisenberg et al., 2009; Liu et al., 2019). Less well documented, but equally powerful, are the scores of well-known and highly successful college graduates who have stepped forward to reveal they struggled with these issues during their college years (e.g., MacPhee, 2023).

With pressure on college health centers to increase mental health services, parents, students, and administrators have changed the dialogue from dealing with deaths to improving awareness, belonging, and prevention (e.g., Lipson et al., 2019; Schwartz & Kay, 2009). While many U.S. institutions are reconsidering what they do provide, often with the expert assistance of organizations such as the Jed Foundation, the recognition that no college or university will be able to meet the level and cyclical nature of unmet needs that we are now seeing on college campuses is nearly universal. Neither can mental health professionals within geographic areas around campuses contend with the overflow, nor do so within the financial or insurance resources available to most college students. According to the National Survey on Drug Use and Health, more than half of Americans who reported the need for mental health services reported they are receiving no treatment with even more who are in care reporting continued unmet needs (Center for Behavioral Health Statistics and Quality, 2017). The burden of fixing a broken mental health system cannot be laid at the feet of higher education. What we see on college campuses simply reflects the state of mental health care in the nation overall.

That said, the criticality of addressing mental health on U.S. college campuses, as well as international ones, can no longer be ignored. Colleges and universities have recognized the challenge and have both reconsidered their mental health service systems (e.g., telehealth options, distributed counseling offices) and built a range of other support systems to address the stressors that can lead to mental health problems (e.g., food pantries, financial education services). The one thing they have not done is to address the social, psychological, and cultural forces that stand in the way of students accessing these novel options. That is, stigma has stood in the way of the uptake of services, whether narrowly defined or more broadly related to triggering mental health problems. Confronting stigma involves strategies ranging from simple mental health literacy (i.e., recognizing mental health issues and knowing what to do about them) to tackling the prejudice and discrimination that typically accompanies mental illness head on.

One viable option, to accompany the reconsideration of services provided, turns the focus to ongoing efforts to change the cultural climate and weave mental health into the social fabric of higher education. Having students take a required course faces the barriers of increasing requirements and the legitimate complaint that other issues might be just as critical. Launching typical anti-stigma media campaigns has been shown to have little effect, and making it part of orientation, while helpful, represents the one-time "inoculation" model that has also been shown to have short-term effects at best (National Academies of Sciences Engineering and Medicine [NASEM], 2016). Rather, by normalizing the idea that college entry can come with novel stressors, providing an understanding of the greater awareness of early signs of stressors that may trigger the onset of mild to serious mental health problems, and empowering students with resources to reduce the stigma of mental illness on an ongoing basis, students can take part in a range of efforts to address issues from inclusion to recognition, seeking care, managing ongoing problems, and providing accommodations. Under the proposed model, the program offers a peer effort that reflects an accepting and welcoming environment and that fosters a community of inclusion and open discussion about struggles and services (Funkhouser et al., 2017; Siegel et al., 2023).

The University Bring Change to Mind (UBC2M) program, developed and piloted at Indiana University's flagship campus in Bloomington, is one such model. In higher education, deploying a supported, evidence-based, peer-to-peer, "high-touch" program avoids most institutional barriers (e.g., curriculum approvals, required training). It can broaden mental health targets to include opportunities for workforce development, professional socialization, advocacy, faculty–student interaction, and leadership training. At Indiana University (IU), this program entailed two development efforts: (1) UBC2M, the peer-led, institutionally supported program; and (2) the College Toolbox Project (CTP), a four-year study of an entering cohort of students at IU, designed and carried out by a cross-disciplinary, volunteer team of staff and scientists, that marked attitudes and behaviors at two points in time. The latter established the evidence base for the program which uses a more contemporary approach to dissemination and implementation elsewhere.

The purpose of this chapter is to introduce the science, logic, and principles behind this one effort to improve the cultural climate toward mental health issues on college campuses. UBC2M targets individuals, groups, and institutional social change by encouraging many parts of the college or university to partner with empowered students to move toward a "safe and stigma-free" campus. In doing so, it not only responds directly to the challenges listed (e.g., spreading awareness of mental health, bolstering connectedness and inclusion, providing social and information resources, and increasing retention) but also enhances the development of a less stigmatizing generation of mental health providers, policy leaders, employers, teachers, parents, and informed citizens. Because current research suggests mental health stigma is higher in older population groups (Pescosolido et al., 2020), there is a sense among social scientists involved in the mental health sector that targeting the next generation may have a greater societal impact and longer lasting effect than targeting the general population. Of course, it remains unclear whether the finding on age represents a conservatizing effect of growing old, a period effect in which current elders grew up (although "the greatest generation" seems to ally more closely with millennials and generations that followed), or a cohort effect of experiences that included greater demonization of individuals and asylums of care. Still, betting on a well-informed, mental health-interested current generation represents an encouraging pathway to sustained improvement.

The current chapter has three parts. First, a "refresher" on the target of the program wherein the stigma attached to mental health, whether mental illness, addiction, or other associated issues (e.g., eating disorders, domestic violence), is provided. This is accompanied by a discussion of classic and contemporary social science research on individual and institutional change, as well as social movements. Second, the guiding principles of the program are laid out. Third, the process of creating a program, looking at its content, and evaluating its impact is provided.

The Science Behind the Architecture of UBC2M

Understanding the Nature of Stigma

The target of UBC2M is the stigma attached to mental illness and related issues (i.e., compounded or layered stigma) such as addictions and other statuses (LGBTQ+, race/ethnicity). The "seed" of stigma, which came from ancient Greek practice of branding slaves captured during warfare, is essentially a mark of "difference," whether physical or social, that produces a stereotype. As summarized in Table 7.1, that mark of difference translates into prejudice (attitudes, beliefs, and cultural constructions with generally negative connotations) and discrimination (behaviors that shun, disregard, and deny social and material resources). While the overall target of UBC2M is public stigma (i.e., the cultural climate on campus), activities, events, and information can target any of the many types of stigma, including self-stigma (internalized), structural stigma (institutionally embedded in

Table 7.1 Basic terms and definitions surrounding the stigma of mental health and illness

Stigma →	Prejudice →	Discrimination
Stereotype: Attribution of a set of characteristics	Negative (often) and positive (sometimes) attitudes	Behaviors
Fixed, apply to all members of the marked group	Knowledge: MI = bad character Beliefs: MI = dangerousness Attitudes: MI = unsuitable employees, supervisors, marriage partners	Reject, exclude, isolate… Coerce, restrain, arrest… Not hire, promote, date, rent to…

policies and laws), courtesy or affiliate stigma (faced by family and providers). Research has provided a solid scientific foundation on current levels of stigma, correlative forces and factors, and effects (Parcesepe & Cabassa, 2013; Pescosolido, 2013; Pescosolido et al., 2013). Understanding the multilevel, complex nature of stigma is essential to determine the targets for stigma change, including messages that work and don't work (NASEM, 2016; Pescosolido et al., 2010; Stuart et al., 2012; Stuart & Sartorius, 2022) and groups, such as men and people of color, that require special attention because related discussion of mental health issues have been problematic and rare (Eylem et al., 2020; Thornicroft et al., 2022; Yamaguchi et al., 2011).

Understanding the Nature of Social Change

Following on its initial connection to Bring Change to Mind, the advocacy group founded by actor Glenn Close, UBC2M built on the dual legs of science and family (in our case, the college "family"), to "end stigma by starting the conversation" (https://www.bringchange2mind.org). UBC2M was developed before many college-targeted programs were developed (except for the National Alliance on Mental Illness [NAMI] and Active Minds) and drew more generally from social science research on successful shifts in individual, group, and societal cultures.

The Theories and Models Included

Cohort Replacement Theory. This theory suggests that documented social and cultural change, often characterized as "changing hearts and minds" was, in reality, a turnover in the attitudes, beliefs, and behaviors of population groups. Since stigma research has consistently documented higher levels of stigma among older individuals, research suggested that focusing on younger populations and reinforcing their more tolerant cultural views may be a better target for a societal shift in stigma over the long run (Burstein & Freudenburg, 1978.) *Take-away message:* Rather than trying to focus on a general campaign, target new members (i.e., students). This does not mean that accompanying shifts could not occur among others on campus, simply that the "engine of change" might more efficiently focus on students.

The Acquired Disposition Model. This model suggests that changing "hearts and minds" is more likely during periods of individuals' lives when they are most open to rethinking their cultural values. College represents just such a developmental period and entry into college represents a key point in emerging adulthood. Engaging college students as they enter a new role and context offers a prime time to focus or refocus their beliefs about "others" (Vaisey & Lizardo, 2010). *Take-away Message:* Focus on students during a key time in their social, emotional, and intellectual development when they are exposing themselves to new ideas.

Institutional Theories of Social Change. These theories suggest effective change can only take hold if efforts focus on changing and integrating with the "social fabric," weaving central beliefs and norms into the larger culture. That is, efforts are more likely to be successful if they are long-term and integrate with the day-to-day, regular activities of a people or place (Blee, 1991). Also, change agents should be part of the group targeted for change. Students are much more likely to understand what will get other students "in the door" to activities, to know what messages they will hear and how they will interpret them, and what mechanisms may be likely to keep this "top of mind" for students. Everything from what events to do, when to do them, what kind of "swag" they will actually use or wear, and how to provide resources that they can access when needed can best be determined by members of that "culture." This kind of local information changes more quickly than faculty and staff can grasp. *Take-away Message:* Avoid stand-alone approaches in favor of ones that tap peers who understand "the moment" and shape engagement where mental health issues can become part of undergraduate and graduate life.

Theories of Social Movements and Sustainable Implementation. These suggest that ownership by the group targeted for change ("nothing about us without us"), at least minimal buy-in from the institution ("skin in the game"), and connection to a larger, stable organization ("high touch") are fundamental for relevant, successful, and long-lasting change, especially in the college environment (Corrigan, 2016; McCarthy & Zald, 1977). *Take-away Message:* Students must be at the center of the effort, leading the strategies for and content of change. However, even with an initial enthusiastic and talented group of students, the natural progress of students to graduation and their lack of familiarity with organizational procedures requires a professional guide above the level of a typical faculty advisor. In other words, thinking ahead about efficient processes requires an advisor with training in student organizations, a focus on sustainable processes for leadership and recruitment, and a clear resourced signal from the larger administration that this is an important activity. While minimal budget resources are needed to support a student-led program, equally important are symbolic signals (e.g., allowing use of the institution logo in branding materials).

The Program

The basis for UBC2M efforts is scientific research, avoiding approaches known to be ineffective, condescending, or narrowly pedantic. A review of existing evidence on stigma change, per se, provided further substantive direction and suggestions for reducing stigma, increasing the acceptance of people with mental health challenges, and supporting the development and use of existing services. Research pointed away from educational-based efforts and lofty public awareness campaigns in favor of long-term, peer-involved efforts (consistent with learning research that supports active versus passive learning, e.g., Yamaguchi et al., 2013). Traditional approaches were increasingly seen as antiquated, inflexible, and unscalable with lengthy curriculum-type modules (e.g., diversity, mental illness, bullying) and a top-down approach that “trained” individuals who often returned to their earlier levels of stigma endorsement over time.

UBC2M targets campus climate and institutional social change, as well as individual change (Fig. 7.1). In higher education, deploying an institution-based program avoids most institutional requirements for curriculum change which is often opposed because it interferes with the increasing requirements for majors. More importantly, by being a program with ownership primarily by students but also welcoming staff and faculty, the goals for creating a “safe and stigma-free” campus can broaden to include opportunities for workforce development, professional socialization, advocacy, and peer leadership. For example, UBC2M leaders have engaged faculty and mental health providers in discussion events to address the stigma that some have faced from family and friends when they express interest in careers in psychiatry, psychiatric social work, or psychiatric nursing. Similarly, events have included leveraging upcoming campus visitors involved in mental health research, advocacy, or philanthropy for special events with the program and bringing students in the program to BC2M galas and scientific conferences.

In the end, five general and five tailored principles derived from stigma and social science research provided a new approach to meet the challenges of stigma reduction and avoid the efficacy–effectiveness dilemma characteristic of training, public service campaigns, and one-shot events. The underlying general principles of change (Panel A) and how they are translated into the specific principles (Panel B) for UBC2M are listed in Table 7.2. Generally speaking, research has documented that launching media or other “campaigns” tends not to gain much attention nor to have much effect. Rather, targeting the more manageable ideas of a group, in this case, an age group, on their concerns and with mechanisms that will garner

Fig. 7.1 The UBC2M Logo

Table 7.2 Basic evidence-based scientific principles about normative and behavioral change and their applications and implications for mental health programming in higher education. (Adapted and updated from Pescosolido et al., 2020)

Panel A: General principles	**Anti-stigma programs**	**Implications for college-based program**
Target a population, clarify message	Do not target generally, but focus on groups open to change and who can take "ownership."	College students stand at a key transition point. Target awareness and changing norms of inclusion.
Choose leaders "of the community" and provide resources	Institutionally required training is less effective than student programs designed, with guidance, by students themselves.	A student group with minimal, but key, assistance from professionals trained in student activities is optimal.
Avoid known, ineffective approaches	Base the program in the research on effective anti-stigma approaches.	Mentoring includes science-based tools and, if possible, integration into the work (teaching and research) of interested faculty.
Leverage existing resources	Avoid common unwillingness among organizations, including mental health organizations, to work together. Break through the tradition to "own" programs to create sharing communities.	Partner with existing student groups and institutional events. Develop a division of labor to enhance resources and avoid redundancy.
Build in change	Flexibility is essential to continue efficacy as communities undergo social change and newer cohorts of students bring new interests and ideas.	Avoid detailed manualized programming and build in flexibility and mechanisms for change.
Panel B: Tailored principles	**Anti-stigma college and university programs**	**Possible strategies**
Start young	Within the college population, deploy a special focus on entering students.	Include all students, but target first-year students. If possible, establish a presence at orientation or "welcome week" type of events.
By students, for students	Organic focus on the campus climate, not institutional requirements or needs. Awareness, inclusion, tolerance, and diversity remain in-scope.	Traditional educational approaches are most effective with younger groups or those with area interest. Leave education to faculty and administration in relevant programs, majors, and extra-curricular activities.

(continued)

Table 7.2 (continued)

"Bait & flip"	Consider the "draw" first. That is, ask what will draw students to an activity, event, or message. Those who attend traditional mental health or anti-stigma events have already been documented to have lower levels of stigma.	Get "outside the choir" to be most effective.
Leverage	Events require resources. More integrated events can provide opportunities for extra resources, and existing special pots of resources allow students to learn about grant applications, writ small, which should be applied for by students with advisor mentoring.	Seek places, other student groups, or college offices with similar goals and pool resources. Infiltrate, share, and build resources.
Evolve	Provide information and guides to events. This includes what it takes to do the event, how to do it (and how to do it better next time), and how/where tailoring to other campuses is possible. Engage students to do simple, summative assessments included in materials. Create shareable resources that build larger efforts. Broaden the student experience to include basic assessment research tools/approaches.	Create and add to a "living library" of each event that includes a blueprint and assessment and allows for other campuses to have ownership.

their attention is more likely to work (Mehta et al., 2015). Often, change efforts have taken the form of education by "higher ups" or by "experts" who lecture on the topic (e.g., https://jedfoundation.org/campus-mental-health-action-planning-guide/). While important and useful, especially for organizational assessment and change, research has indicated that education and training work best for very young age groups of individuals who have no awareness of the topic at all (e.g., middle school and younger) (Song et al., 2023). Formal programming will likely only draw in those students already interested in the topic (i.e., those "in the choir"). Activities and events must attract individuals to the event who do not think this is a topic relevant to them. Then, through creative and often fun activities, programs can integrate awareness, learning, and dissemination of resource materials to those "outside the choir." Further, having ideas and efforts come from like-individuals has greater acceptance and resonance, especially when innovative, engaging efforts align both with evidence-based approaches and the interests of the target group, especially as they enter a new context (e.g., during orientation). Because one problem highlighted in the NASEM report (2016) is that mental health groups are siloed, rarely work together, and share meager resources (as opposed to cancer or heart disease), another message for a college program lies in leveraging other student groups advocating on relevant generational issues. For example, early in the pilot years, UBC2M students were asked to be part of a "trash" fashion show where students created and modeled outfits made from entirely recycled materials. While environmental change was the initiating focus, students brought in Ashley Graham, the first plus-sized winner of *America's Top Model*, so that issues of body positivity were acknowledged; UBC2M students provided mental health supporting presence and materials. Finally, traditional change models (typically small-scale, randomized clinical trials with required fidelity to the model) are hard to scale, often ill-fit to new contexts and likely become stale over time. In the underlying model presented here, fidelity to the *principles* of change is key to longevity, tailoring, and greater impact (for greater detail, see NASEM, 2016; Stuart & Sartorius, 2022).

UBC2M conceptualizes the college campus as a "community" in which using active, participatory events designed and carried out by students can achieve social and educational goals. Drawing from the energy and knowledge of the students themselves facilitates the relevance of events, drawing in a broader audience, especially among students who are neither interested in nor aware of the salience of mental health to their lives (See Fig. 7.2). While the focus remains on the larger cultural context of the stigma of mental illness, specific events may focus on different groups (e.g., first-year students, students of color, faculty, the larger community) or simultaneously address other issues of prejudice and discrimination (see Fig. 7.3). Thus, leveraging other student groups, special campus events, or other important campus goals translates to efforts with a wider draw that includes the possibility of intersectional or multiple stigmas. Student leaders can integrate, share, and leverage campus resources for greater impact and some campus administrative leaders have innovated student inclusion in the mental health crisis (e.g., student mental health councils) which multiplies the potential of an anti-stigma program to have important effects. Finally, events can integrate with students' other interests, taking advantage of the many facets of student life and providing them with leadership opportunities across their college activities (see Fig. 7.4).

In sum, UBC2M aims for an approach with flexibility to change, continually drawing from student and community energy, and moving in alignment with sociodemographic and cultural trends. The wealth of energy and enthusiasm among the students, administrators, and faculty who donated their time and resources to the IU program was demonstrated in both the programmatic and research components of the pilot effort. The list of brochures available at this point and a sample of their

Fig. 7.2 An example of an event that translated a popular trend into an integrative, participatory event with mental health translation of "clues" to escape

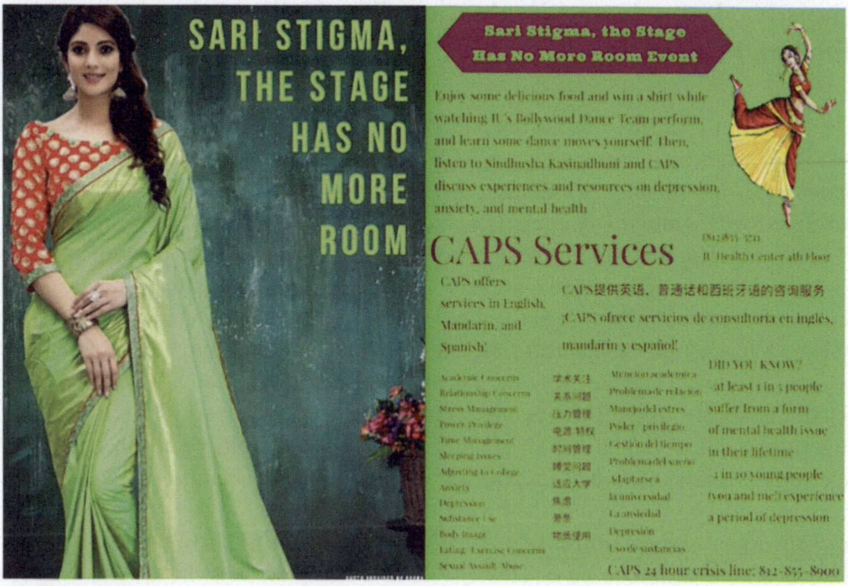

Fig. 7.3 An example of an event that leverages other student groups and targets intersectional issues in stigma

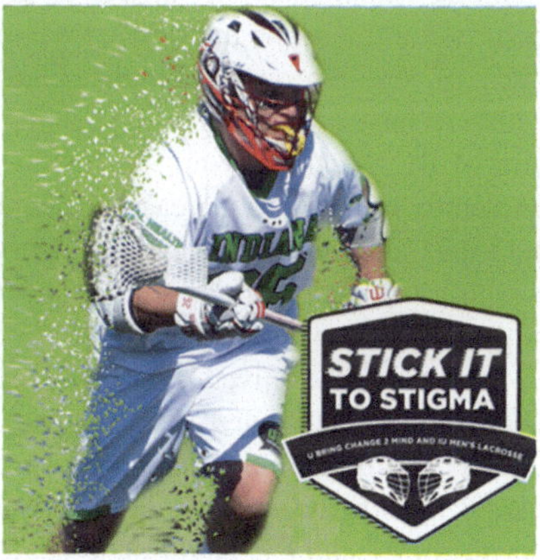

Fig. 7.4 An example of an event that integrates students' other activities, in this case, a club sport, with efforts to reduce stigma

content, provided in Table 7.3 and Fig. 7.7 in the Appendix 7.1, reveals the range of activities, from large to small, and the cooperation of groups from the campus cinema to the local coffee shops. The goal is to continue to build these and, on request of students, will now include a "legacy page" that lists the campus that developed the event, now that the program has disseminated to all nine campuses of Indiana University. A living library of events, from IU and other campuses that become involved, provides direct existing ideas, and more importantly, a springboard for more and different ideas as well as campus pride.

Logistics, Launch, and Evaluation: The College Toolbox Project

The launch of UBC2M was accompanied by the College Toolbox Project (CTP), a two-wave, web-based survey during IU Bloomington's students' first and third academic years to establish an evidence base. From April 14 to 17, 2013, the Program Advisor for Cognitive Disorders (Banbury Center) hosted a planning meeting at Cold Spring Harbor Labs to design both the program and the assessment plan. Eighteen IU undergraduate and graduate students, national and international stigma researchers, mental health organization leaders (e.g., the Jed Foundation), founder (Glenn Close), and members of BC2M programs spent 2 days developing the "bones" of a novel college program. The meeting was organized by the author as the scientific advisor of BC2M. Faculty were selected by their research in the area of stigma or related mental health areas (e.g., health psychology, health equity) or relevant research methods (e.g., survey methodology, evaluation research). Staff were asked to be involved if they were centrally involved in student activities, or relevant organizational offices (e.g., First Year Experience, Dean of Students Office). Student recruitment focused on closely related existing student efforts (e.g., Culture of Care student group), students developing research agendas on stigma or student organizing, or students involved in classes with a focus on the stigma of mental illness. The meeting resulted in the development of the initial logo (see Fig. 1), understanding which university offices would be critical for success (e.g., legal office for permission to use the university logo on UBC2M merchandise and events), a summary of research on what makes change efforts work, and a preliminary plan of action to have a program pilot year starting in fall 2014. UBC2M, the "U"niversity arm of BC2M, then, would be a student-led club (initially, now transformed to a university program to increase sustainability) planning and carrying out anti-stigma activities and advocating for change. UBC2M was relaunched in fall 2015 as an institutionally supported, student-led organization to make campuses "safe and stigma-free zones."

The role of the university was minimal but critical (IRB approval for the research, licensing for activities). Faculty participation was heaviest in the early design aspects and in the much later analysis and write-up of the evaluation. The heaviest load is now on the students themselves to decide on and carry out events, hold regular meetings, and pay attention to leadership succession and recruitment. However, without the early, heavy investment of the lead faculty to pave the way with research and program needs (e.g., purchasing and approvals), the work of both the students and the half-time staff person would have been impossible. This was to be expected in developing an entirely new approach. At this point, many of these details have been worked out with information provided in program materials. However, the key element of a half-time staffer remains; the program would be untenable without the dedicated staff position. This represents the only cost to the institution for the program materials and continual "high-touch" communication with the national UBC2M infrastructure which is still being built. For the new, seven additional campus programs on other IU campuses, current reports indicate it can take at least a semester or two to get going and find the fit with the campus culture, determine what kinds of events from the living library are exciting to student leadership, and to develop their own uniquely tailored events (i.e., working alongside a student food pantry) which later can be submitted to become a part of the living library. A fall 2023 meeting of staffers and students from those campuses held at the Irsay Institute on the Bloomington campus indicated initial successes and some ripples in their launch. We anticipate this fall gathering will become a yearly event to exchange ideas, report issues, and collaborate on finding solutions. If UBC2M garners sufficient endowment, the goal is to follow this yearly conversation by state, region, or other relevant community definitions.

The College Toolbox Project, funded by Bring Change to Mind, was carried out with volunteer faculty and students designing the study, submitting IRB approval forms, analyzing data, and producing scientific and public-facing materials. The cross-disciplinary faculty team also provided mentorship and worked with institutional officials to clear administrative hurdles. The university did not subsidize their work in either time-release or salary. For example, the pre-post evaluation would be survey-based, focused on an entering cohort of first-year students and repeated in the third year. Given regulations that discourage or even prohibit cash incentives, students were given a "swag bag" of university and program-branded materials as well as donated materials from local and national organizations. Students were critical in determining the content of specifically produced materials. Their requests (e.g., tank tops and fanny packs, among other items) clearly reinforced the principle that students have ideas on incentives that almost mystify faculty and staff and that change quickly across cohorts.

Initially, UBC2M was housed and launched in a research center that was most connected to the national organization (the Indiana Consortium for Mental Health Services Research led by BC2M's Scientific Advisor [author] and the Academic Specialist in that center). We served as faculty advisors but having a half-time person who was trained in student organizations and having knowledge of mental health issues was (and continues to be) essential. We believe the key element to program success is an institutional home at the college or university in an appropriate program (e.g., office of student success, counseling center, wellness office). Having faculty involved, including IU faculty who include UBC2M-related assignments in their classes, is a bonus that enriches the program, but institutional buy-in of staff ensures the sustainability of the program.

More specifically, the CTP Outcomes Assessment (IU-IRB Protocol #1407536121) was based on online surveys administered in two waves during years two and four. Year one involved human subject approvals, the development of materials in concert with an initial student group, and the piloting of events and activities. Overall, the learning experience of the initial year was critical. Barriers were encountered and strategies were developed to overcome them. For example, an IU Technologies data manager needed to be recruited to provide access to restricted student data that is not open to researchers and satisfy the IU Council of Data Stewards' concerns that the project complied with IU data policies. Access to restricted data was necessary to confirm the first-year status of survey participants and resulted in the participation of more than half of the entering student cohort (in contrast to the very low response rates usually received from campus-based surveys). Students were invited to the survey at their orientation visit, programming that had not previously allowed research data collection (see Fig. 7.5). Activities were tried, sometimes failing with too broad a scope, too little dissemination to the student body, or overlapping with other (more attractive) student events. Unanticipated successes were also encountered, including the most effective recruiting device: a student-designed wrap for one of the campus buses. Initially designed with a different ending to the message (i.e., student messaging often had double-edged, slightly salacious, humorous, or cutting-edge cultural messaging more aligned with youth than adult tastes), it was denied approval by the Provost's Office but then redesigned to meet approval. The bright, neon green that students chose (over IU colors or the more sober green of the mental health ribbon), became a point of discussion by faculty and staff (see Fig. 7.6). College students showed remarkable leadership and enthusiasm, facing logistic and institutional challenges successfully. Over time, student leadership developed normative standards or expectations for their semester activities specific to IU permissions, pilot events, and instrument testing. To be clear, the CTP aim was for the research to establish an evidence base, directing program changes and developing instruments that could be used by any campus. It is not a requirement of the program—to meet high scientific standards, substantial resources are required to engage and follow an entering cohort of students and to do the post-data collection coding, analysis, and dissemination.

All Class of 2015 students (N = 7376) were eligible to participate at baseline (Time One; T1). The research group in IU's Office of Enrollment Management sent survey invitation emails, queued confidential reminders to non-respondents, and provided limited socio-demographic data for consented subjects. Students completing the survey (N = 3287; response rate = 44.6%) received a student-designed

Fig. 7.5 Students taking the Time 1 (T1) survey at stations throughout campus

Fig. 7.6 UBC2M Bus Wrap Design, 2016

"swag bag" (described above). Two years later, those same students were sent invitations to the follow-up survey (Time Two; T2 N = 1832; response rate = 27.6%). In the assessment, we focused on the 1193 students who completed both waves since intra-individual comparison lessens response bias inherent in comparing responses of all panel respondents.

Scientific Findings

The analysis of the two waves of the survey data provided evidence of the utility of this approach. Overall, active engagement in UBC2M appears to be the key to lowering prejudice, increasing inclusive behaviors, and reporting positive perceptions of campus mental health culture. While detailed framing, methods, and scientific results appear in the *Journal of the American Academy of Child and Adolescent Psychiatry* (Pescosolido et al., 2020), reporting the most basic findings here will shed some light on how change works. In brief, we documented that statistically significant positive changes in attitudes and behavioral predispositions emerged. Stigma was lower at T2 across all measures with the magnitude of change ranging from a 10.9% to 13.8% decrease. This is in line with changes in well-funded, national campaigns over a similar period (e.g., Evans-Lacko et al., 2014). In addition, while stigma levels among college students are much lower than seen in the general population, they are more in line with Americans' stigma attitudes toward child and adolescent mental health problems (see US National Stigma Studies, e.g., Martin et al., 2000; Pescosolido et al., 2008). Further, active engagement was associated with lowering prejudice. All UBC2M engagement measures, whether active or passive, were significantly positively related to more favorable perceptions of campus mental health culture. Finally, students who self-reported having a mental illness were more likely to have positive views of the program. These findings provided the basic support for the utility of the UBC2M approach.

However, in a series of working papers, the research team also accumulated a set of findings important for understanding how the program worked by examining typical questions around logistical issues, mechanisms, and effectiveness that underlay the development of UBC2M. For example, investigating whether and how language matters, the survey at both time points used four forms, randomly assigned to students. This is an often-raised point among communities that deal with mental health and illness. The different forms each used person-first language but described the person as having “mental illness,” “mental health problems,” “a history of mental illness,” or a “history of mental health problems.” No effects of language were found. The larger social concerns about the labels used to describe the specific target of stigma do not appear to result in differential reporting of stigma, so data are collapsed across forms (Krendl & Pescosolido, 2023).

Another analysis comparing the respondents who participated in both waves showed that the stigma level drop effects were greater for men, Black students, students without a mental illness diagnosis, and those with low levels of social contact with people. However, when looking at all respondents at both points, which measures not individual change but change in overall cultural climate, the drop in stigma was not limited to particular social groups. Nonetheless, there were baseline differences in stigma that persisted in T2 (e.g., higher levels of stigma in BIPOC and cishet populations; Manago et al., 2023). Digging deeper into the potential mechanisms, results from other analyses suggest social networks and connectedness/interactions are the underlying mechanisms of change, consistent with the long-held contact hypothesis. Students who report gaining ties to people with mental illness/health problems also report more tolerant attitudes in follow-up. Further, gaining a tie to a friend receiving mental health treatment at follow-up was associated with lowered levels of stigma across all stigma measures compared to baseline (Pullen et al., 2023). Finally, certain segments of the student population were more likely to actively engage. For example, women and students who were white, reported lower socioeconomic status, and identified as LGBTQ were more likely among college students to discuss these issues with others. These key “nodes” or “early adopters” of change also reported lower levels of stigmatizing attitudes, prior contact with people with mental illness, or a mental illness diagnosis in follow-up (Ekl et al., 2023).

Overall, the analyses of the survey data provided not only a scientific foundation for taking a peer-to-peer approach girded by institutional support but also offered directions for where the program could be improved. For example, if the early adopters described above could be recruited as “game changers” to promote other effective interventions (Bogart et al., 2020), the positive effects may be both wider and deeper.

Conclusion: Looking Back and Pushing Forward

Unlike the heavily manualized interventions of the past that required 100% fidelity to an unchanging, top-down protocol, UBC2M is a twenty-first-century, sustainable, peer-led, and flexible intervention, based in science, which fosters the engagement, leadership, and retention of students. A community-based, student empowerment approach with institutional supports represents a promising avenue to reduce stigma on college campuses, develop the next generation of mental health workers and leaders, and reduce societal levels of stigma in the long run. CTP provides evidence that both contact and contextual visibility matter and that UBC2M offers a nationally longer-run strategy, with the advantage of potentially creating a new generation of medical, political, and social leadership in mental illness, including stigma. Through the process and assessment of UBC2M, the research findings and continual collaboration with other anti-stigma efforts nationally and internationally, three things became clear to the building of a college network nationally.

First, programs that do not require "institutional buy-in" in the form of a paid advisor located in a university office (e.g., Dean of Students, Provost Office) tend to come and go. Enthusiastic students start a program and get a faculty advisor, but over time, students graduate, and faculty advisors are overwhelmed with other service obligations or leave for one reason or another. As a result, the group disappears. This has happened several times at IU to our knowledge: once with the NAMI college program, and once with an Active Minds group. It has not happened with UBC2M, even without major funding, because UBC2M built major institutional support into the program. However, the absence of a program director who has the training and the charge to guide and assist students puts the program at risk. In addition, the "high-touch" nature of the program, including but not limited to the professional advisors and interaction with the national BC2M program requires a national home/office. For UBC2M to disseminate, a clear requisite for a high-touch program with sophisticated and continuing materials being produced and shared among colleges and universities, it must have a supported base.

Second, the goal of UBC2M is to be free of charge. Other groups with demonstrated success (Sontag-Padilla et al., 2018) that have a national presence use a funding model that charges for materials. For example, UBC2M used Active Mind's Post-Secret, an event that has students write secrets they have never told others that they feel are stigmatizing. These are posted for a time period, followed by an open discussion event, and have the possibility of bringing in the speaker who developed the event. We were able to "buy" the postcards and instruction materials from Active Minds for $500, but students did not have, nor would we have provided, the 10K required for the speaker. The goal of UBC2M is to have sufficient resources to provide base materials for the toolbox, free of charge, and develop a set of national advisors who would support program events at other partner programs for minimal honoraria and travel costs.

Third, there is no need to duplicate efforts. The National Academy of Sciences' report (2016) made clear that duplication of efforts, and the unwillingness to work together has been a stumbling block in stigma reduction in the United States. By collaborating with programs and drawing on their strengths, a national college network can be built better and stronger. For example, Active Minds has a successful summer college summit. It makes no sense for UBC2M to do the same; rather if UBC2M disseminates nationally, partnering with Active Minds to make their college summit THE college summit to which UBC2M or any other student group members could attend is a more efficient and effective path. College programs can coexist and even strengthen the outcomes on any college campus.

Acknowledgments Funding for the student program and survey costs were provided by Bring Change to Mind. The author provided research services pro bono, except for travel to BC2M meetings as required. I would like to thank Alex Capshew, Melanie Payne, Pamela Harrington, and Susan Barnett Purrington who were there from the beginning and all the way through. I would also like to thank the many faculty who provided their labor and skills pro bono and many members of the IU administration who cleared the road on legal, financial, and logistical barriers. Finally, I would like to thank Laurie McRobbie, former first lady of IU, for her steadfast support, and most of all Glen Close for her vision and many efforts on behalf of those with mental health issues.

Appendix 7.1 Illustration and Listing of UBC2M "Living Library"

Table 7.3 College toolbox event booklets

Panel A: Education event programs	**Event description**
Mental health matters	Trivia night
"13 reasons" understood	A dinner and discussion
Panel B: Drop-in event programs	**Event description**
De-stress fest	De-stress event
Memory Monday	De-stress event
Something bigger	Mural creation
Stigma can suck my popsicle	Awareness event
The duck pond	Awareness event
Panel C: Entertainment event programs	**Event description**
An illuminated mind	Art show
Bring in the booty	Scavenger Hunt
Escape the stigma	Escape room
Kick stigma in the balls	Kickball
Love the skin you're in	Fashion show
UBC2M block party	Recreational day

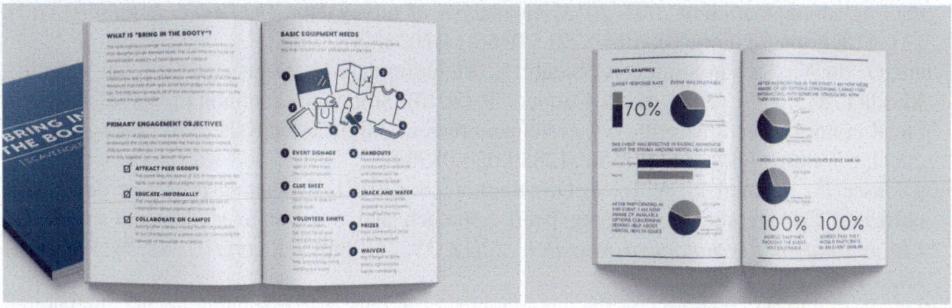

Fig. 7.7 The brochures include a description and rationale for the event, plans, timelines, and original budget for guidance

References

Blanco, C., Okuda, M., Wright, C., Hasin, D. S., Grant, B. F., Liu, S. M., & Olfson, M. (2008). Mental health of college students and their non–college-attending peers: Results from the National Epidemiologic Study on alcohol and related conditions. *Archives of General Psychiatry, 65*(12), 1429–1437. https://doi.org/10.1001/archpsyc.65.12.1429

Blee, K. M. (1991). Women in the 1920s' Ku Klux Klan movement. *Feminist Studies, 17*(1), 57–77. https://doi.org/10.2307/3178170

Bogart, L. M., Matovu, J. K. B., Wagner, G. J., Green, H. D., Storholm, E. D., Klein, D. J., Marsh, T., Mac Carthy, S., & Kambugu, A. (2020). A pilot test of game changers, a social network intervention to empower people with HIV to be prevention advocates in Uganda. *AIDS and Behavior, 24*(9), 2490–2508. https://doi.org/10.1007/s10461-020-02806-4

Burstein, P., & Freudenburg, W. (1978). Changing public policy: The impact of public opinion, antiwar demonstrations, and war costs on senate voting on Vietnam war motions. *American Journal of Sociology, 84*(1), 99–122. https://doi.org/10.1086/226742

Busby, D. R., Horwitz, A. G., Zheng, K., Eisenberg, D., Harper, G. W., Albucher, R. C., Roberts, L. W., Coryell, W., Pistorello, J., & King, C. A. (2020). Suicide risk among gender and sexual minority college students: The roles of victimization, discrimination, connectedness, and identity affirmation. *Journal of Psychiatric Research, 121*, 182–188. https://doi.org/10.1016/j.jpsychires.2019.11.013

Center for Behavioral Health Statistics and Quality. (2017). *2016 National Survey on drug use and health: Detailed tables*. Substance Abuse and Mental Health Services Administration.

Corrigan, P. W. (2016). Lessons learned from unintended consequences about erasing the stigma of mental illness. *World Psychiatry, 15*(1), 67–73. https://doi.org/10.1002/wps.20295

de Girolamo, G., McGorry, P. D., & Sartorius, N. (2019). Introduction: Relevance of the age of onset of mental disorders to research in psychiatry and to the organization of services for people with mental illness. In G. de Girolamo, P. D. McGorry, & N. Sartorius (Eds.), *Age of onset of mental disorders: Etiopathogenetic and treatment implications* (pp. 1–13). Springer International Publishing. https://doi.org/10.1007/978-3-319-72619-9_1

Eisenberg, D., Golberstein, E., & Hunt, J. B. (2009). Mental health and academic success in college. *The B.E. Journal of Economic Analysis & Policy, 9*(1), 40. https://doi.org/10.2202/1935-1682.2191

Ekl, E. A., Perry, B. L., Pullen, E., & Pescosolido, B. (2023). *Who "starts the conversation"? How individual, relationship and social network contacts shape discussion of mental health stigma [Unpublished manuscript]*. Irsay Institute, Indiana University.

Evans-Lacko, S., Corker, E., Williams, P., Henderson, C., & Thornicroft, G. (2014). Effect of the time to change anti-stigma campaign on trends in mental-illness-related public stigma among the English population in 2003–2013: An analysis of survey data. *The Lancet Psychiatry, 1*(2), 121–128. https://doi.org/10.1016/S2215-0366(14)70243-3

Eylem, O., de Wit, L., van Straten, A., Steubl, L., Melissourgaki, Z., Danışman, G. T., de Vries, R., Kerkhof, A. J. F. M., Bhui, K., & Cuijpers, P. (2020). Stigma for common mental disorders in racial minorities and majorities: A systematic review and meta-analysis. *BMC Public Health, 20*(1), 879. https://doi.org/10.1186/s12889-020-08964-3

Funkhouser, C. J., Zakriski, A. L., & Dee Spoltore, J. (2017). Evaluating peer-peer depression outreach: College students helping peers approach and respond to students in crisis. *Psi Chi Journal of Psychological Research, 22*(1), 19–28. https://doi.org/10.24839/2325-7342.JN22.1.19

Harvey, B. C. (2021). Teetering on the demographic cliff, part 1: Prepare now for the challenging times ahead. *Planning for Higher Education, 49*(4), 1–12.

Hinshaw, S., & Kranz, R. (2009). *The triple bind: Saving our teenage girls from today's pressures*. Ballantine Books.

Hurst, C. S., Baranik, L. E., & Daniel, F. (2013). College student stressors: A review of qualitative research. *Stress and Health, 29*(4), 275–285. https://doi.org/10.1002/smi.2465

Kadison, R., & DiGeronimo, T. F. (2004). *College of the overwhelmed: The campus mental health crisis and what to do about it*. Jossey-Bass.

Krendl, A. C., & Pescosolido, B. (2023). *What's in a name? Examining the effect of mental health labels on stigma [Unpublished manuscript]*. Irsay Institute, Indiana University.

Lipson, S. K., Abelson, S., Ceglarek, P., Phillips, M. L., & Eisenberg, D. (2019). Investing in student mental health: Opportunities & benefits for college leadership. American Council on Education Reports. https://www.acenet.edu/Documents/Investing-in-Student-Mental-Health.pdf

Liu, C. H., Stevens, C., Wong, S. H. M., Yasui, M., & Chen, J. A. (2019). The prevalence and predictors of mental health diagnoses and suicide among U.S. college students: Implications for addressing disparities in service use. *Depression and Anxiety, 36*(1), 8–17. https://doi.org/10.1002/da.22830

Mac Phee, J. (2023, January 30). I struggled with mental health as a division I athlete. Here's how colleges should help. Higher Ed Dive. https://www.highereddive.com/news/mental-health-student-athletes-jed-foundation/641146/

Manago, B., Perry, B. L., & Pescosolido, B. (2023). *Are the stigma-reducing effects consistent across social groups? Examining the effects of critical sociodemographic characteristics on outcomes of UBC2M [Unpublished manuscript]*. Irsay Institute, Indiana University.

Martin, J. K., Pescosolido, B. A., & Tuch, S. A. (2000). Of fear and loathing: The role of disturbing behavior, labels, and causal attributions in shaping public attitudes toward persons with mental illness. *Journal of Health and Social Behavior, 41*(2), 208–233. https://doi.org/10.2307/2676306

McCarthy, J. D., & Zald, M. N. (1977). Resource mobilization and social movements: A partial theory. *American Journal of Sociology, 82*(6), 1212–1241. http://www.jstor.org/stable/2777934

Mehta, N., Clement, S., Marcus, E., Stona, A. C., Bezborodovs, N., Evans-Lacko, S., Palacios, J., Docherty, M., Barley, E., Rose, D., Koschorke, M., Shidhaye, R., Henderson, C., & Thornicroft, G. (2015). Evidence for effective interventions to reduce mental health-related stigma and discrimination in the medium and long term: Systematic review. *British Journal of Psychiatry, 207*(5), 377–384. https://doi.org/10.1192/bjp.bp.114.151944

National Academies of Sciences Engineering and Medicine [NASEM]. (2016). *Ending discrimination against people with mental and substance use disorders: The evidence for stigma change*. The National Academies Press. https://doi.org/10.17226/23442

Parcesepe, A. M., & Cabassa, L. J. (2013). Public stigma of mental illness in the United States: A systematic literature review. *Administration and Policy in Mental Health and Mental Health Services Research, 40*(5), 384–399. https://doi.org/10.1007/s10488-012-0430-z

Pescosolido, B. A. (2013). The public stigma of mental illness: What do we think; what do we know; what can we prove? *Journal of Health and Social Behavior, 54*(1), 1–21. https://doi.org/10.1177/0022146512471197

Pescosolido, B. A., Jensen, P., Martin, J. K., Perry, B. L., Olafsdottir, S., & Fettes, D. L. (2008). Public knowledge and assessment of child mental health problems: Findings from the National

Stigma Study--Children. *Journal of the American Academy of Child & Adolescent Psychiatry, 47*(3), 339–349. https://doi.org/10.1097/CHI.0b013e318160e3a0

Pescosolido, B. A., Martin, J. K., Long, J. S., Medina, T. R., Phelan, J. C., & Link, B. G. (2010). "A disease like any other"? A decade of change in public reactions to schizophrenia, depression, and alcohol dependence. *American Journal of Psychiatry, 167*(11), 1321–1330. https://doi.org/10.1176/appi.ajp.2010.09121743

Pescosolido, B. A., Medina, T. R., Martin, J. K., & Long, J. S. (2013). The 'backbone' of stigma: Identifying the global core of public prejudice associated with mental illness. *American Journal of Public Health, 103*(5), 853–860. https://doi.org/10.2105/AJPH.2012.301147

Pescosolido, B. A., Perry, B. L., & Krendl, A. C. (2020). Empowering the next generation to end stigma by starting the conversation: Bring change to mind and the college toolbox project. *Journal of the American Academy of Child & Adolescent Psychiatry, 59*(4), 519–530. https://doi.org/10.1016/j.jaac.2019.06.016

Pullen, E., Perry, B., & Pescosolido, B. A. (2023). *Is the effect really about change in social networks? Examining the effects of changing contact on creating safe and stigma free college campuses [Unpublished manuscript]*. Irsay Institute, Indiana University.

Schwartz, V., & Kay, J. (2009). The crisis in college and university mental health. *Psychiatric Times, 26*(10), 32–34.

Siegel, K. R., Mobley, T. P., & Sanderson, C. A. (2023). Addressing the college mental health crisis: Training students to become effective bystanders. *Psychological Services, 20*(3), 410–422. https://doi.org/10.1037/ser0000720

Song, N., Hugh-Jones, S., West, R. M., & Mir, G. (2023). The effectiveness of anti-stigma interventions for reducing mental health stigma in young people: A systematic review and meta-analysis. *Cambridge Prisms: Global Mental Health, 10*(e39), 1–16. https://doi.org/10.1017/gmh.2023.34

Sontag-Padilla, L., Dunbar, M. S., Ye, F., Kase, C., Fein, R., Abelson, S., Seelam, R., & Stein, B. D. (2018). Strengthening college students' mental health knowledge, awareness, and helping behaviors: The impact of active minds, a peer mental health organization. *Journal of the American Academy of Child & Adolescent Psychiatry, 57*(7), 500–507. https://doi.org/10.1016/j.jaac.2018.03.019

Stuart, H., Arboleda-Florez, J., & Sartorius, N. (2012). *Paradigms lost: Fighting stigma and the lessons learned.* Oxford University Press.

Stuart, H., & Sartorius, N. (2022). *Paradigms lost, paradigms found: Lessons learned in the fight against the stigma of mental illness*. Oxford University Press.

Thornicroft, G., Sunkel, C., Alikhon Aliev, A., Baker, S., Brohan, E., el Chammay, R., Davies, K., Demissie, M., Duncan, J., Fekadu, W., Gronholm, P. C., Guerrero, Z., Gurung, D., Habtamu, K., Hanlon, C., Heim, E., Henderson, C., Hijazi, Z., Hoffman, C., et al. (2022). The *lancet* commission on ending stigma and discrimination in mental health. *The Lancet, 400*(10361), 1438–1480. https://doi.org/10.1016/S0140-6736(22)01470-2

Vaisey, S., & Lizardo, O. (2010). Can cultural worldviews influence network composition? *Social Forces, 88*(4), 1595–1618. https://doi.org/10.1353/sof.2010.0009

Yamaguchi, S., Mino, Y., & Uddin, S. (2011). Strategies and future attempts to reduce stigmatization and increase awareness of mental health problems among young people: A narrative review of educational interventions. *Psychiatry and Clinical Neurosciences, 65*(5), 405–415. https://doi.org/10.1111/j.1440-1819.2011.02239.x

Yamaguchi, S., Wu, S.-I., Biswas, M., Yate, M., Aoki, Y., Barley, E. A., & Thornicroft, G. (2013). Effects of short-term interventions to reduce mental health–related stigma in university or college students: A systematic review. *The Journal of Nervous and Mental Disease, 201*(6), 490–503. https://doi.org/10.1097/NMD.0b013e31829480df

Zhou, S., & Eisenberg, D. (2022). College student mental health: Current trends and implications for higher education. In M. Elliott (Ed.), *Research handbook on society and mental health* (pp. 325–347). Edward Elgar Publishing. https://doi.org/10.4337/9781800378483.00024

Bernice A. Pescosolido, Ph.D., is a distinguished and chancellor's professor of sociology at Indiana University. Along with Brian Powell, she founded and directed sociology's Preparing Future Faculty Program. She is currently the co-chair of Bring Change to Mind's Scientific Advisory Council with psychologist Stephen Hinshaw. She is an elected member of both the National Academy of Sciences and the National Academy of Medicine.

Chapter 8
Self-Stigma and Strategic Disclosure Among College and University Students: Honest, Open, Proud-College

K. Amanda Maranzan, Grishma Dabas, Kristin Kosyluk, Nele Loecher, and Patrick Corrigan

Abstract Internalized or self-stigma is a significant concern for college students, especially those experiencing mental distress. It negatively affects self-esteem, empowerment, and hope, leading to the "why try" effect, which undermines functioning and deters students from seeking support or fully engaging in their academic and social environments. This chapter discusses a regressive model of self-stigma within the college context. Drawing from social psychology literature, we highlight how disclosure can counteract the negative effects of secrecy. With the primary aim of alleviating stigma stress and supporting informed decision-making regarding disclosure, Honest, Open, Proud—College (HOP-C) is an effective anti-stigma approach implemented on campuses in the United States and Canada. It consists of three sessions led by trained peer facilitators, targeting groups of six to ten students.

The authors have no conflicts of interest to declare that are relevant to the content of this chapter. Dr. Amanda Maranzan is supported in part by funding from the Social Sciences and Humanities Research Council. The contents of this book chapter were partially developed under a grant from the National Institute on Disability, Independent Living, and Rehabilitation Research (NIDILRR grant number 90IFRE0056) awarded to Dr. Kristin Kosyluk. NIDILRR is a Center within the Administration for Community Living (ACL), Department of Health and Human Services (HHS). The contents of this book chapter do not necessarily represent the policy of NIDILRR, ACL, or HHS, and you should not assume endorsement by the Federal Government.

K. A. Maranzan (✉) · G. Dabas
Psychology Department, Lakehead University, Thunder Bay, ON, Canada
e-mail: kamaranz@lakeheadu.ca

K. Kosyluk
Department of Mental Health Law & Policy, University of South Florida, Tampa, FL, USA

N. Loecher
College of Community and Behavioral Sciences, University of South Florida, Tampa, FL, USA

P. Corrigan
Department of Psychology, Illinois Institute of Technology, Chicago, IL, USA

© The Author(s), under exclusive license to Springer Nature Switzerland AG 2025

K. M. Brennan, K. S. Gorman (eds.), *A University-Wide Approach to Changing Campus Cultures of Mental Illness Stigma*, Knowledge Studies in Higher Education 18, https://doi.org/10.1007/978-3-031-86496-4_8

HOP-C helps participants evaluate the pros and cons of disclosing their mental health status, teaches relatively safe ways to disclose, should the student decide to do so, and guides students in crafting narratives that align with their disclosure goals. The chapter concludes by summarizing the growing evidence supporting HOP-C and offering recommendations for its implementation and future research directions.

Keywords Disclosure · Mental illness · Stigma · Anti-stigma

This chapter focuses on the *Honest, Open, Proud* (HOP) program to address self-stigma of mental illness, which occurs when a person with a mental illness internalizes prejudice (Link et al., 2001).[1] First, we unpack the self-stigma experience, especially as it applies to college and university students. We then discuss the special role of strategic disclosure in self-stigma change; HOP was developed to facilitate this kind of disclosure. We briefly review HOP and its adaptation for postsecondary settings (*Honest, Open, Proud—College*; HOP-C), followed by a review of several outcome studies on which HOP-C rests. We end by examining case studies from two funded projects currently assessing HOP-C's impact in these settings.

Self-stigma can be understood via a regressive model, which identifies how the roots of self-stigma (perceptions of public stigma) may lead to harming self-esteem, self-efficacy, and shame (Corrigan et al., 2011; Corrigan & Watson, 2002). The model focuses on four stages: awareness, agreement, application, and harm. People with mental distress are first *aware* of the stigma of mental distress (also called perceived stigma: "The public thinks people who experience mental distress are incompetent"; Phelan et al., 2000). This awareness influences *agreeing* with the stigma ("Yep; that's right. People who experience mental distress are incompetent!"), followed by self-*application* ("I experience mental distress so I must be incompetent."). It is this application which negatively *harms* self-esteem ("I am less of a person because I experience mental distress and am incompetent.") and self-efficacy ("I am less able to accomplish my goals because I experience mental distress and am incompetent."), leading to shame. Self-stigma also yields the "why try" effect, a sense of behavioral futility (Corrigan et al., 2009a). This leads to beliefs such as: "Why try to get a degree? Someone like me is not worthy or able."

Research has consistently shown self-stigma to yield negative outcomes with an especially pernicious impact on self-esteem, self-efficacy, and hope (Link et al., 2001; Livingston & Boyd, 2010; Mashiach-Eizenberg et al., 2013). For college and university students, self-stigma can be a barrier to integration in the campus environment (Salzer, 2012). It may include feelings of incompetence, self-blame, and shame (Markoulakis & Kirsch, 2013; Stein, 2012). In navigating their social sphere, students often need to consider what aspects of their mental health experiences to

[1] See Chap. 1 for a list of fundamental stigma concepts and their definitions.

share in what situations, while navigating concerns they will be judged, stigmatized, and discriminated against (Ennals et al., 2015; Wada et al., 2019). As a result, students may restrict their social circles and engagement, leading to feelings of isolation, disconnection, alienation, and exclusion (Wada et al., 2019).

There are several programs on college campuses which are meant to challenge public stigma, and many are presented in this volume. We propose tackling *self-stigma* through strategic disclosure, with a focus on reducing stigma stress, increasing self-efficacy of coping with stigma, and thus ultimately supporting student well-being and recovery. By addressing self-stigma, we propose an empowering approach to helping students to manage the stigma-related barriers they encounter in university settings.

Disclosure and Self-Stigma

While a variety of approaches have been developed to address self-stigma, they can be broadly categorized into three strategies: psychoeducation, cognitive therapy, and strategic disclosure. Psychoeducation provides information to individuals and communities about the nature and symptoms of mental illness, as well as the horrendous effects of stereotypes. It teaches participants to recognize and challenge negative attitudes and stereotypes toward people with mental illnesses (e.g., Lucksted et al., 2017; McCay et al., 2006, 2007). There is mixed evidence to support this approach, with some demonstration of reduced self-stigma compared to a waitlist control group (Ivezić et al., 2017) and a treatment-as-usual group (Uchino et al., 2012). Other trials reported no impact on self-stigma but improvements in self-concept, quality of life, and hope (McCay et al., 2007).

Psychoeducation is often combined with cognitive therapy approaches, aimed to help the person to identify and challenge negative thoughts and beliefs that contribute to self-stigma such as feelings of shame and guilt. This approach also focuses on developing coping strategies to manage the negative emotions and thoughts associated with self-stigma (e.g., Fung et al., 2011; Yanos, et al., 2012, 2015). As with psychoeducation, there are also mixed outcomes associated with cognitive therapy techniques, with some trials showing reduced self-stigma compared to treatment-as-usual groups (e.g., Lucksted et al., 2017; Young, 2018; Young et al., 2020) and others showing no improvements compared to groups receiving psychoeducation only (e.g., Drapalski et al., 2021; Wood et al., 2018) or treatment-as-usual (Morrison et al., 2016).

The third approach, strategic disclosure, is a process of selectively sharing information about one's mental illness. This involves careful consideration of who to disclose to, what to disclose, how much to disclose, and the potential risks and benefits of disclosing which will vary with context (Lucksted & Drapalski, 2015). This approach aims to reduce feelings of secrecy and shame and increase feelings of control and empowerment, thus enhancing participants' ability to *cope with* rather than *eliminate* stigma. Conceptualizing empowerment as the opposite of self-stigma, improving empowerment may also reduce self-stigma (Corrigan et al., 2009a).

Programs on strategic disclosure are based on social psychology research, which point to the harmful effects of "secrets," including self-concealment (Pachankis, 2007; Smart & Wegner, 1999). In contrast to other objects of stigma such as race, gender, and age, mental illness is essentially concealable (Jones et al., 1984). This means students are confronted with important decisions about disclosure: there are a range of types of disclosure in which students may participate and choose from, which vary by setting. For example, a student could engage in social avoidance by not disclosing their mental illness to anyone and avoiding situations where others may find out about it. They may choose secrecy, where their mental illness is a secret but important settings within the university community are not avoided. A student may use selective disclosure (i.e., disclosing to select persons such as a professor, friend, or disability services, but not to everyone) or indiscriminate disclosure (i.e., making the decision to no longer conceal their mental illness). And/or, a student may decide to broadcast their experience by actively seeking out and educating others about their experience.

Of course, disclosure decisions depend on a student's individual preferences, needs, and the specific context at a given point in time. This means students' disclosure decisions are dynamic and context-dependent. Because college and university students are uniquely impacted by how emerging adulthood and the postsecondary context influence distress and, by extension, stigma experiences, these disclosure decisions are especially relevant. Students must navigate a variety of contexts related to disclosure. For example, disclosure decisions in academic contexts might consider how instructors or academic advisors might respond, impacts on one's major or trade, whether accommodations or supports are available, and performance evaluation. Students might also consider how disclosure may impact social contexts related to roommates, residence advisors, classmates, and romantic partners. The employment context is also relevant for students who seek part-time jobs and practical/internships, and how disclosure might impact future career goals. Family and healthcare/treatment contexts are also pertinent disclosure contexts for college and university students. On the one hand, concealment might seem to be an advantageous choice because family, friends, acquaintances, and a general public that is unaware of a person's mental illness are less likely to discriminate against them. On the other hand, secrecy has malignant effects (Smart & Wegner, 1999). It can lead to hypervigilance in situations (e.g., "who can tell I have a mental illness?") which may worsen distress (Hopper, 2007; Lysaker et al., 2007; Pachankis, 2007) and deepen social isolation (Link & Phelan, 2001; Link et al., 2001).

Disclosure is one way to reduce secrecy's harm (Chaudoir & Fisher, 2010; Chaudoir & Quinn, 2010). There are several benefits for people who have disclosed concealable conditions, such as increases in empowerment and self-esteem, quality of life, recovery, and supportive relationships (e.g., Corrigan et al., 2010; Mayer et al., 2022; Rüsch et al., 2019). A higher comfort with disclosure is related to better mental well-being and reduced stigma-related stress (Rüsch et al., 2014a). In college and university students specifically, mental illness disclosure is associated with psychological well-being in the domains of self-esteem, environmental mastery, and life satisfaction (Taniguchi, 2020). Overall, disclosure appears to positively impact the life domains that tend to be harmed by self-stigma.

Disclosure needs to be tempered by understanding the risks of coming out, which may include shame, pressure to conform, and discrimination from those who know (Chaudoir & Fisher, 2010; Corrigan et al., 2009b). Individuals are often concerned about potential stigma and discrimination in response to disclosure of their mental health status (e.g., Chaudoir & Fisher, 2010; Mulfinger et al., 2017). These concerns are associated with less willingness to disclose (Watson et al., 2007). Agreement with stigma (perceived legitimacy) is also associated with less willingness to disclose (Watson et al., 2007). In contrast, social support, especially to support autonomous decisions, makes disclosure less problematic.

Given these findings, two approaches have emerged relevant to disclosure. The first focuses on decision-making: disclosure is influenced by consideration of the pros and cons of disclosure in different contexts (Pahwa et al., 2017). The second approach uses peers as an important source of support, drawing on the links between disclosure, increased social support, and increase resources for dealing with stigma (Bos et al., 2009; Pahwa et al., 2017; Weisz et al., 2016). Based on these social psychology findings, HOP was developed to reduce stigma stress and to support individuals in their decision-making about disclosure.

Honest, Open, Proud (HOP)

HOP (formerly called "*Coming Out Proud (COP) to Erase the Stigma of Mental Illness*") was developed by a group of advocates and researchers to address key mediators of self-stigma and its harmful impacts (Corrigan et al., 2013). It is a peer-led, manualized group intervention designed to empower individuals through self-efficacy in coping with stigma, reducing self-stigma, and lessening stigma-related stress (Corrigan et al., 2013; Scior et al., 2020). Note the goal of HOP is *not* to convince people to disclose. Rather, the goal is to reduce stigma stress and support people in their decision-making about disclosure. It recognizes disclosure decision-making is mainly an ongoing process and thus there is a need to support participants in reaching a decision that feels right at a given point in time within a given setting (Scior et al., 2020).

The original version of HOP was developed for working adults living with significant mental illnesses, based on a chapter about disclosure in Corrigan and Lundin's (2001) book about coping with stigma. HOP was ultimately developed into a stand-alone program through a process involving input from people with mental illnesses along with collaboration with partners from around the globe to consider cultural sensitivity and relevance. It has since been adapted for use in a variety of contexts (e.g., adolescents, suicide attempt survivors, military veterans, active soldiers, mental health professionals, parents of children with mental health issues, and people with specific conditions) and countries (e.g., Australia, Germany,

UK, Chile, China, Israel, and Italy) (Corrigan et al., 2018; Rüsch & Kösters, 2021; Scior et al., 2020).

The HOP Program and Lessons

HOP is a manualized intervention for which the manual and workbook are freely available on the HOP website (www.hopprogram.org). Although there are several adaptations for different context and countries (such as HOP-C), there are many elements that are present across adaptations and which are described here. HOP includes three lessons to address disclosure and factors related to self-stigma and its impact. It is delivered by trained peer facilitators in three weekly workshop sessions (groups of six to ten participants) and can be followed by a booster session (for example, after 1 month). The sessions are largely based on completing worksheets followed by discussions and role-plays. HOP thus provides group members with an opportunity to share their experiences, thoughts, and concerns around disclosure with other peers.

Table 8.1 summarizes the three HOP lessons and booster session. At the start of every session, facilitators and group members discuss and establish ground rules to foster an open, safe space within HOP sessions. Session one is focused on evaluating the pros and cons of disclosing. Since motivators have important and dynamic effects on disclosure and self-stigma (Chaudoir & Quinn, 2010), group members identify the costs and benefits of disclosure. As the balance of costs and benefits are likely to vary by setting (e.g., work versus neighbors versus school), group members complete cost-benefit analyses in terms of specific settings. Other topics for the first session include one's identification with mental illness and the concept of self-stigma.

Session two coaches group members to learn ways to identify safe people to disclose to. Given the importance of social support in disclosure, group members learn strategies to assess the likelihood that specific people in specific settings (e.g., a professor or peer at school) are likely to react positively to disclosure. Major topics in session two include types of disclosure (ranging from secrecy or telling no one, to broadcasting or sharing widely with the intent to advocate for stigma change), disclosing on social media (a topic specifically added in the HOP-C adaptation), deciding who to disclose to, and how others might respond to disclosure.

Finally, in session three, participants craft a disclosure story. Roe et al. (2014) have shown the quality of story and personal narrative is relevant to decreasing self-stigma, so group members are taught about elements of an effective disclosure story. They then use this information to write their own story. Elements of an effective story include relaying challenges with symptoms and the negative effects of stigma and sharing one's strengths, coping strategies, and goals for disclosure. Group members also practice sharing this narrative with other participants and learn how to evaluate the outcomes of disclosure interactions. Session three also asks participants to reflect on their learning from previous sessions and consider their future directions in terms of disclosure.

Table 8.1 Summary of Honest, Open, Proud—College lessons

Lesson	Main objective	Tasks	Learning objectives
1	Consider the pros and cons of disclosing	Do you identify yourself as a person with mental illness?	• Understand whether and how you identify yourself with respect to mental illness. • Consider how you label your experiences leading to stigma (e.g., mental illness; mental health challenge; other terms). • Challenge personally hurtful self-stigma, if relevant.
		Consider the pros and cons of disclosing	• Discuss the benefits and costs to disclosing. • Frame personal choice in disclosure decisions. • Consider how the costs and benefits differ depending on the setting (e.g., in a classroom versus among roommates).
2	Identify that there are different ways to disclose	Different ways to disclose	• Discuss how people disclose mental illness experiences and corresponding treatments in different ways. • Understand the costs and benefits of disclosing in the five different ways. • Identify different costs and benefits associated with each of the five ways. Identify that costs and benefits may vary by setting. • Discuss using social media to disclose to someone versus face-to-face disclosure.
		To whom might you disclose?	• Identify that some people are better to disclose to compared to others. • Learn how to identify a good person to whom you might disclose. • Understand the procedure for "testing out" a person before disclosing.
		How might others respond to your disclosure?	• Understand that disclosure will impact others. • Consider the different ways people may respond to your disclosure.

(continued)

Table 8.1 (continued)

Lesson	Main objective	Tasks	Learning objectives
3	Learn to tell your story	Learn a way to tell your story in a personally meaningful way	• Read through an example of how to tell a story of one's experience with mental illness. • Use the provided guide to construct your own story. • Understand the values and issues related to telling your own story.
		Review how telling your story felt	• Learn how to evaluate a specific instance of disclosure.
		Put together all you've learned to move forward	• Summarize insights from the worksheets provided in the workbook. • Decide how you wish to move forward with the issue of disclosure.
Booster	Review your decision to disclose since completing HOP-C	Review previous intentions to disclose after completing HOP-C	• Review your intentions to disclose (including to whom, when, and where) as well as what you expected from the disclosure.
		Discuss whether you disclosed, and help evaluate how it went and how it may impact future disclosures	• If you disclosed, describe how it went and rate the quality of the exchange. • Explain how the experience changed your mind about disclosing.

Note: the HOP-C Manual and Workbook are freely available at www.hopprogram.org; Al-Khouja et al., 2017a, 2017b

If the optional booster session is implemented, participants reflect on their disclosure decisions following the last session by discussing their intentions to disclose (or not disclose) (i.e., who, when, where, what?) with a peer. If they did disclose, participants describe how it went and rate the quality of the exchange using a worksheet. Participants also revisit their disclosure cost-benefit analysis relevant to future disclosure decisions, comparing the costs and benefits of disclosure as they see them now, with those brainstormed before. Finally, participants consider how their personal disclosure narrative may have changed post-intervention. Participants may consider questions such as: "What worked and what did not work when telling your story?" "What things would you add and eliminate from your story?"

The HOP programs also include a fidelity measure for lessons one to three, as well as for the booster session. The fidelity measure is in the form of a checklist. It contains items to verify facilitators cover the group ground rules, provide an overview of each lesson, and hit on the key learning objectives, worksheets, and discussion questions for each task. Typically completed by a research assistant who observes the group and completes the measure or reviews a video or audio recording of the group, the fidelity measure can be used to assess the consistency of content presented across the HOP lessons. It can also be used to provide feedback to the peer facilitators, who can incorporate this feedback to further refine content coverage and increase fidelity to the intervention.

Two of the important strengths of the HOP program are the group setting and peer facilitation. More specifically, participants value peer facilitators' first-hand experience in disclosing their mental health difficulties (Rüsch et al., 2014b) and see the facilitators as inspiring role models (Mulfinger et al., 2017). Participants also value the opportunity to share their thoughts and concerns and hear the stories of other people who have similar experiences as them, in a safe, open, trusting, and respectful group space (Mulfinger et al., 2017; Rüsch et al., 2014b). Participants have reported a decreased sense of isolation with their experiences with stigma and disclosure (Rüsch et al., 2014b). HOP can therefore be characterized as a "structured, manualized, time-limited mutual support group" with peer facilitation as a critical component (Rüsch & Kösters, 2021, p. 1523).

Outcomes for HOP

There is a growing research base in support of HOP's theory of change. This theory posits that supporting disclosure decisions can reduce stigma stress and fear of being "found out," reduce self-stigma, and increase self-efficacy for coping with stigma (Corrigan et al., 2013). Table 8.2 highlights the study features and key outcomes for the HOP randomized controlled trials (RCTs) completed in 2024, including HOP adult, adolescent, and college versions. Notably, a recent meta-analysis compared HOP for adults or adolescents with mental illness or adult survivors of suicide attempts to a waitlist control group (Rüsch & Kösters, 2021). There was a significant medium effect of HOP on stigma-related stress, largely driven by an increase in perceived resources to cope with stigma. While the program's impact on self-stigma was not significant post-intervention, it did demonstrate a small effect at three- to four-week follow-up. There was no program impact on symptoms of depression at either post-intervention or follow-up.

Honest, Open, Proud—College (HOP-C)

HOP was adapted to address the stigma concerns specific to college and university students yielding *Honest, Open, Proud—College* (HOP-C) (Al-Khouja et al., 2017a, 2017b). Students with mental illnesses were recruited through a campus Active Minds group (a mental health advocacy organization focused on college mental health and suicide prevention). They participated in four 120-minute focus groups focused on adapting HOP to the student context. This community-based participatory research (CBPR) approach is central to the HOP approach (Scior et al., 2020). It involves active participation and collaboration between researchers and members of a community (students with mental illnesses), with the aim of producing a

Table 8.2 Summary of randomized controlled trials (RCTs) for Honest, Open, Proud

Study, year, country	Participant sample	Comparators (N)	Key HOP outcomes (Relative to comparator)
Rüsch et al. (2014a, 2014b); Switzerland	Adults	HOP (50); treatment-as-usual (50)	• Decrease in stigma stress, disclosure-related distress, and secrecy. • Increase in perceived benefits of disclosure.
Corrigan et al. (2015); USA	Adults	HOP (51); waitlist control (75)	• Decrease in self-stigma, stigma stress, and depressive symptoms (females only). • Increase in perceived coping resources.
Conley et al. (2020); USA	Postsecondary students	HOP-C (63); waitlist control (55)	• Decrease in self-stigma and harm from stigma stress. • Increase in perceived coping resources and disclosure self-efficacy.
Modelli et al. (2021); Brazil	Adults with depression and bipolar disorders	HOP (30); psychoeducation (31)	• Decrease in cognitive appraisals of stigma-related harm, stigma harm, and self-alienation. • Increase in perceived coping resources.
Mulfinger et al. (2017); Germany	Adolescents	HOP adapted for adolescents (49); treatment-as-usual (49)	• Decrease in self-stigma, stigma stress, disclosure-related distress, and depression. • Increase in perceived quality of life, attitudes toward disclosure, and intentions to seek help.
Qin et al. (2024); China	Adults with serious mental illness	HOP (68); waitlist control (67)	• Decrease in self-stigma. • Increase in disclosure self-efficacy.
Sheehan et al. (2023); USA	Adults with at least one lifetime suicide attempt	HOP (16); control (19)	• Decrease in self-stigma and depression. • Increase in self-esteem.

Note: HOP = Honest, Open, Proud (formerly Coming Out Proud); HOP-C = Honest, Open, Proud—College relevant, meaningful, and useful program that promotes change and improves stigma outcomes for college/university students.

Several themes were identified through this CBPR process, including an interest in focusing on depression and anxiety rather than serious mental illness, a need to focus on relationships relevant to postsecondary settings (e.g., family, peers, professors) rather than work settings that is a key focus of the original version of HOP, and a desire to include content about disclosure through social media. Based on these recommendations, HOP-C includes an entire section on social media disclosure. It also includes new vignettes to incorporate elements of mental illness and disclosure that are more appropriate to postsecondary environments, such as family, peers, and professors. HOP-C also has a focus on anxiety and depression.

Outcomes for HOP-C

One published randomized controlled trial compared HOP-C to a waitlist control condition among college students and included a booster session 2 to 3 weeks after completion of the main HOP-C program (Conley et al., 2020; Table 8.2). University students (mean age = 21 years) self-reporting experiences with mental illness(es) or mental health challenges were recruited from three university campuses in the United States. Peer facilitators were recruited from relevant student groups and email listservs and completed a two-day training before facilitating the groups. Student participants were randomly assigned to HOP-C or a waitlist control group. Relative to the waitlist control group, students in the HOP-C program reported reduced harms related to self-stigma, specifically, reduced harm from self-applied stereotypes. They also reported improved self-efficacy about disclosure and perceived resources to cope with stigma stress post-intervention. After the booster session, disclosure self-efficacy and stigma stress coping effects remained significant (Conley et al., 2020). These gains were maintained through a two-month follow-up period, when examined in a sub-sample of 55 students. During the follow-up period there was additional improvement in the domain of perceived harm from stigma (Hundert et al., 2022). This peer-led intervention for self-stigma in college and university students can therefore have lasting effects.

HOP-C Case Study (Lakehead University, Canada)

The Mental Health Research Lab at Lakehead University, Thunder Bay, Ontario, is testing the efficacy of HOP-C for college and university students across Canada (project end date: December 2024). This project is funded by the Social Sciences and Humanities Council of Canada (SSHRC), through a three-year Insight Grant. Herein we describe some practical considerations for others wishing to implement HOP-C on their campus. The focus herein includes training and supporting peer facilitators, determining who to recruit for the HOP-C groups, and special considerations in using an online video platform.

This project initially planned for in-person groups; however, university operational changes due to the COVID-19 pandemic precipitated a move to online groups. This created an opportunity to recruit from a larger pool of potential participants. We recruited students from across Canada through social media and student organization listservs. As participant recruitment can be a challenge for programs such as HOP-C, this larger pool of potential participants was an advantage. Other benefits of an online platform are increased accessibility, reduced participant and administrative burden, and knowledge exchange amongst students from various geographical locations. Relative to other technological options, using a video communication platform may better support group discussions of sensitive topics while being more discreet than in-person groups for individuals especially impacted by self-stigma. However, video platforms may also pose some unique challenges. It is difficult to guarantee confidentiality on the part of group members for any support group, and this issue is compounded when using a video platform. Before every session, we remind our group members to ensure they have access to a private space and/or use headphones to increase their comfort in sharing their own experiences and to protect what other group members share as well. Facilitators also discuss video conference etiquette as part of the ground rules at the start of each session (e.g., taking breaks, keeping cameras and mic on vs. off, using the chat, etc). Further, facilitators will need to learn how to use the chosen video platform to ensure groups run smoothly (e.g., functions such as sharing screens, creating breakout rooms, and moderating chats). As such, having a co-facilitator for online HOP-C groups may support running the group and managing technological aspects. Other considerations for online groups include costs of participant recruitment (paying for social media recruitment, which is our best recruitment tool but also expensive) and coordinating groups across potentially six time zones. Also unknown is the impact of online versus in-person HOP-C groups, which this project aims to clarify.

Facilitator Recruitment and Training

A significant strength of the HOP approach is the peer facilitation component (Mulfinger et al., 2017; Rüsch et al., 2014b; Rüsch & Kösters, 2021), and this is an aspect of the program that requires initial as well as ongoing time and resource investment. We try to recruit four peer facilitators, which allows us to run two HOP-C groups simultaneously, if needed. It also builds a team to support one another and fill in if needed (e.g., for illness). Facilitators are students with self-reported lived experience of mental illness and/or distress; we have selected students from health and social science courses through an application and interview process. The facilitator training first involves completion of a set training program with a HOP-C master trainer (online training was available). This training focuses on the ideas and concepts contained in the HOP-C program as well as training on group facilitation and troubleshooting. During the training, facilitators can experience the group as participants and see the group run by an experienced facilitator.

We then hold our own practice sessions with the facilitators to support greater familiarity with the HOP-C material and practice facilitating sessions within time constraints. These practice sessions work well as facilitators can benefit from watching other facilitators in addition to receiving feedback from the group. We use a fidelity check to ensure facilitators are covering the necessary material. Facilitators are required to run through a practice session with 80% fidelity before they start running groups independently.

When running groups, our team holds debriefing meetings with the facilitators to discuss how the session went, any difficult situations that arose, and troubleshooting if needed. This might include how to respectfully engage if a group participant is quiet or using one's personal examples to invite dialogue. Following this, we shift to having monthly debriefing meetings, so facilitators continue to have a support forum. We also compensate our facilitators with a $50 (Canadian) honorarium per group cycle for contributing their time and experience. Considering all the resources invested to train and support our facilitators, ideally, we would like to retain them for a long time. However, because we prefer facilitators to be at least in their second year of study, most of our facilitators can run groups for 2 to 3 years before they are no longer students and lose their "peer" status. Those looking to implement HOP-C programs may choose to have a permanent staff member receive training to become a master trainer themselves so that they can more continuously train incoming facilitators.

Participant Recruitment

Another practical consideration when preparing to offer the HOP-C program is who to recruit for the groups. For our research project, we wanted to keep the eligibility criteria as open as possible to reach a diverse population while recruiting students who may benefit more from the program. As such, we chose to limit the groups to students aged 17–29 years because this age represents the *emerging adulthood* life stage, and emerging adults may share more similar experiences compared to older individuals (Arnett, 2015). Shared lived experiences may be especially important for HOP-C, where group discussions are foundational to the program. Further, we required students to self-identify as experiencing mental health challenges, but not necessarily diagnosed/diagnosable mental illness(es), and endorse experiencing at least a moderate level of self-stigma. As HOP-C is primarily an anti-stigma program, these criteria shift the focus from the type/severity of mental health challenges to students' relationship with those experiences.

HOP-C Case Study (University of South Florida, USA)

The STigma Action Research (STAR) Lab at the University of South Florida is currently conducting a feasibility, acceptability, and preliminary effectiveness trial of the HOP-C intervention with students (project end date: August 2025) supported by a three-year grant from the National Institute on Disability, Independent Living, and Rehabilitation Research (NIDILRR). In addition to the outcomes documented in previous HOP-C research, our study examines outcomes aligned with Tinto's well-supported model of student departure from college (Tinto, 1993). This model highlights engagement in higher education as key to student retention and comprises formal and informal academic and social integration. Students with mental health challenges who are experiencing stigma report not feeling included on their college campuses (Salzer, 2012), which according to Tinto's model impacts degree attainment. HOP-C may increase inclusion and therefore support college student persistence in higher education. Community participation and inclusion-related outcomes measured as a part of this trial include student engagement (measured by academic and social integration), service engagement (i.e., use of academic accommodations and mental health supports that might be availed through disclosure), and sense of campus belonging and satisfaction with one's college. We hypothesize the traditionally measured HOP-C outcomes variables, including self-stigma and appraisals of stigma as a stressor, will have mediating effects on these community participation and inclusion outcomes, and ultimately on postsecondary persistence and achievement. These are outcomes of keen interest to those working in higher education.

Language Considerations

We also carefully considered feedback from people with lived experience with mental illness in making decisions around program implementation, including the name of the intervention. For this study, STAR Lab has used an alternative name for the HOP-C program, calling it *Up To Me*, a name originally adopted for the youth version of the program adapted by the Wisconsin Initiative on Stigma Elimination (WISE). We chose to use this name for the program based on feedback from individuals living with mental health conditions who felt the name *Honest, Open, Proud* implied if one ultimately chose not to disclose at the end of the intervention, one was not being honest and should not be proud. This feedback is an indicator of possible considerations around program acceptability to the postsecondary population. We chose the name *Up To Me* to emphasize the disclosure decision is ultimately up to the individual, and the goal of the program is to empower them in the decision-making process, a previously documented disclosure-related outcome (Corrigan et al., 2010).

One important lesson our team learned early in the implementation of *Up To Me* at USF centered around language. We began our effort to recruit student program participants by asking students two questions: "Do you identify as living with a mental health challenge?" and "Do you feel a sense of shame about your mental health challenges and feel a need to keep them a secret?" Using this language, very few interested students were deemed to be eligible to participate because many answered "no" to one of these two questions. To remedy this, we expanded the language in our eligibility questionnaire to ask additional questions with variations of shame/self-stigma language. We asked a series of five questions to determine if a student might benefit from the program: (1) Do you feel *ashamed* of disclosing your mental health challenge? (2) Do you feel *nervous* about disclosing your mental health challenge? (3) Do you feel *embarrassed* about disclosing your mental health challenge? (4) Do you feel *self-conscious* about disclosing your mental health challenge? and (5) Do you feel *judged* when disclosing your mental health challenge?

Using this strategy, we were able to identify many more students who might benefit from *Up To Me*. One lesson herein may be the experience of shame itself being stigmatized. Most students have indicated feeling judged when disclosing their mental health challenges. Interestingly, some students have completed our eligibility questionnaire who answered "yes" to questions about shame, nervousness, embarrassment, self-consciousness, and judgment around disclosing their mental health challenges, but indicated they do not identify as living with a mental health challenge. This may again relate to the importance of language choice when implementing programs meant to address stigma. We have heard in previous work (Mizock et al., 2022) the term "mental health challenges" may be preferred by college students to "mental illness," but for some college students, the term "mental health challenges" may also not resonate. Fortunately, the HOP-C/*Up To Me* program accounts for this, including a segment in lesson one on language.

Summary and Future Directions

There are various departments or organizations that could house HOP-C on a post-secondary campus, depending on the specific focus and resources available, and this may include collaboration among multiple departments, groups, and individuals. Some common campus places where this anti-stigma program could be housed include counseling centers or mental health services, student health services or wellness centers, health promotion offices, diversity and inclusion offices, student organizations (e.g, dedicated to mental health advocacy, disability rights, or other related issues), student housing or residence life, and academic departments. The research examples provided above (Lakehead University; University of South Florida) are examples of research initiatives that house HOP-C at their respective institutions.

Our team has found having an institutional "champion" for HOP-C to be one key to its successful implementation and longevity. In the college/university context specifically, peer facilitator turnover is an important consideration, as peers eventually graduate. This means that having a master trainer on site (i.e., someone who can regularly train new peer facilitators) is important. Campuses may wish to consider having a staff member trained as a master trainer, with the ability to train new peer facilitators as needed, provide support to the peer facilitator team, and hold responsibility for organizing and recruiting for the HOP-C groups. Partnering with other campus departments and groups is also critical to HOP-C sustainability. We have found that partnering with student clubs (e.g., mental health advocacy clubs; peers support clubs) has been a great way to advertise for peer facilitator positions. We have also had success advertising peer facilitator positions among students taking health and behavioral sciences majors, where the opportunity to gain peer facilitation skills is attractive to students studying to work in health care and related fields.

A challenge and paradox for self-stigma programs such as HOP-C occurs if stigma keeps students from participating, particularly in face-to-face interventions focused on stigma and disclosure (Conley et al., 2020). Despite strong evidence for the effectiveness of strategies to reduce self-stigma, commitment to and retention in evidence-based interventions like HOP and *Up To Me* is challenging. This is where partnerships and administrative endorsement can again be helpful. HOP-C participants can be recruited from the general student population, but we have found it additionally helpful to advertise through student groups, university departments such as student health and counseling, as well as national student mental health groups (an example being Active Minds in the USA). Campuses may wish to run a larger anti-stigma campaign and have HOP-C situated as one component of the anti-stigma work. Administrative endorsement (such as leaders talking about and promoting HOP-C) is also helpful to recruitment. Such endorsement can signal a supportive and empowering environment that encourages students to participate in HOP-C by enhancing its credibility, visibility, and resources, while also setting a positive example for the campus community.

Another approach to address recruitment and retention issues may be to adapt HOP-C for mobile health technologies (which are treatments provided to people during their everyday lives, in real-time and real-world; Heron & Smyth, 2010). Leveraging the momentum generated around *Up To Me*, the STAR Lab is currently working to adapt the intervention to chatbot delivery. A prototype has been developed to guide participants through the three *Up To Me* lessons, and preliminary data suggests students find the chatbot an acceptable way to deliver the intervention. The benefits of using technology include increased access and fewer concerns about associating with the program due to stigma, while drawbacks include challenges with incorporating peer support, an essential component of the intervention. One way we have addressed this disadvantage is by having the chatbot guide users to videos of a student facilitator leading them through the intervention. During these videos, the student facilitator shares his own lived experience. This is a component of peer support but it is not mutual, two-way support which is a component of the live, synchronous program.

In addressing self-stigma on college and university campuses, we must be careful to not suggest that stigma is the person's fault. Rather, stigma is a form of social injustice and a societal problem, and therefore a problem that society must take responsibility for and prioritize. Campuses may wish to include HOP-C among a variety of anti-stigma efforts to address culture change. While HOP-C is more narrowly focused on helping students who are impacted by self-stigma, empowerment is, in a sense, the opposite of stigma and a broad manner by which we can reduce stigma (Corrigan & Rao, 2012). Thus, addressing self-stigma is crucial in combating public stigma on college and university campuses.

HOP-C is a promising program to address the challenge of self-stigma, and student well-being and recovery can ultimately be supported through this empowering approach to helping students to manage the stigma-related barriers they encounter in postsecondary settings. Strengths of HOP-C include the community-based participatory model and empowerment, which are central tenets to the overall HOP programs. Additional published research in the postsecondary context will benefit this program, such as understanding the impact of HOP-C on the wider campus culture, adapting and testing for other postsecondary contexts like trade and vocational schools, and including students from diverse ethnic and cultural backgrounds. There is also a need to test whether HOP-C's intended targets (the regressive stages of self-stigma, affirming attitudes, and disclosure decisions/activities) are engaged and whether identified change mechanisms are operative in the context of this program. Technology adaptations, such as the *Up to Me* chatbot, are a promising future development for HOP-C and may increase the uptake and retention of postsecondary students in this evidence-based anti-stigma program.

References

Al-Khouja, M. A., Corrigan, P. W., & Nieweglowski, K. (2017a). Honest, Open, Proud to eliminate the stigma of mental illness on college campuses*:* Manual. https://hopprogram.org/wp-content/uploads/2022/04/HOP_college_manual_FINAL.pdf

Al-Khouja, M. A., Corrigan, P. W., & Nieweglowski, K. (2017b). *Honest, Open, Proud to eliminate the stigma of mental illness on college campuses: Workbook for program facilitators and participants*. https://hopprogram.org/wp-content/uploads/2022/04/HOP_college_workbook_FINAL.pdf

Arnett, J. J. (2015). *Emerging adulthood: The winding road from the late teens through the twenties*. Oxford University Press.

Bos, A. E. R., Kanner, D., Muris, P., Janssen, B., & Mayer, B. (2009). Mental illness stigma and disclosure: Consequences of coming out of the closet. *Issues in Mental Health Nursing, 30*, 509–513. https://doi.org/10.1080/01612840802601382

Chaudoir, S., & Fisher, J. D. (2010). The disclosure process model: Understanding disclosure decision making and post-disclosure outcomes among people living with a concealable stigmatized identity. *Psychological Bulletin, 136*(2), 236–256. https://doi.org/10.1037/a0018193

Chaudoir, S. R., & Quinn, D. M. (2010). Revealing concealable stigmas: The impact of disclosure motivations and positive first-disclosure experiences on fear of disclosure and Well-being. *Journal of Social Issues, 66*(3), 570–584. https://doi.org/10.1111/j.1540-4560.2010.01663.x

Conley, C. S., Hundert, C. G., Charles, J. L. K., Huguenel, B. M., Al-Khouja, M., Qin, S., Paniagua, D., & Corrigan, P. W. (2020). Honest, open, proud–college: Effectiveness of a peer-led small-group intervention for reducing the stigma of mental illness. *Stigma and Health, 5*(2), 168–178. https://doi.org/10.1037/SAH0000185

Corrigan, P. W., Kosyluk, K. A., & Rüsch, N. (2013). Reducing self-stigma by coming out proud. *American Journal of Public Health, 103*(5), 794–800. https://doi.org/10.2105/AJPH.2012.301037

Corrigan, P. W., Larson, J., & Rüsch, N. (2009a). Self-stigma and the "why try" effect: Impact on life goals and evidence-based practices. *World Psychiatry, 8*(2), 75–81. https://doi.org/10.1002/j.2051-5545.2009.tb00218.x

Corrigan, P. W., Larson, J. E., Hautamaki, J., Matthews, A., Kuwabara, S., Rafacz, J., Walton, J., Wassel, A., & O'Shaughnessy, J. (2009b). What lessons do coming out as gay men or lesbians have for people stigmatized by mental illness? *Community Mental Health Journal, 45*(5), 366–374. https://doi.org/10.1007/s10597-009-9187-6

Corrigan, P. W., & Lundin, R. (2001). *Don't call me nuts: Coping with the stigma of mental illness.* Recovery Press.

Corrigan, P. W., Morris, S., Larson, J., Rafacz, J., Wassel, A., Michaels, P., Wilkniss, S., Batia, K., & Rüsch, N. (2010). Self-stigma and coming out about one's mental illness. *Journal of Community Psychology, 38*(3), 259–275. https://doi.org/10.1002/jcop.20363

Corrigan, P. W., Rafacz, J., & Rüsch, N. (2011). Examining a progressive model of self-stigma and its impact on people with serious mental illness. *Psychiatry Research, 189*(3), 339–343. https://doi.org/10.1016/j.psychres.2011.05.024

Corrigan, P. W., & Rao, D. (2012). On the self-stigma of mental illness: Stages, disclosure, and strategies for change. *Canadian Journal of Psychiatry, 57*(8), 464–469. https://doi.org/10.1177/070674371205700804

Corrigan, P. W., Larson, J. E., Michaels, P. J., Buchholz, B. A., Del Rossi, R., Fontecchio, M. J., Castro, D., Gause, M., Krzyzanowski, R., & Rusch, N. (2015). *Diminishing the self-stigma of mental illness by coming out proud. Psychiatry Research, 229*, 148–154. https://doi.org/10.1016/j.psychres.2015.07.053

Corrigan, P. W., Rüsch, N., & Scior, K. (2018). Adapting disclosure programs to reduce the stigma of mental illness. *Psychiatric Services, 69*(7), 826–828. https://doi.org/10.1176/APPI.PS.201700478

Corrigan, P. W., & Watson, A. C. (2002). The paradox of self-stigma and mental illness. *Clinical Psychology: Science and Practice, 9*(1), 35–53. https://doi.org/10.1093/clipsy.9.1.35

Drapalski, A. L., Lucksted, A., Brown, C. H., & Fang, L. J. (2021). Outcomes of ending self-stigma, a group intervention to reduce internalized stigma, among individuals with serious mental illness. *Psychiatric Services, 72*(2), 136–142. https://doi.org/10.1176/appi.ps.201900296

Ennals, P., Fossey, E., & Howie, L. (2015). Postsecondary study and mental ill-health: A meta-synthesis of qualitative research exploring students' lived experiences. *Journal of Mental Health, 24*(2), 111–119. https://doi.org/10.3109/09638237.2015.1019052

Fung, K. M., Tsang, H. W., & Cheung, W. M. (2011). Randomized controlled trial of the self-stigma reduction program among individuals with schizophrenia. *Psychiatry Research, 189*(2), 208–214. https://doi.org/10.1016/j.psychres.2011.02.013

Heron, K. E., & Smyth, J. M. (2010). Ecological momentary interventions: Incorporating mobile technology into psychosocial and health behaviour treatments. *British Journal of Health Psychology, 15*(Pt 1), 1–39. https://doi.org/10.1348/135910709X466063

Hopper, K. (2007). Rethinking social recovery in schizophrenia: What a capabilities approach might offer. *Social Science & Medicine, 65*, 868–879. https://doi.org/10.1016/j.socscimed.2007.04.012

Hundert, C. G., Hareli, M., & Conley, C. S. (2022). Honest, open, proud—College: Follow-up effects of a peer-led group for reducing the stigma of mental illness. *Stigma and Health, 7*, 122–125. https://doi.org/10.1037/sah0000326

Ivezić, S. Ŝ., Sesar, M. A., & Mužinić, L. (2017). Effects of a group psychoeducation program on self-stigma, empowerment and perceived discrimination of persons with schizophrenia. *Psychiatria Danubina, 29*(1), 66–73.

Jones, E. E., Farina, A., Hastorf, A. H., Markus, H., Miller, D. T., & Scott, R. A. (1984). *Social stigma: The psychology of marked relationships*. Freeman.

Link, B. G., & Phelan, J. C. (2001). Conceptualizing stigma. *Annual Review of Sociology, 27*, 363–385. https://doi.org/10.1146/annurev.soc.27.1.363

Link, B. G., Struening, E. L., Neese-Todd, S., Asmussen, S., & Phelan, J. C. (2001). Stigma as a barrier to recovery: The consequences of stigma for the self-esteem of people with mental illnesses. *Psychiatric Services, 52*, 1621–1626. https://doi.org/10.1176/appi.ps.52.12.1621

Livingston, J. D., & Boyd, J. E. (2010). Correlates and consequences of internalized stigma for people living with mental illness: A systematic review and meta-analysis. *Social Science & Medicine, 71*(12), 2150–2161. https://doi.org/10.1016/j.socscimed.2010.09.030

Lucksted, A., & Drapalski, A. L. (2015). Self-stigma regarding mental illness: Definition, impact, and relationship to societal stigma. *Psychiatric Rehabilitation Journal, 38*(2), 99–102. https://doi.org/10.1037/prj0000152

Lucksted, A., Drapalski, A. L., Brown, C. H., Wilson, C., Charlotte, M., Mullane, A., & Fang, L. J. (2017). Outcomes of a psychoeducational intervention to reduce internalized stigma among psychosocial rehabilitation clients. *Psychiatric Services, 68*(4), 360–367. https://doi.org/10.1176/APPI.PS.201600037

Lysaker, P. H., Davis, L. W., Warman, D. M., Strasburger, A., & Beattie, N. (2007). Stigma, social function and symptoms in schizophrenia and schizoaffective disorder: Associations across 6 months. *Psychiatry Research, 149*, 89–95. https://doi.org/10.1016/j.psychres.2006.03.007

Markoulakis, R., & Kirsh, B. (2013). Difficulties for university students with mental health problems: A critical interpretive synthesis. *The Review of Higher Education, 37*(1), 77–100. https://doi.org/10.1353/rhe.2013.0073

Mashiach-Eizenberg, M., Hasson-Ohayon, I., Yanos, P. T., Lysaker, P. H., & Roe, D. (2013). Internalized stigma and quality of life among persons with severe mental illness: The mediating roles of self-esteem and hope. *Psychiatry Research, 208*(1), 15–20. https://doi.org/10.1016/j.psychres.2013.03.013

Mayer, L., Corrigan, P. W., Eisheuer, D., Oexle, N., & Rüsch, N. (2022). Attitudes towards disclosing a mental illness: Impact on quality of life and recovery. *Social Psychiatry and Psychiatric Epidemiology, 57*(2), 363–374. https://doi.org/10.1007/S00127-021-02081-1

McCay, E. A., Beanlands, H., Leszcz, M., Goering, P., Seeman, M., Ryan, L., Johnston, N., & Vishnevsky, T. (2006). A group intervention to promote healthy self-concepts and guide recovery in first episode schizophrenia: A pilot study. *Psychosocial Rehabilitation Journal, 30*(2), 105–111. https://doi.org/10.2975/30.2006.105.111

McCay, E., Beanlands, H., Zipursky, R., Roy, P., Leszcz, M., Landeen, J., Ryan, K., Conrad, G., Romano, D., Francis, D., Hunt, J., Costantini, L., & Chan, E. (2007). A randomized controlled trial of a group intervention to reduce engulfment and self-stigmatisation in first episode schizophrenia. *Australian e-Journal for the Advancement of Mental Health, 6*(3), 212–220. https://doi.org/10.5172/jamh.6.3.212

Mizock, L., Dilts, G., Sotilleo, E., & Cherry, J. (2022). Preferred terminology of people with serious mental illness. *Psychological Services, 21*(1), 184–197. https://doi.org/10.1037/ser0000717

Modelli, A., Candal Setti, V. P., van de Bilt, M. T., Gattaz, W. F., Loch, A. A., & Rössler, W. (2021). Addressing mood disorder diagnosis' stigma with an honest, open, proud (HOP)-based intervention: A randomized controlled trial. *Frontiers in Psychiatry, 11*, 582180. https://doi.org/10.3389/FPSYT.2020.582180

Morrison, A. P., Burke, E., Murphy, E., Pyle, M., Bowe, S., Varese, F., Dunn, G., Chapman, N., Hutton, P., Welford, M., & Wood, L. J. (2016). Cognitive therapy for internalised stigma in people experiencing psychosis: A pilot randomised controlled trial. *Psychiatry Research, 240*, 96–102. https://doi.org/10.1016/J.PSYCHRES.2016.04.024

Mulfinger, N., Müller, S., Böge, I., Sakar, V., Corrigan, P. W., Evans-Lacko, S., Nehf, L., Djamali, J., Samarelli, A., Kempter, M., Ruckes, C., Libal, G., Oexle, N., Noterdaeme, M., & Rüsch, N. (2017). Honest, open, proud for adolescents with mental illness: Pilot randomized controlled trial. *Journal of Child Psychology and Psychiatry, 59*, 684–691. https://doi.org/10.1111/jcpp.12853

Pachankis, J. E. (2007). The psychological implications of concealing a stigma: A cognitive-affective-behavioral model. *Psychological Bulletin, 133*(2), 328–345. https://doi.org/10.1037/0033-2909.133.2.328

Pahwa, R., Fulginiti, A., Brekke, J. S., & Rice, E. (2017). Mental illness disclosure decision making. *The American Journal of Orthopsychiatry, 87*(5), 575–584. https://doi.org/10.1037/ORT0000250

Phelan, J. C., Link, B. G., Stueve, A., & Pescosolido, B. A. (2000). Public conceptions of mental illness in 1950 and 1996: What is mental illness and is it to be feared? *Journal of Health and Social Behavior, 41*(2), 188–207. https://doi.org/10.2307/2676305

Qin, S., Sheehan, L., Yau, E., Chen, Y., Wang, Y., Deng, H., Lam, C., Chen, Z., Zhao, L., CBPR Team, & Corrigan, P. (2024). Adapting and evaluating a strategic disclosure program to address mental health stigma among Chinese. *International Journal of Mental Health and Addiction, 22*, 1029–1046. https://doi.org/10.1007/s11469-022-00911-0

Roe, D., Hasson-Ohayon, I., Masiach-Eizenberg, M., Derhy, O., Lysaker, P. H., & Yanos, P. T. (2014). Narrative enhancement and cognitive therapy (NECT) effectiveness: Quasi-experimental study. *Journal of Clinical Psychology, 70*(4), 303–312. https://doi.org/10.1002/jclp.22050

Rüsch, N., Abbruzzese, E., Hagedorn, R., Hartenhauer, D., Kaufmann, I., Curshellas, J., Ventling, S., Zuaboni, G., Bridler, R., Olschewski, M., Kawohl, W., Rössler, W., Kleim, B., & Corrigan, P. W. (2014b). Efficacy of coming out proud to reduce stigma's impact among people with mental illness: Pilot randomized controlled trial. *British Journal of Psychiatry, 204*(5), 391–397. https://doi.org/10.1192/bjp.bp.113.135772

Rüsch, N., Brohan, E., Gabbidon, J., Thornicroft, G., & Clement, S. (2014a). Stigma and disclosing one's mental illness to family and friends. *Social Psychiatry and Psychiatric Epidemiology, 49*(7), 1157–1160. https://doi.org/10.1007/S00127-014-0871-7

Rüsch, N., & Kösters, M. (2021). Honest, open, proud to support disclosure decisions and to decrease stigma's impact among people with mental illness: Conceptual review and meta-analysis of program efficacy. *Social Psychiatry and Psychiatric Epidemiology, 56*(9), 1513–1526. https://doi.org/10.1007/S00127-021-02076-Y

Rüsch, N., Malzer, A., Oexle, N., Waldmann, T., Staiger, T., Bahemann, A., Wigand, M. E., Becker, T., & Corrigan, P. W. (2019). Disclosure and quality of life among unemployed individuals with mental health problems: A longitudinal study. *The Journal of Nervous and Mental Disease, 207*(3), 137–139. https://doi.org/10.1097/NMD.0000000000000914

Salzer, M. S. (2012). A comparative study of campus experiences of college students with mental illnesses versus a general college sample. *Journal of American College Health, 60*(1), 1–7. https://doi.org/10.1080/07448481.2011.552537

Scior, K., Rüsch, N., White, C., & Corrigan, P. W. (2020). Supporting mental health disclosure decisions: The honest, open, proud programme. *The British Journal of Psychiatry, 216*(5), 243–245. https://doi.org/10.1192/BJP.2019.256

Sheehan, L., Oexle, N., Bushman, M., Glover, L., Lewy, S., Armas, S. A., & Qin, S. (2023). To share or not to share? Evaluation of a strategic disclosure program for suicide attempt survivors. *Death Studies, 47*(4), 392–399. https://doi.org/10.1080/07481187.2022.2076266

Smart, L., & Wegner, D. M. (1999). Covering up what can't be seen: Concealable stigma and mental control. *Journal of Personality and Social Psychology, 77*(3), 474–486. https://doi.org/10.1037/0022-3514.77.3.474

Stein, K. F. (2012). DSS and accommodations in higher education: Perceptions of students with psychological disabilities. *Journal of Postsecondary Education and Disability, 26*(2), 145–161.

Taniguchi, E. (2020). The roles of mental illness disclosure and disclosure strategies on Well-being among college students. *Journal of American College Health, 70*(3), 929–939. https://doi.org/10.1080/07448481.2020.1781868

Tinto, V. (1993). *Leaving college: Rethinking the causes and cures of student attrition* (2nd ed.). University of Chicago Press.

Uchino, T., Maeda, M., & Uchimura, N. (2012). Psychoeducation may reduce self-stigma of people with schizophrenia and schizoaffective disorder. *The Kurume Medical Journal, 59*(1–2), 25–31. https://doi.org/10.2739/KURUMEMEDJ.59.25

Wada, M., Suto, M. J., Lee, M., Sanders, D., Sun, C., Le, T. N., Goldman-Hasbun, J., & Chauhan, S. (2019). University students' perspectives on mental illness stigma. *Mental Health & Prevention, 14*, 200159. https://doi.org/10.1016/j.mph.2019.200159

Watson, A. C., Corrigan, P. W., Larson, J. E., & Sells, M. (2007). Self-stigma in people with mental illness. *Schizophrenia Bulletin, 33*(6), 1312–1318. https://doi.org/10.1093/schbul/sbl076

Weisz, B. M., Quinn, D. M., & Williams, M. K. (2016). Out and healthy: Being more "out" about a concealable stigmatized identity may boost the health benefits of social support. *Journal of Health Psychology, 21*, 2934–2943. https://doi.org/10.1177/1359105315589392

Wood, L., Byrne, R., Enache, G., & Morrison, A. P. (2018). A brief cognitive therapy intervention for internalised stigma in acute inpatients who experience psychosis: A feasibility randomised controlled trial. *Psychiatry Research, 262*, 303–310. https://doi.org/10.1016/J.PSYCHRES.2017.12.030

Yanos, P. T., Luksted, A., Drapalski, A. L., Roe, D., & Lusaker, P. (2015). Interventions targeting mental health self-stigma: A review and comparison. *Psychiatric Rehabilitation Journal, 38*(2), 171–178. https://doi.org/10.1037/prj0000100

Yanos, P. T., Roe, D., West, M. L., Smith, S. M., & Lysaker, P. H. (2012). Group-based treatment for internalized stigma among persons with severe mental illness: Findings from a randomized controlled trial. *Psychological Services, 9*(3), 248–258. https://doi.org/10.1037/a0028048

Young, D. K. W. (2018). Cognitive behavioral therapy group for reducing self-stigma for people with mental illness. *Research on Social Work Practice, 28*(7), 827–837. https://doi.org/10.1177/1049731516681849

Young, D. K. W., Ng, P. Y. N., Corrigan, P., Chiu, R., & Yang, S. (2020). Self-stigma reduction group for people with depression: A randomized controlled trial. *Research on Social Work Practice, 30*(8), 846–857. https://doi.org/10.1177/1049731520941594

K. Amanda Maranzan, Ph.D., C. Psych., is an associate professor at Lakehead University in Ontario, Canada. Dr. Maranzan's primary research is related to mental illness stigma with additional interests in mental health outcome measurement, professional psychology and training. She teaches courses about mental illness, ethics, and clinical supervision. As a registered (licensed) psychologist, she also engages in clinical practice.

Grishma Dabas, is a Ph.D. student in clinical psychology at Lakehead University, Ontario, Canada. Her research interests include mental illness stigma and mental healthcare systems and policies. Under the supervision of Dr. Maranzan, Grishma's doctoral research is examining the outcomes associated with HOP-C, an anti-stigma intervention for post-secondary students.

Kristin Kosyluk, Ph.D., is an associate professor of mental health law & policy at the University of South Florida and Director of the STigma Action Research (STAR) Lab. Dr. Kosyluk's research focuses on understanding and addressing the stigma surrounding mental illness, with much of her work focused on stigma in higher education settings. She is currently the principal investigator of a grant from the National Institute on Disability, Independent Living, and Rehabilitation Research (NIDILRR), which supports a feasibility, acceptability, and preliminary effectiveness trial of Up To Me (also known as Honest, Open, Proud-College Version [HOP-C]).

Nele Loecher, Ph.D., is a postdoctoral research fellow at St. Jude Children's Research Hospital. Her research focuses on stigma, health behaviors, and the transition off active treatment for childhood cancer survivors. Her dissertation work in the STigma Action Research (STAR) Lab under Dr. Kosyluk focused on stigma in chronic disease and mental illness. During her graduate training, she was the research coordinator of a grant investigating the feasibility, acceptability, and preliminary effectiveness of the Up To Me (also known as HOP-C) intervention.

Patrick Corrigan, Ph.D., is a distinguished professor of psychology at the Illinois Institute of Technology as well as director of the Center for Health Equity, Education, and Research (www.iit.edu). He has authored more than 500 journal articles and 20 books. He is also the editor of *Stigma and Health*, an APA journal.

Chapter 9
Using Social Marketing Tactics to Impact Mental Illness Stigma on Campus

Marie A. Yeh

Abstract One strategy for shifting higher education culture around mental illness stigma involves the use of social marketing campaigns. These well-intentioned campaigns must be developed strategically so they are effective and do not create more stigma on campuses. This chapter outlines steps for creating effective campaigns to change mental illness stigma cultures on college campuses. The chapter concludes with a case study demonstrating how the steps can be used to assess, target, and implement a comprehensive social marketing campaign to reduce mental illness stigma.

Keywords Mental illness · Stigma · Social marketing · Marketing campaigns

Changing the culture surrounding mental illness stigma is no easy task. Indeed, it is not just one task. As this book represents, it requires several different cultural shifts be achieved among several different constituencies on campus. One strategy for shifting culture around mental illness stigma is the use of social marketing campaigns on campus. Social marketing applies marketing principles and strategies to influence target audience behaviors for the benefit of society (Kotler & Lee, 2008). The goal is to promote voluntary behavior and attitudinal change toward a social issue (Grier & Bryant, 2005).

Marketing involves a multi-step process to create strategies for selling a product and, in the case of social marketing, selling a message, behavior, value, attitude, or ideal. Marketing campaigns can be used to transmit the desired cultural change and transform the campus environment. Using a marketing strategy engages several different tactics to maximize return on investment. This chapter discusses these tactics

The author has no conflicts of interest to declare that are relevant to the content of this chapter.

M. A. Yeh (✉)
Marketing Department, Loyola University Maryland, Baltimore, MD, USA
e-mail: mayeh@loyola.edu

© The Author(s), under exclusive license to Springer Nature Switzerland AG 2025

K. M. Brennan, K. S. Gorman (eds.), *A University-Wide Approach to Changing Campus Cultures of Mental Illness Stigma*, Knowledge Studies in Higher Education 18, https://doi.org/10.1007/978-3-031-86496-4_9

with a step-by-step planning process for developing a social marketing campaign to address mental illness stigma on campus.

Marketing campaigns should not be used in isolation. They can only contribute to cultural change in concert with other efforts to decrease stigma (National Academies of Sciences, Engineering and Medicine, 2016). While they can result in short-term positive attitude change, social marketing campaigns in and of themselves do not result in long-term behavioral change (Walsh & Foster, 2021). Other tactics need to be implemented in conjunction with a social marketing campaign to fully address stigma on campus.

Understanding the stigmatization process and the related stigma attitudes and behaviors is necessary to inform the creation of social marketing campaigns aimed to disrupt and reverse the process. Stigmatization occurs on societal, interpersonal, and individual levels with dynamically interrelated manifestations of different stigmas such as structural, public, and self-stigma (Bos et al., 2013).[1] The focus of stigma reduction in social marketing efforts has centered most frequently on combatting public stigma. The target attitudes and behaviors to be changed are the cognitions and feelings that comprise these types of stigma.

Link and Phelan (2001) suggest the process of mental illness stigma consists of beliefs, which include stereotypes, affective reactions to the stereotype, the phenomenon of othering those with mental illness, and behavioral endorsements about how stigmatizers might treat people with mental illness. Researchers have found a clear, consistent, and persistent consensus about stigmatized beliefs of those with mental illness; these beliefs associate mental illness with dangerousness, unpredictability, and incompetency. People with mental illness are also blamed for their illness, causing them to feel shame and hide their illness (Angermeyer & Matschinger, 2003; Evans-Lacko et al., 2013; Kobau et al., 2010; Pescosolido et al., 2013). Combined with an expectation of a negative prognosis for recovery from mental illness, these beliefs lead to affective reactions like fear, pity, and anger (Angermeyer & Matschinger, 2003; Corrigan et al., 2003; Evans-Lacko et al., 2013). Together these affective responses and cognitive beliefs cause people without mental illness to consider those with mental illness to be "other," leading to an "us" versus "them" mentality among those who stigmatize. These beliefs also lead to endorsement of behaviors toward people with mental illnesses, such as coercive treatment. These cognitions cause others to avoid and socially distance themselves from people with mental illness. But not all components are negative; behavioral endorsements can be positive, leading those who stigmatize to have concern for and a desire to help those with mental illness.

By endorsing these negative beliefs about themselves, people with mental illness often experience diminished self-esteem and self-efficacy (Corrigan & Rao, 2012). For example, whereas stigmatizers believe those with mental illness should feel shame, those with mental illness are ashamed and feel distress, disgrace, and/or humiliation for having a mental illness. While those who stigmatize believe people

[1] These terms are defined in Chap. 1.

with mental illness may harm others, those with mental illness may internalize that fear, thereby making them afraid they will hurt others or themselves. While stigmatizers will keep their distance from people with mental illness, people with mental illness may keep their distance from others believing others do not want to associate with someone with mental illness and/or fearing being judged or patronized. Being aware that people may discriminate against them, they may remove themselves from social situations to avoid putting themselves in the line of discriminatory behavior. This may also be exacerbated by a belief they are incompetent as others believe them to be.

Social marketing campaigns aim to change these attitudes and behaviors. Campaigns may target changing perceptions of people with mental illness as dangerous, unpredictable, incompetent, to be feared or pitied, to be blamed, incapable of recovery from the illness, and as "other." How to address these beliefs effectively will be discussed next.

Steps for Using Social Marketing to Combat Mental Illness Stigma

Social marketing differs from other cultural change strategies such as education or policy implementation. Educational programming seeks generally to target change at the individual level through improvements in knowledge while policy often uses coercion or threat of punishment to manage behavior (e.g., codes of conduct). While social marketing campaigns can educate, the goal is more to persuade and influence as well as to create an environment where the change can be seen as consistent with one's self-interest and the culture of the campus (Grier & Bryant, 2005). The messaging and campaigns themselves are a tool for creating and maintaining a culture of acceptance and welcome on campus for people with mental illness.

One important means of creating such a campus culture is to use a community-based participatory approach which involves inviting a cross-section of individuals from campus, especially students and faculty/staff with mental illness, in the planning and implementation of the campaign (Israel et al., 1998; Schulz et al., 2002). By engaging individuals across campus, social marketing campaigns can build on the strengths and resources of all involved while also activating and mobilizing the social processes, networks, and supports needed to make cultural change happen. Community-based participatory approaches are critically important when tackling issues related to marginalized groups who suffer from ingrained societal and cultural inequities (Suarez-Balcazar et al., 2020). Including people with mental illness in the process of campaign development ensures they have been given a voice on the issue and empowers them in the process. It also ensures that campaigns, in their effort to change those who stigmatize, do not inadvertently harm those with mental illness.

Step One: Conduct Audience Research

The first step in good marketing is to understand the customer. In the case of transforming culture around mental illness stigma, this translates to understanding the beliefs, attitudes, and behaviors of constituencies on campus. Questions to be addressed include "Whose behavior and attitudes require change?" and "What aspect of the stigmatization process should be targeted?" While most campuses might initially focus these efforts on the student body, staff and faculty should be targeted as well as they often set the tone and influence the culture on campus.

Once the targeted group is determined broadly, research on the chosen audience needs to be conducted to segment the group properly. For instance, if a campus is targeting students, it is important to recognize "students" refers to a set of heterogeneous-comprised individuals who will vary in how they endorse stigmatizing beliefs, attitudes, and behaviors. Studies show 60–75% of college students have one or more mental illnesses (American College Health Association, 2022; Lipson et al., 2022). At the very least, one needs to determine whether to target students with mental illness, students without mental illness, or students at risk for mental illness with your campaign.

Stigma is a complex, multidimensional construct. As such, not all people will endorse the dimensions of stigma similarly. Yeh et al. (2017) demonstrated when one uses all the components of stigma to evaluate a group, different groups emerge in their endorsement of stigma beliefs. Their work demonstrated the need to segment and target very specifically around the stigma dimensions relevant to each group to impact the stigma surrounding mental illness. They found the measures used in mental illness stigma research loaded onto six factors: menace, nurturance, blame, shame, difference, and incompetence. Each factor included several different stigma dimensions. For instance, menace as a factor included these stigma dimensions: dangerousness, unpredictability, fear, and anger. Their study also separated those with mental illness into their own distinct segment as a part of a cluster analysis. Separating out people with mental illness in analyzing segments is important because it allows deeper understanding of how those who have mental illness also engage in the stigmatizing process. Stigma reduction efforts for those with mental illness should be different than campaigns targeting those without mental illness.

Yeh et al. (2017) found stigmatizers varied in the stigma dimensions they endorsed and, thus, identified groups as either allies, adversaries, blamers, shamers, or ambivalents. *Allies* did not endorse the stigma beliefs, attitudes, and behaviors. Indeed, allies held more favorable thoughts and feelings toward people with mental illness than did people with mental illness. *Adversaries* comprised individuals who endorsed almost all the stigma dimensions. *Blamers* thought people with mental illness were to blame for their illness. *Shamers* strongly believed people with mental illness should hide their mental illness, which they used as a proxy for shame. Shamers also scored high on nurturance. *Ambivalents* had mixed feelings toward people with mental illness, having identical levels of nurturance but also endorsing them as different. Segmenting groups based on what type of stigma they hold allows marketers to target messaging directly and effectively. See Appendix 9.1 for the assessment used by Yeh et al. (2017) as one example of how assessment can be used to segment groups.

A survey assessment should be conducted anonymously to protect the privacy of all participants. One should also take steps to not collect information that could potentially be used to identify respondents. For example, if a campus does not employ a very diverse staff or faculty, the collection of race/ethnicity, department, and college information could potentially be used to identify respondents; this might dissuade them from participating and result in an inaccurate picture of the campus constituents. Understanding who on campus has close friends and/or family members with mental illness is also important to know. Messaging used in a social marketing campaign can tap into people's existing experiences with mental illness in their family. Having this general understanding of who has experience with mental illness either on a first- or second-hand basis is valuable information for the campaign creation.

In addition, one needs to measure and understand other important information about these campus constituents (segments) such as their media consumption, living situation, major, undergraduate/graduate class year, and demographics. Knowing the segment's media consumption (e.g., Instagram, Facebook, Snapchat, BeReal, YouTube, etc.) and living arrangements (e.g., living on or off campus) can help inform decisions on how to reach a segment with the campaign's messaging. One example is to use postings on the university's Instagram account to target those who follow it. Posting messaging in the residence halls and enlisting resident assistants in getting the messages out to those who live on campus is another effective strategy. Social marketing could become a part of the specific programming that occurs on campus for first-year students, for example, who live in residence halls specific to their needs or take required first-year courses.

Data regarding stigma levels on campus before campaign implementation can be used to evaluate the campaign's effectiveness. Questions that assess attitudes toward people with mental illness and social distance (i.e., the degree to which people might avoid people with mental illness) can also be included. These are often asked using a series of questions such as "would you be friends with someone with mental illness?" and "would you date someone with mental illness?" (Yeh et al., 2013, 2017). After a campaign is implemented, another study can be conducted to assess changes in the endorsement of the stigma dimensions.

Step Two: Targeting and Positioning a Message

With this understanding of the audience, segments of these potential audiences are chosen as the targets of the campaign. Having a clear focus aimed at these targeted groups will help develop the campaigns to be specific to the beliefs, attitudes, and behaviors around mental illness stigma held by those segments targeted.

In social marketing, positioning is about creating the most appropriate message for the selected targets. The marketing funnel, a familiar concept to marketers, is

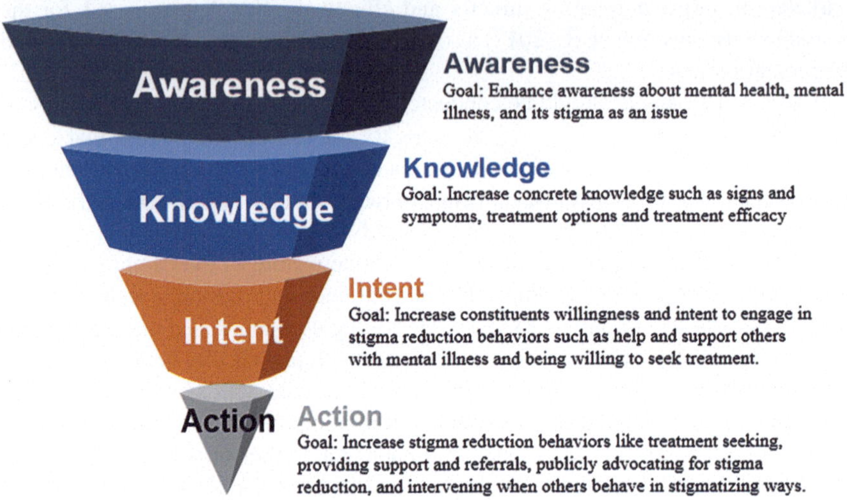

Fig. 9.1 Stigma reduction social marketing funnel

also used in social marketing. Figure 9.1 illustrates the marketing funnel, components, and goals. It is important to consider that where one positions a message depends on the target audience, the behavior change sought, and the depth of the audience's existing knowledge, behavior, and attitudes. The following sections discuss specific ways to use these components as part of a social marketing campaign to reduce mental illness stigma.

Step Three: Campaign Message Development

Once one has decided upon the targeted goal in the funnel, campaign message content needs to be developed for the campaign to position the issue in the minds of consumers. If a campus has the resources and expertise, original campaigns can be created. Existing social marketing campaigns, both at the larger population/country level as well as those specific to college campuses, can also be used so one need not start from scratch in creating campaigns. Examples of existing campaign ideas and how they might target different segments and different stages of the funnel follow.

Campaigns to Raise Awareness and Increase Knowledge

Educational messaging can be positioned as a part of campaign strategies. Common messaging can focus on:

- Common signs and symptoms of anxiety, depression, eating disorders, bipolar, schizophrenia, and others.

- Understanding the mental health continuum.
- Understanding the impact of stigma and discrimination.
- How to talk about mental health.
- Skills and suggestions for offering support.
- Self-care.
- Resources and treatment options and efficacy.

While these strategies are ostensibly about creating allies for people with mental illness, these messages and campaigns can also help those with mental illness and those at risk for developing a mental illness. Those struggling with anxiety or depression symptoms may be able to obtain enough support and assistance to prevent progression to diagnosable symptoms. Some may not realize the symptoms they are having are signs of an illness. Others may be aware they have an illness but do not know about treatment options. And all people can benefit from knowing how to talk to others about mental health (whether it affects another's or their own) and how to care for themselves.

Raising awareness and education are also the goals of activities created for mental illness awareness week (first week in October), mental health awareness month (May), suicide prevention week (second week of September), or World Suicide Prevention Day (Sept. 10). Many organizations have toolkits available to implement these awareness activities (see Appendix 9.2). These activities help bring attention to everyone's mental health on campus. Social marketing campaigns tied to these activities can supplement and complement other university methods such as educational programming.

Changing Perceptions of Incompetence

Campaigns can educate around specific beliefs pervasively held about people with mental illness. Two beliefs with significant impact on stigmatized groups are warmth and competence. Derived from Fiske et al.' (2002) stereotype content model, the model proposes stereotypic beliefs serve the functional purposes of identifying (1) the stereotyped group's intent (positive/warm or negative/cold) and (2) the group's capability or competence in meeting its goals. The combination of intent (warmth/coldness) and competence influences discriminatory behavior. Studies show people with mental illness are perceived as both cold and incompetent (Allstadt Torras et al., 2023). To counter these dimensions, a campaign can message around warmth and competence.

Both those with and those without mental illness endorse the belief that people with mental illness have a lack in abilities (Angermeyer & Matschinger, 2003; Evans-Lacko et al., 2013; Kobau et al., 2010; Pescosolido et al., 2013). One strategy the Northern Lakes Community Mental Health Authority (2023) uses to educate about mental illness is to create a poster showcasing the multitude of highly successful and influential individuals throughout history who had mental illness such as Abraham Lincoln and Charles Darwin.

Reducing Othering and Perceptions of Difference

Studies have also examined general tactics used in stigma reduction around mental illness comparing the effect of education versus contact versus protest. Contact strategies facilitate exchanges between people with lived experience discussing their experiences with mental illness and recovery (Corrigan & Fong, 2014; Corrigan & Penn, 1999). Meta-analyses suggest contact strategies are more effective than educational strategies (Corrigan et al., 2012). While these studies looked at more significant programming involving real person contact events, campaign messaging can and has utilized the basic premise of portraying real people living with mental illness in a marketing campaign to reduce othering and perceptions of difference.

For example, Active Minds' (2023) exhibit, Send Silence Packing, showcases the real stories of people living with mental illness. A visual interactive display of backpacks with over 250 personal stories and messages attached helps expose people to the lived experience of mental illness. Public service announcements (PSAs) have also portrayed the ordinary, daily lives of people with mental illness to counter perceptions of them as "other." One of Bring Change 2 Mind's (2013) PSAs, Schizo, starts as if it is a promo for a horror movie and then moves toward a scary door which opens to find someone living with schizophrenia engaging in daily routines with their family. OC87RecoveryDiaries.org (2023) serves as a vehicle for those with mental health concerns telling their stories of recovering from mental illness to empower those with mental illness and to bust stigma.

Contact also underlies why celebrities sharing about having mental illness can be influential in reducing stigma as well. If someone who is highly admired has a mental illness and shares their challenges with it, this directly contests the shame associated with having a mental illness. Ferrari (2021) found using celebrity case materials in the teaching of a psychology class did indeed reduce public stigma and the stigma of help-seeking; these changes persisted over 3 months.

Othering can also be reduced by showcasing how many people have close friends and family members with mental illness even if they themselves do not. Bring Change 2 Mind's (2009) first PSA Grand Central Terminal showcased this in a video with people wearing t-shirts with their mental illness on it and their loved one wearing a t-shirt with their relation to the other person on it. The PSA also emphasizes the statistic that one in six people have a mental illness. Simply focusing on a statistic which showcases the frequency of occurrence of mental illness plays a role in normalizing mental illness. Indeed, rates of mental illness have been reportedly at an all-time high with the 2021–2022 Healthy Minds survey indicating 44% of students with symptoms of depression, 37% experiencing anxiety, and 15% having seriously considered suicide (Alonso, 2023). A serious outcome of having a mental illness is feelings of social isolation. Messaging showcasing the prevalence of mental illnesses can help reduce the feeling of isolation and the sense that they are alone.

Research supports these methods, particularly when they are paired with peer education efforts. Ahmad and co-authors (2020) conducted a randomized trial on the effects of an anti-stigma high school club program. The study was based on the Bring Change to Mind campaign's focus on support for contact-based efforts which sought to humanize those with mental illness. While the club's messaging varied from school to school, the focus was on contact, both direct and indirect, through media. They found these activities served to reduce the perception of people as "others" while also increasing knowledge and enhancing attitudes toward people with mental illness. Sontag-Padilla et al. (2018) found similar efficacy at the college level for their Active Minds program, which provides similar activities.

Destigmatizing Treatment and Treatment Efficacy

Focusing on the importance of treatment seeking and treatment effectors as normative is another strategy for social marketing campaigns. Social norms marketing involves using the discrepancy between perceived social norms (attitudes and behaviors perceived to be held or performed by most of their peers within a given context) and actual norms (the attitudes and behaviors people actually hold and enact) to influence those attitudes or behavior (Perkins & Berkowitz, 1986). Downs and Eisenberg (2012) found study participants tended to overestimate how negatively others viewed mental health seeking, demonstrating a discrepancy between perceived and actual norms. Acting on this discrepancy, Silk et al. (2017) created a social norms campaign around help-seeking for university counseling center services. Example messages included "72% of students would seek help if they felt overwhelmed by stress or depression" and "2/3's of students would tell a friend to go the university counseling center if they thought their friend needed help." Those who were in the intervention condition were more likely to seek help, more likely to recommend seeking help to others, and more likely to have more accurate perceptions of whether other students would do the same.

Campaigns to Increase Intent and Engender Action

Using the above-noted tactics will hopefully not only raise awareness and increase knowledge about treatment but also engender action. Desired actions can target multiple groups. Those with mental illness may feel more hopeful about their prognosis as well as less "stigmatized" because they realize they are not alone; this may lead to higher treatment adherence. Those who may be experiencing symptoms for the first time will be more likely to seek treatment. Friends of those who are experiencing symptoms may also be more likely to encourage their friends to seek treatment and be supportive of them in general.

Indeed, a major component of many social marketing campaigns around mental illness center around being supportive of those with a mental illness to reduce social distancing and enhance skills around providing support. Using support as a major campaign message can also target the shame associated with stigma; this messaging can also help connect those with mental illness to support. By fostering people's willingness to help those with mental illness, the campaign fosters connections and relationships. The ultimate goal is to enlist more allies for those with mental illness.

For example, Seize the Awkward, created by the Ad Council, the JED Foundation, and the American Foundation for Suicide Prevention, encourages friends to check in on their friends (seizetheawkward.org, 2020). The goal is to give people the resources they need to learn how to support a friend. The focal message: start a conversation about mental health with your friends as a first step on a journey to support each other. This campaign directly targets the stigma dimension of "othering." By encouraging people to continue to invite their friends to social gatherings as well as actively reaching out to their friends, they maintain that their friend is still just that: their friend. It also directly seeks to address the outcome of stigmatization: social isolation. The campaign also emphasized the development of skills with concrete suggestions for what to do to help a friend. While not developed specifically for use on college campuses as the campaign is national in focus, its messaging targets the college demographic, making it an appropriate one to use on campus. Another example of this type of campaign is #DoYourShare, sponsored by the Pan American Health Organization (n.d.) which emphasizes the importance of doing your part by talking about the stigma of mental illness.

Support as a campaign message can and should also increase the audiences' knowledge about mental health resources on campus as well as those available nationally such as 988, the US Suicide and Crisis Lifeline. Similar international numbers can be found at www.iasp.info.

Incorporating such knowledge of on-campus and other resources can also tackle the stigma dimension of treatment effectiveness. Treatment efficacy as a messaging tactic should target all constituents on campus, encouraging those with mental illness to seek treatment and/or stay the course of treatment and those without mental illness to recommend resources and treatment options in support of those living with mental illness.

Campaigns can also target the entire social marketing funnel. For example, the National Alliance on Mental Illness's (2023) campaign, StigmaFree, raises awareness about mental illness. This program encourages people to take the StigmaFree pledge, committing to: (1) be educated on mental illness, (2) see the person, not the illness, and (3) act against stigma. Interestingly, this campaign seeks to obtain people's commitment mimicking the way one would wish to move people through the social marketing funnel (see Fig. 9.1). Active Minds has a similar program, Spirit Week (held in October annually), which uses a model of five pillars of change: awareness, education, advocacy, connection, and community. These pillars follow the tenants of the marketing funnel (Active Minds, 2024).

Points of Caution for Social Marketing Campaigns

Targeting all stigma dimensions is not recommended. Blame is perhaps one of the most well-studied stigma beliefs. Thus, it seems to make sense to create messaging to reduce the blame people place on people with mental illness for their illness. Since blame is related to cause and controllability, the most common messaging used to tackle the issue of blame has been biogenetics as the cause. That is, by educating the public about mental illness being biologically and genetically determined, one can reduce the blame incurred by those with mental illness. Messaging to this effect has indeed reduced the blame placed upon those with mental illness; however, studies have shown this messaging exacerbates other aspects of stigma, in particular social distancing and perceptions of dangerousness (Angermeyer et al., 2011; Kvaale et al., 2013).

In addition, not all message formats for social marketing campaigns are effective. A common message format used to combat mental illness stigma is the myth/fact message format. In this message format, myths about an issue—common misconceptions about a topic—are followed by correct information. While the myth/fact message format did change attitudes toward people with mental illness, it did so through the peripheral route using the message format as a cue for the change in attitude instead of actually cognitively processing the message (Yeh & Jewell, 2015). That is, individuals are not actually processing the message itself and therefore have not had the myth corrected. Presenting the myth may also reinforce the myth rather than refute it and therefore should not be included in campaign messaging. Instead, when correcting for a myth, the myth should not be mentioned and instead the correct information should be presented alone. For example, Bring Change 2 Mind's (2013) PSA, Schizo, is designed to refute the myth that people with mental illnesses are dangerous; however, their use of horror movie music and motifs at the beginning of the PSA may reinforce the association of dangerousness with people with mental illness.

Step Four: Distribute a Campus Campaign Through Multiple Channels

Common marketing lore suggests one use the rule of seven which states a prospect needs to hear an advertiser's message at least seven times before they will take action to buy that product or service. A campaign needs to use multiple channels to "spread the word." A variety of channels can and should be used to distribute a campaign to the audience. Often used strategies, including posters, fliers, signage, and table tenting, are older but effective ways to disseminate messages by posting them in areas and routes frequented by students. Posters displayed outside of different large lecture halls across campus can expose hundreds of students who have classes in those rooms every day. If allowed on campus, chalked messages on sidewalks on frequent routes can also be an effective strategy. Digital signage and electronic message boards are also potential channels.

With its ubiquitous use among college students, many believe social media to be a primary way to reach audiences. Certainly, university health and counseling centers may have social media channels which could be used to circulate messages. However, social media often requires students to follow those department's social media channels, something students may be unlikely to do given the stigmatization that doing so may engender. University administrators may also be reluctant to use main university channels to deliver campaign messages for fear of how such messaging on mental health and mental illness might appear to prospective students and their families. This reluctance is an example of the perpetuation of stigma by administrators who can and should also be targeted.

A better (and free) potential channel strategy for using social media is to recruit students to serve as brand ambassadors. Companies have utilized students as brand ambassadors for years. For example, Red Bull regularly recruits college students as brand ambassadors whose job is to praise, publicize, and push their products. They do so by giving away products for free at campus events as well as regularly creating content incorporating their brand and products on their own social media. A similar program could be created where students are recruited and trained to publicize and push messages about mental illness stigma out to their social networks. The Seize the Awkward campaign has downloadable resources for ready-made GIFS, Instagram posts, and videos that can be used as a part of distributing a message over social media as well as more traditional channels like posters. In addition, if a campus has an Active Minds chapter or similar student organization, that group could run campaigns on their social channels. They can also have their members recruit partnerships with other student organizations to amplify the message. This can occur by having the organizations use the campaign's hashtag and to like, comment on, and share the campaign's social media content via their own personal social media platforms. By actively sharing a campaign on social media, students are not just passively receiving the campaign but also actively pushing the campaign's messages to their peers who then, in turn, can push the message to their peers. Other steps to spread the message include running a social media contest encouraging organization members to share and repost campaign content on their own social media platforms, spreading the message even farther.

Should funding exist, messaging could also be pushed over social media using a paid advertising strategy. Instagram, for example, allows for any post to be turned into a pushed advertisement. These posts can be very specifically targeted to a relevant audience. That is, when targeting students on a specific campus, a campaign on Instagram may be able to tell who specifically has ties to that university.

Campaigns should use a multi-channel approach so that the campaign's message is viewed with a website presence, a social media presence, and with offline traditional methods like posters and fliers. This multi-channel approach might include the use of social media, the distribution of posters/flyers/swag in welcome packets, residential hall floor meetings, dining establishments, sporting events, classrooms, pop-up galleries, art displays, live streaming, PSA screenings, and during mental health discussions/programming.

Step Five: Test the Campaign

Before running the campaign, it is important to conduct audience testing, even if the messaging has been used successfully on other campuses. Social marketing campaign effectiveness can differ based on the context within which it is run. Universities can differ drastically regarding their culture, demographic makeup, and political atmosphere generally which influences the culture on campus related to mental health concerns. People responding positively on one campus may not respond positively on another. Testing each campaign before it is issued is a critically important step.

To test a campaign, the first step is to convene several focus groups of the targeted audience. In the focus groups, all aspects of the campaign are presented. This is followed by asking about their insights and reactions. If the campaign targets students, testing could occur in a class such as a psychology or marketing class where it could also be tied to a discussion relevant to the class content. More formal testing could be done by sending out a survey to a sample of the targeted audience and asking for their feedback in survey questions. Other stakeholder feedback should also be solicited such as subject matter experts (e.g., counseling center staff) and administrators.

Step Six: Evaluate and Adjust the Campaign with a Long-Term View

Effective marketers evaluate and measure the impact their campaigns have on desired outcomes. Those results will allow for changes and/or revisions to be made. It is important to continue to solicit feedback utilizing the community participatory approach to supplement and revise the campaigns. If research had been conducted on the target audience as discussed in the first step above, a post-campaign measure/survey can be conducted to determine the campaign's impact. A word of caution though. Do not expect quick results. The stigma of mental illness is pervasive and entrenched. One social media marketing campaign will likely not have a strong impact against such well-established attitudes. In addition, one should not rely solely on outcome measures like attitudes toward people with mental illness as an indication of success. Other options to determine campaign effectiveness include questions focused on the awareness of the campaign and the messages utilized in the campaign. The next step is to analyze how this awareness may impact stigma outcomes on campus. Successful media campaigns are sustained and repeated. One example of this approach is England's "A Time to Change" anti-stigma campaign which took place over a five-year period (Sampogna et al., 2017).

Step Seven: Take a Portfolio Approach

A single campaign will likely not be effective long-term even if short-term outcomes are effective (i.e., attitudes toward people with mental illness improve) (Gronholm et al., 2017; Walsh & Foster, 2021). A campus' culture is created by the students, staff, faculty, and administrators who work at the university. While students are often the focus of mental health stigma efforts on a college campus, stigma in the workplace is also a serious problem (Jones, 2011). While most of the tactics discussed above were positioned to target students, social marketing campaigns should also be created to target faculty, staff, and the campus administration.

Social marketing campaigns should also be implemented in conjunction with other strategies on campus. Campaign effectiveness can be amplified by other programmatic efforts to change culture. Some strategies can even strengthen the campaign. For example, peer health educators can act as brand ambassadors serving as a channel for campaign messaging in addition to their traditional educational role. Students, faculty, and staff can also be recruited as mental health first aid responders where they receive training to provide support to students in crisis. These participants can be recruited to be channels serving as messengers for social marketing campaigns. They can also be formally recruited as allies having either signage or other methods (e.g., wearing a green bandana) that conveys their status as ally to others.

A comprehensive assessment and implementation of services for those with mental health concerns should also be conducted. This means it is important to conduct an evaluation of the process through which a campus makes help available to students. Are counseling center services hidden in the basement of a very old building? Is it difficult for a person in crisis to obtain immediate help? Are the public safety/campus police adequately trained to deal with a student in crisis? A social marketing campaign to reduce stigma and enhance help-seeking will not change the campus culture around stigma if the process a student goes through to seek help has barriers and/or is a stigmatizing experience.

Case Example

The following case study shows how the steps mentioned above can be used to assess, target, and implement a comprehensive social marketing campaign to reduce stigma.

Dr. Rachel Harvey, Director of the Counseling Center, has been tasked to do something about the reports from faculty and staff regarding the growing number of students who have reported mental health problems. In fact, she has just written a report about the data found from a student survey implemented on campus that measured mental health and wellness. She thought far enough ahead to include measures of stigma and is pleased with the level of support and acceptance many students exhibit toward people with a mental illness. More problematic is that many do not know what to do when a friend or acquaintance is having difficulty. Additionally, the study indicates that a group of students do not appear to be as supportive toward those with mental illness. These students appear to be more involved in Greek life on campus.

Before making any decisions, Dr. Harvey pulls together a small committee of individuals to help her. The committee comprises staff who work in her office, staff that work in student life, and students who volunteer as peer health educators who are trained to do programming on a variety of issues, including mental health. She also involves a student who sits on the advisory board of Counseling Services who self-identified that she has received services for her depression and anxiety. After meeting to go over the mission and soliciting input, it is decided that a campaign targeting fraternity and sorority

(continued)

members will be conducted alongside a campaign to improve general messaging around campus.

Given Dr. Harvey believes programming should target those involved in Greek life, she adds members of the Panhellenic and Interfraternity Councils in vetting the campaign and involves them in the decision-making process.

Messaging will target increasing awareness and knowledge of mental illness and treatment services. There is also a need to increase supportive attitudes toward people with mental illness. The committee examines existing campaigns and decides on a number of different messaging to include, primarily using NAMI's StigmaFree (2023). They ask Greek leaders to implement activities that solicit stigma-free pledges on campus. They utilize materials to educate on topics like ten common warning signs for mental illness. They also use StigmaFree materials that encourage people to support their friends by showing interest and consideration for their friends and asking them specifically to "see the person, not the illness." The campaign also asks people as a part of the pledge to take action both encouraging them to use stigma-free language themselves and intervening when they see others making hurtful comments to those with mental illnesses. StigmaFree also explicitly asks people to commit to learning about mental illness. As a part of their annual report to the governing councils, the fraternities and sororities will report on the number of their members who take the pledge.

Conversations with Greek leaders reveal that posters in Greek housing would be effective in raising awareness. Sorority and fraternity leaders also agree to use their social media channels to push out messaging on a regular schedule. The Interfraternity and Panhellenic councils also hold a social media competition to encourage members to push out messaging on their own personal social media platforms. The organizations with the most shares and reposts using the campaign's hashtags will win prizes.

Peer health educators will also table during rush and at other major Greek life events like their annual "Olympics" where they compete in different contests against each other. They provide information about mental health resources to all members and all students who are rushing.

In addition, to the social marketing efforts, Greek leaders agree to have all officers and staff participate in Mental Health First Aid training. Some also engage peer health educators to have more extensive educational programming be conducted at their monthly member meetings.

After a year of implementation, Dr. Harvey conducts a follow-up survey among Greek life members to assess impact on attitudes about mental health and support. While she finds positive movement, more needs to be done. In open-ended questions, members report the stressful environment that can be created due to some fraternities and sororities' hierarchical structures and hazing-like activities for new members. She discusses this with the committee to help create programming for another more specific campaign. She also works with leaders to combat hazing activity that violates campus policies.

Conclusion

Social marketing is simply one tool that can be used on campus to dismantle the stigma that mental illness stigma. When done incorrectly, social marketing can further exacerbate stigma. To be effective, social marketing must be conducted in a thorough and purposeful way in conjunction with other strategies. When done correctly, social marketing campaigns can contribute to creating a culture of acceptance on campus for those with mental illness, foster helpfulness and help-seeking, and educate campus constituencies about mental illness and its treatment.

Appendices

Appendix 9.1 Example Stigma Assessment/Evaluation Tool (Yeh et al., 2017)

Beliefs	
Dangerousness	• …how dangerous do you think they are likely to be? • …how violent do you think they are likely to be?
Unpredictability	• …to what extent do you think that they are difficult to deal with? • …to what extent do you think that they are unpredictable.
Incompetent	• …how intelligent do you think that they are likely to be? • …to what extent do you think that they are creative? • …how successful do you believe they can be at work compared to others?
To blame	• How responsible do you think a person is for causing their own mental illness? • …to what extent do you think they are able to pull themselves together without treatment? • How much control do you think a person has over the cause of his or her own mental illness?
Shame	• How much do you believe that once you have been treated for mental illness, the best thing to do is keep it a secret? • How likely would you be to advise a close friend or relative with a mental illness that he or she should not tell anyone about his or her mental illness?
Treatment ineffectiveness	• …to what extent do you believe that they would improve if given treatment and support? • …to what extent do you believe they can eventually recover?
Affective reactions	
Pity	• …to what extent do you feel pity for them?
Fear	• …to what extent do you feel frightened by them? • …to what extent do you feel threatened by them?
Anger	• …to what extent do feel anger toward them? • …to what extent do you feel irritation toward them?

Behaviors and behavioral endorsements	
Othering	• To what extent do you perceive yourself and people with mental illness to be a part of the same group? • …to what extent do you believe that they feel differently from a person without mental illness? • How similar do you think people with mental illness generally are to you? • …to what extent do you believe they feel the same way we all do at times?
Willingness to coerce	• How much do you believe that people with mental illness should be hospitalized because they pose a risk to the general public? • How much do you believe that hospitalizing people with mental illness would reduce crime?
Willingness to help	• …how much concern do you feel toward them? • …to what extent do you feel the desire to help them?

Measured using a 7-point semantic differential scale anchored at strongly disagree (1) and strongly agree (7).
Items prefaced with ellipses (…) begin with "When you think of people with mental illness generally…".

Appendix 9.2 Campaign Resource Websites

Organization	Website
The Ad Council Mental Health Toolkit	https://www.adcouncil.org/our-impact/mental-health-initiative/mental-health-toolkit
Ad Council, American Foundation for Suicide Prevention & The Jed Foundation—Seize the Awkward	https://seizetheawkward.org/
The Jed Foundation	https://jedfoundation.org/our-work/higher-ed/
National Alliance on Mental Illness (2023)	https://www.nami.org/Get-Involved/Awareness-Events/
NAMI On Campus (2023)	https://www.nami.org/NAMI/media/Extranet-Education/NoC-Advocacy-Guide.pdf
Mental Health America (2023)	https://www.mhanational.org/mental-health-month
US Substance Abuse and Mental Health Services Administration (2023)	https://www.samhsa.gov/mental-health-awareness-month/toolkit https://www.samhsa.gov/newsroom/suicide-prevention-month
The US National Institute of Mental Health (2023)	https://www.nimh.nih.gov/get-involved/digital-toolkit-for-suicide-prevention-month
The US Centers for Disease Control (2023)	https://www.cdc.gov/suicide/resources/partner-toolkit.html
Minnesota's Department of Health (2023)	https://www.health.state.mn.us/communities/suicide/documents/suicideprevam23.pdf
Pan American Health Organization	https://www.paho.org/en/campaigns/do-your-share#:~:text=On%20social%20media%2C%20the%20%23DoYourShare,PAHO's%20Regional%20Mental%20Health%20Advisor

References

Active Minds. (2023). *Send silence packing traveling exhibit.* https://www.activeminds.org/programs/send-silence-packing/

Active Minds. (2024). *Active minds spirit week.* https://support.activeminds.org/campaign/active-minds-spirit-week/c405782

Ahmad, S. I., Leventhal, B. L., Nielsen, B. N., & Hinshaw, S. P. (2020). Reducing mental-illness stigma via high school clubs: A matched-pair, cluster-randomized trial. *Stigma and Health, 5*(2), 230–239. https://doi.org/10.1037/sah0000193

Allstadt Torras, R. C., Scheel, C., & Dorrough, A. R. (2023). The stereotype content model and mental disorders: Distinct perceptions of warmth and competence. *Frontiers in Psychology, 14*, 1069226. https://doi.org/10.3389/fpsyg.2023.1069226

Alonso, J. (2023, March 16). Student mental health worsens, but more are seeking help. *Inside Higher Ed.* https://www.insidehighered.com/quicktakes/2023/03/17/student-mental-health-worsens-more-are-seeking-help

American College Health Association. (2022). *American College Health Association-National College Health Assessment III: Reference Group Executive Summary Fall 2021.* Retrieved from https://www.acha.org/documents/ncha/NCHA-III_FALL_2021_REFERENCE_GROUP_EXECUTIVE_SUMMARY.pdf

Angermeyer, M. C., Holzinger, A., Carta, M. G., & Schomerus, G. (2011). Biogenetic explanations and public acceptance of mental illness: Systematic review of population studies. *British Journal of Psychiatry, 199*(5), 367–372. https://doi.org/10.1192/bjp.bp.110.085563

Angermeyer, M. C., & Matschinger, H. (2003). Public beliefs about schizophrenia and depression: Similarities and differences. *Social Psychiatry and Psychiatric Epidemiology, 38*(9), 526–534. https://doi.org/10.1007/s00127-003-0676-6

Bos, A. E., Pryor, J. B., Reeder, G. D., & Stutterheim, S. E. (2013). Stigma: Advances in theory and research. *Basic and Applied Social Psychology, 35*(1), 1–9. https://doi.org/10.1080/01973533.2012.746147

Bring Change 2 Mind. (2009, October 21). *Grand Central Terminal: 60* [Video]. YouTube. https://www.youtube.com/watch?v=WUaXFlANojQ&t=3s

Bring Change 2 Mind. (2013, May 14). *Schizo: 90 (Bring Change 2 Mind's Second PSA)* [Video]. YouTube. https://www.youtube.com/watch?v=21U4sa187GY

Corrigan, P. W., & Fong, M. W. (2014). Competing perspectives on erasing the stigma of illness: What says the dodo bird? *Social Science & Medicine, 103*, 110–117. https://doi.org/10.1016/j.socscimed.2013.05.027

Corrigan, P., Markowitz, F. E., Watson, A., Rowan, D., & Kubiak, M. A. (2003). An attribution model of public discrimination towards persons with mental illness. *Journal of Health and Social Behavior, 44*, 162–179. https://doi.org/10.2307/1519806

Corrigan, P. W., Morris, S. B., Michaels, P. J., Rafacz, J. D., & Rüsch, N. (2012). Challenging the public stigma of mental illness: a meta-analysis of outcome studies. *Psychiatric Services, 63*, 963–973. https://doi.org/10.1176/appi.ps.201100529

Corrigan, P. W., & Penn, D. L. (1999). Lessons from social psychology on discrediting psychiatric stigma. *American Psychologist, 54*, 765–776. https://doi.org/10.1037/0003-066x.54.9.765

Corrigan, P. W., & Rao, D. (2012). On the self-stigma of mental illness: Stages, disclosure, and strategies for change. *The Canadian Journal of Psychiatry, 57*(8), 464–469. https://doi.org/10.1177/070674371205700804

Downs, M. F., & Eisenberg, D. (2012). Help-seeking and treatment use among suicidal college students. *Journal of American College Health, 60*, 104–114. https://doi.org/10.1080/07448481.2011.619611

Evans-Lacko, S., Henderson, C., & Thornicroft, G. (2013). Public knowledge, attitudes and behaviour regarding people with Mental Illness in England 2009–2012. *The British Journal of Psychiatry. Supplement, 55*(Apr), s51–s57. https://doi.org/10.1192/bjp.bp.112.112979

Ferrari, A. (2021). The persistence of stigma reduction after teaching abnormal psychology using celebrity narratives. *Teaching of Psychology, 48*(3), 191–196. https://doi.org/10.1177/00986283209798

Fiske, S. T., Cuddy, A. J., Glick, P., & Xu, J. (2002). A model of (often mixed) stereotype content: competence and warmth respectively follow from perceived status and competition. *Journal of Personality and Social Psychology, 82*(6), 878. https://doi.org/10.1037/0022-3514.82.6.878

Grier, S., & Bryant, C. A. (2005). Social marketing in public health. *Annual Review of Public Health, 26*, 319–339. https://doi.org/10.1146/annurev.publhealth.26.021304.144610

Gronholm, P. C., Henderson, C., Deb, T., & Thornicroft, G. (2017). Interventions to reduce discrimination and stigma: The state of the art. *Social Psychiatry and Psychiatric Epidemiology, 52*(3), 249–258. https://doi.org/10.1007/s00127-017-1341-9

Israel, B. A., Schulz, A. J., Parker, E. A., & Becker, A. B. (1998). Review of community-based research: Assessing partnership approaches to improve public health. *Annual Review of Public Health, 19*, 173–202. https://doi.org/10.1146/annurev.publhealth.19.1.173

Jones, A. M. (2011). Disclosure of mental illness in the workplace: A literature review. *American Journal of Psychiatric Rehabilitation, 14*(3), 212–229. https://doi.org/10.1080/15487768.2011.598101

Kobau, R., DiIorio, C., Chapman, D., Delvecchio, P., & SAMHSA/CDC Mental Illness Stigma Panel Members. (2010). Attitudes about mental illness and its treatment: Validation of a generic scale for public health surveillance of mental illness associated stigma. *Community Mental Health Journal, 46*, 164–176. https://doi.org/10.1007/s10597-009-9191-x

Kotler, P., & Lee, N. (2008). *Social marketing: Influencing behaviors for good*. Sage.

Kvaale, E. P., Gottdiener, W. H., & Haslam, N. (2013). Biogenetic explanations and stigma: A meta-analytic review of associations among laypeople. *Social Science & Medicine, 95*, 95–103. https://doi.org/10.1016/j.socscimed.2013.07.017

Link, B. G., & Phelan, J. C. (2001). Conceptualizing stigma. *Annual Review of Sociology, 27*, 363–385. https://doi.org/10.1146/annurev.soc.27.1.363

Lipson, S. K., Zhou, S., Abelson, S., Heinze, J., Jirsa, M., Morigney, J., Patterson, A., Singh, M., & Eisenberg, D. (2022). Trends in college student mental health and help-seeking by race/ethnicity: Findings from the national healthy minds study, 2013–2021. *Journal of Affective Disorders, 306*, 138–147. https://doi.org/10.1016/j.jad.2022.03.038

National Academies of Sciences, Engineering and Medicine. (2016). *Ending discrimination against people with mental and substance use disorders: The evidence for stigma change*. The National Academies Press. https://doi.org/10.17226/23442

National Alliance on Mental Illness. (2023). *StigmaFree on campus*. https://www.nami.org/Get-Involved/Pledge-to-Be-StigmaFree/StigmaFree-Community/StigmaFree-on-Campus

Northern Lakes Community Mental Health Authority. (2023). *Famous people who have had a mental illness*. https://www.northernlakescmh.org/learn/general-mental-health-topics/famous-people-who-have-had-a-mental-illness/

OC87recoverydiaries. (2023). *OC87 recovery diaries: Stories of mental health, empowerment, and change*. https://oc87recoverydiaries.org/

Pan American Health Organization. (n.d.). #DoYourShare. *Mental Health Stigma Reduction Campaign*. https://www.paho.org/en/campaigns/do-your-share#:~:text=On%20social%20media%2C%20the%20%23DoYourShare,PAHO's%20Regional%20Mental%20Health%20Advisor

Perkins, H. W., & Berkowitz, A. D. (1986). Perceiving the community norms of alcohol use among students: Some research implications for campus alcohol education programming. *International Journal of Addiction, 21*, 961–976. https://doi.org/10.3109/10826088609077249

Pescosolido, B. A., Medina, T. R., Martin, J. K., & Long, J. S. (2013). The "backbone" of stigma: Identifying the global core of public prejudice associated with mental illness. *American Journal of Public Health, 103*(5), 853–860. https://doi.org/10.2105/AJPH.2012.301147

Sampogna, G., Bakolis, I., Evans-Lacko, S., Robinson, E., Thornicroft, G., & Henderson, C. (2017). The impact of social marketing campaigns on reducing mental health stigma: Results from the 2009–2014 time to change programme. *European Psychiatry, 40*, 116–122. https://doi.org/10.1016/j.eurpsy.2016.08.008

Schulz, A. J., Krieger, J., & Galea, S. (2002). Addressing social determinants of health: Community-based participatory approaches to research and practice. *Health Education & Behavior, 29*(3), 287–295. https://doi.org/10.1177/109019810202900302

Silk, K. J., Perrault, E. K., Nazione, S. A., Pace, K., & Collins-Eaglin, J. (2017). Evaluation of a social norms approach to a suicide prevention campaign. *Journal of Health Communication, 22*(2), 135–142. https://doi.org/10.1080/10810730.2016.1258742

Sontag-Padilla, L., Dunbar, M. S., Ye, F., Kase, C., Fein, R., Abelson, S., Seelam, R., & Stein, B. D. (2018). Strengthening college students' mental health knowledge, awareness, and helping behaviors: The impact of active minds, a peer mental health organization. *Journal of the American Academy of Child & Adolescent Psychiatry, 57*(7), 500–507. https://doi.org/10.1016/j.jaac.2018.03.019

Suarez-Balcazar, Y., Francisco, V. T., & Rubén Chávez, N. (2020). Applying community-based participatory approaches to addressing health disparities and promoting health equity. *American Journal of Community Psychology, 66*(3–4), 217–221. https://doi.org/10.1002/ajcp.12487

Walsh, D. A. B., & Foster, J. L. H. (2021). A call to action: A critical review of mental health related anti-stigma campaigns. *Frontiers in Public Health, 8*, 1–15. https://doi.org/10.3389/fpubh.2020.569539

Yeh, M. A., & Jewell, R. D. (2015). The myth/fact message frame and persuasion in advertising: Enhancing attitudes toward the mentally ill. *Journal of Advertising, 44*(2), 161–172. http://www.jstor.org/stable/24749798

Yeh, M. A., Jewell, R. D., & Hu, M. Y. (2013). Stereotype processing's effect on the impact of the myth/fact message format and the role of personal relevance. *Psychology & Marketing, 30*, 36–45. https://doi.org/10.1002/mar.20587

Yeh, M. A., Jewell, R. D., & Thomas, V. L. (2017). The stigma of mental illness: Using segmentation for social change. *Journal of Public Policy and Marketing, 36*(1), 97–116. https://doi.org/10.1509/jppm.13.125

Marie A. Yeh, Ph.D., is an associate professor of marketing at Loyola University Maryland. Her scholarship tackles deeply entrenched societal issues such as mental illness, stigma, and sexual violence. Her translational work sits at the intersection of theory, policy, and marketing to find solutions that can be applied in the real world. Her work has been published in the *Journal of Public Policy and Marketing (JPPM), Journal of Consumer Affairs (JOCA), Journal of Marketing Management,* and the *Journal of Advertising*. She serves on the ERB of JPPM and JOCA.

Chapter 10
Solidarity, Substance Use, and Stigma

Dylan Dunn, Kimberly Boulden, and Sydney Cheifetz

Abstract On college campuses, a noteworthy shift is underway: alcohol consumption among students seems to be on the decline, marking a positive turn spurred by years of candid conversations, data-driven harm reduction initiatives, and targeted awareness efforts. Yet, amidst this progress, another trend persists—a rise in the self-reported use of other drugs among students. This increase takes on added gravity against the backdrop of the United States' escalating overdose crisis, which has claimed more than a million lives since 2008. Despite the clear efficacy of harm reduction strategies in mitigating alcohol-related harm, institutions of higher education have been slow to adopt similar approaches for broader substance use issues on campus. This chapter delves into the pervasive influence of stigma on campus policies and cultures surrounding substance use. It underscores the need for a paradigm shift, advocating for a move away from moralistic judgments toward a compassionate, strengths-based approach centered on safety and recovery. By dismantling stigma and fostering empathy, campus stakeholders can promote lasting change. As campus professionals strive to improve the well-being of their communities, embracing a culture of empowerment emerges as a vital imperative in confronting the challenges of campus substance use.

Keywords Substance use · College students · Mental illness · Stigma · Campus policies

---

The authors have no conflicts of interest to declare that are relevant to the content of this chapter.

D. Dunn (✉) · S. Cheifetz
SAFE Campuses, SAFE Project, Arlington, VA, USA
e-mail: dylan.dunn@safeproject.us

K. Boulden
SAFE Campuses, SAFE Project, Arlington, VA, USA

MATTERS Network, Buffalo, NY, USA

© The Author(s), under exclusive license to Springer Nature Switzerland AG 2025
K. M. Brennan, K. S. Gorman (eds.), *A University-Wide Approach to Changing Campus Cultures of Mental Illness Stigma*, Knowledge Studies in Higher Education 18, https://doi.org/10.1007/978-3-031-86496-4_10

Jamie[1] came through the front door of the Collegiate Recovery Community—a support space for students with a relationship to addiction and recovery. The office had been established that year after another student died of a fentanyl-laced heroin overdose. He stated simply, "I need help and I need to call my mom." The staff meeting at the dining room table quickly shifted gears. One staff member sat with the student, welcomed him with coffee, and kept him talking; the other staff member began contacting treatment options.

Jamie shared that he had bounced between recovery and active addiction during his 2 years on campus. He introduced himself by explaining that for months, he had watched the new recovery support program being built right outside of his window. He recalled moments when, while using drugs in his room, he would watch the office as it transitioned from a construction site to a place of recovery and healing. Jamie said he cried when he read the building's nameplate, finding hope that the campus cared about, or even acknowledged, students like him and offered a space for him to seek positive change.

Jamie survived an overdose the night before and was certain he would not survive another. While he had not been ready to connect with the space before, he knew there was support available when the time came. With the help of university staff, Jamie was able to successfully enter treatment and found sustainable recovery.

On the same campus where stigma and lack of understanding preceded one student loss via overdose, meaningful steps forward directly created an opportunity to save another. Stories like Jamie's continue to unfold at universities across the country yet not all of them have such happy endings. It is our responsibility to ensure students know they belong and they matter. In this chapter, we will outline the contours of substance use culture and stigma in college; provide examples of where stigma impacts campuses and students; and discuss lessons learned from implementing harm reduction and recovery-support initiatives at institutions around the United States. Finally, we will reflect on the cultural implications for student affairs professionals and the field of higher education overall.

Substance Use Culture in Higher Education

The college student experience in the United States has had a tight-knit relationship with drinking alcohol and partying dating back to the early years of the nation's history. For example, Harvard originally built and operated its own brewery to satisfy early students' expectations for beer (Barber, 2011). The brewery at Harvard could not keep up with student demand, and ongoing student complaints eventually led to the firing of Harvard's President in 1639 (Munk, 2014). This deeply rooted culture of college drinking continues today and is reflected in the popularity of rankings and

[1] Pseudonym used for anonymity.

Internet searches for party schools. About half of all traditionally aged college students reported drinking alcohol in the past month, with about half of those students self-reporting that they engaged in binge drinking (Substance Abuse and Mental Health Services Administration [SAMHSA], 2022). Additionally, nearly 1 in 13 college students aged 18–24 reported binge drinking five or more days last month (SAMHSA, 2022). While collegiate drinking culture does not exist in a vacuum and is reflective of the place of alcohol in the broader beliefs and norms of the United States, substance use in the lives of college students takes a unique shape.

Within what is commonly referred to as a "work hard, play hard" culture where high-achieving young adults under great academic pressure seek equally intense methods of unwinding with peers, student affairs professionals are well aware of the negative impacts of drinking on student success. 696,000 students each year are physically assaulted by another student who has consumed alcohol (Hingson et al., 2005). It is estimated that a majority of sexual assaults in college involve substance use (Carey et al., 2015; Lawyer et al., 2010). Approximately one-quarter of all students report academic consequences from drinking. Finally, about 13% of college students meet the criteria for alcohol use disorder (Blanco et al., 2008). The criteria for alcohol use disorder can be summarized through four themes: consuming increasing amounts of alcohol to achieve the intended level of intoxication, experiencing physical or psychological problems when stopping or slowing use, clear consequences stemming from use, and struggling to stop or slow drinking behaviors despite a desire to do so (American Psychiatric Association [APA], 2022). Research shows that binge drinking rates among college students have decreased over time, but rates still remain generally high with college students reporting more binge drinking and more alcohol-related problems than their non-college-going peers (Krieger et al., 2018). While alcohol use disorder is a diagnosable condition that benefits from research-informed intervention and treatment, it is regularly normalized and accepted as a part of collegiate culture, with a small number of staff present on most campuses dedicated to managing student drinking.

Substance Use and Campus Safety

When it comes to drinking, student affairs professionals approach students with compassion and care whenever possible. College administrators largely understand that if punitive measures are the primary response to alcohol issues on campus, these behaviors will be pushed further into the private domain and away from the educators in a position to help (Barber, 2011). As a response, many, if not most, campuses have incorporated educational components in their campus response to underage drinking, including safer consumption strategies; how to count drinks; how to intervene in concerning situations; and how to ask for help if someone is struggling or actively in danger. Today, alcohol education is often a required annual component of programming as students begin or re-enter their relationship with a campus, especially if they are underage. Instead of punitive action, campuses create a 4-to-6-year experience where students feel empowered, and even expected, to experiment safely with substances. Ideally, students develop a healthy and personalized relationship with alcohol (and increasingly cannabis) products as they near the age of legal consumption. As a society, however, this more lenient approach is typically reserved for emerging adults who can gain access to, and are thus protected by, a college campus. Research indicates that this privilege is not experienced equitably within the college-aged population (Marconi et al., 2022). For example, students of color who experiment with alcohol and cannabis will experience greater harm and are more likely to face punitive action than their white peers at the same institution (Drug Enforcement Agency, 2020).

Since 1989, institutions of higher education in the United States have been required to comply with the Drug-Free Schools and Communities Act (DFSCA). This piece of legislation plays a simple role: to ensure college campuses have policies addressing the unlawful possession, use, and distribution of alcohol and other drugs (Drug Free Schools and Communities Act of 1989, 1989). Failure to comply with this regulation could have implications for federal funding of programs such as financial aid. While the original legislation indeed intended to encourage punitive enforcement of drug laws, the Department of Education has since begun promoting DFSCA compliance as an opportunity to invest in substance use prevention and recovery programming. While core components of compliance have remained unchanged, the legislation has been updated to allow for a more wellness-focused interpretation rather than an anti-crime one. Updates to the legislation in 2006 noted that failure to comply deprived both students and the institution of necessary information. Students need the relevant information to make knowledgeable decisions about their substance use based on law, policy, and research. Similarly, institutions need data to understand the efficacy of their own wellness programming (Custer & Kent, 2018).

In all, campuses have largely embraced a drinking culture that prioritizes student safety first, while also maintaining campus policy aligning closely with federal, state, and local laws. The underlying message is not hard to recognize: if you use the substances we talk about, please use responsibly and stay out of trouble. For the students who may struggle or face consequences stemming from drinking, parents and peers may wonder if that student simply may not "be able to handle college." Students, and even staff, who do not participate in campus drinking rituals or traditions are questioned, assumed to have had a problem, and required to navigate social situations as an outsider.

More than Alcohol

But it is important to ask, what about other drugs? If it is within our scope as educators to share safer alcohol consumption strategies with underage students who are consuming despite their behaviors being in violation of the law, why does it typically seem so far-fetched for a campus to offer tips, for example, for safer psychedelic consumption or properly testing a pill or powder for fentanyl? It is fair to assume the reason for this inequity is that a greater percentage of students use alcohol and more than half of students can consume alcohol legally. Still, it is worth considering how much of an impact drug use needs to have on a campus before staff, faculty, and administrators arrive at a duty to properly educate and prevent harm.

The challenge of the moment is campuses are experiencing an impact of drug use that cannot be ignored: fatal overdose. Opioid overdose has emerged as a leading cause of death among our nation's youth (National Safety Council, n.d.; Friedman et al., 2022); over one million people in the United States have died of overdose since 1999, and more and more students are arriving on campus with an understanding that drugs can be deadly. Yet, when most students search their institution for resources to prevent or address overdose, they are left wanting.[2] The silence is a signal and a symptom of the culture.

College often symbolizes a period of experimentation and learning about things such as one's own relationship with substance use. Unfortunately, fentanyl's unpredictable presence throughout the illicit drug supply has seemingly destroyed the gentle "on-ramp" where substance use-naive young adults can try a variety of substances without much risk of fatal consequences. In response, a minority of campuses have chosen to mitigate these increased risk factors by educating students and equipping them with naloxone and fentanyl testing strips, some even finding that they are unable to keep up with student demand (Ketterer, 2022; Knox, 2022).[3] While we often see students experience unintended consequences of risky behaviors due to feeling near invincible, the emerging fentanyl crisis found institutions reflecting the same attitude—sure, overdoses happen, but they would never happen to "us." Institutions have long arrived at a point where we need to take responsibility for what we can do, but it can be helpful to first come to terms with why most campuses have waited so long.

---

[2] In 2024, NASPA, HECAOD, and SAFE Project released a checklist to assist campuses in guiding their opioid overdose prevention and response efforts. This guide can be accessed at: https://naspa.org/blog/opioid-overdose-on-campus-key-steps-to-expand-harm-reduction-efforts.

[3] As an increasing number of campuses begin to implement naloxone education and distribution programs in response to tragedies and changes to state and local law, the diversity of ways to implement these programs also grows. Strong examples include West Virginia Collegiate Recovery Network's "Be The One" campaign, the Ohio Department of Health's Project DAWN, and the Coalition of Colorado Campus Alcohol & Drug Educator's partnership with SAFE Project to implement naloxone programs on campuses across the state of Colorado.

The Heart of the Matter: Stigma

While serving as Surgeon General, Jerome Adams remarked, "I'm often asked what I think the biggest killer is out there, whether it is cigarettes, or obesity, or fentanyl." Instead, he stated, "I feel the biggest killer out there is actually stigma" (US Department of Health and Human Services [USDHHS], n.d.). Such a statement, coming from a leader in the highest ranks of the US government, reflected the relationship Adams had with substance use in his own family. During his tenure, Adams was open about the fact that his brother was incarcerated for crimes related to his substance use. Step by step throughout his brother's life there had been opportunities for connection and intervention, but these opportunities were superseded by a progression deeper into his substance use disorder. This continued descent led to increasing ostracism and social exclusion, including 10 years of incarceration (USDHHS, n.d.). Stigma manifests by positioning particular traits or experiences as existing outside of the realm of acceptable, normal, or allowable behaviors (Goffman, 1963). At the root of stigma is an "us versus them" dichotomy, defined by social normalcy and deviance. For substance use, normalized behaviors associated with belonging often include drinking alcohol at sporting event tailgates, utilizing prescription stimulants as study aids, and happy hours after a challenging day. Deviant behaviors, according to what is stigmatized, often include partaking in substances at a rate far higher or far lower than your peers in social events, seeking support or making changes around previous habits of use, or simply using in a way that is outside of the traditions and norms of your environment. These norms can be confusing, unclear, and even sometimes contradictory. Despite this ambiguity, campus cultures often establish a range of acceptable substance use, where deviating from the perceived norm, whether by using more or less, can result in social consequences ranging from exclusion to criminalization.

Sources and Outcomes of Stigma

Stigma does not materialize on its own. There are complex social systems that author, maintain, and enforce stigma. Stereotypes (the things we believe), prejudices (the judgments we make), and discrimination (the actions we take), all inform larger societal stigma surrounding drugs and the people who use them (Corrigan et al., 2014). Our collective understanding of substance use is riddled with misinformation, mythology, and perspectives that most of us understand are outdated or problematic. The challenge is that stigma survives through inaction and lack of consideration. For example, one could poll individuals at a bar about their support for safe-consumption sites, places where individuals can go to receive access to regulated and safer substances in a controlled and supportive environment. Would the respondents scoff and rail against the idea of these resources, while consuming a regulated substance (alcohol) in a controlled environment (a bar), surrounded by the support of coworkers during an after-work happy hour? Bars are normalized and socially sanctioned, but this was not always the case: the United States has a long history of morally and legally rebuking alcohol. Prohibition was lifted partly due to changes in public opinion, but also due to the increasing harm of unregulated products in the illegal market (such as "bathtub gin" or bootlegged liquor). This reversal in public opinion shows that, with concerted and directed effort, societal stigma can be mitigated.

Campus practitioners contend with the impacts of societal stigma (in that students may feel shame around seeking help) as well as internalized stigma (in that students may not feel worthy of help to begin with). Like many mental health conditions and modes of oppression, an internalization of the negative beliefs of the greater culture can form within individuals. This internalized stigma and shame can be incredibly challenging to overcome and unravel and they have dire consequences. First, stigma leads individuals to not seek care, even after identifying their own need for help. Approximately 10% of adults in 2021 who self-identified as needing substance use support did not pursue treatment for fear of attracting judgment (SAMHSA, 2022). In a college context, these decreased rates of support-seeking behaviors may be even more dire, as college students are less likely to identify their own substance use as cause for concern. One study found that while nearly 47% of 3rd-year students on a campus met the criteria for a substance use disorder at some point in college, less than 4% ever felt a need for support despite 16% being recommended to seek resources for change. Interestingly, despite the general distancing of themselves from the need for support, 90% of students in the aforementioned study did seek help once they believed they had a problem (Caldeira et al., 2009).

Another impact of stigma comes through individuals concealing their substance use. If stigma is perpetuated by labeling certain behaviors or traits as socially unacceptable, revealing substance use while seeking help may feel like a considerable risk for emerging adults as they strive to establish themselves within their peer community. College students' understanding of their peers' substance use varies significantly from the data that students report about their own use, with the average student greatly overestimating use among their peers (Cox et al., 2019). Emerging research suggests student perceptions of community substance use are greatly influenced by, and more reflective of, the habits of their closest peers (Russell et al., 2021). One could assume that greater openness to discussing substance use, rather than limiting these discussions to our closest peers, could help right-size our understanding of the behaviors of our larger community. Instead, stigma encourages silence.

Finally, students may actually increase their substance use in response to stigma. The guilt and shame associated with developing a substance use disorder are deeply tied to belonging for many students. Students may blame themselves for their own problems and internalize the stigma their culture enforces about others. In turn, substance-seeking behavior can result as a coping mechanism or even a mode of self-harm (Volkow, 2020).

In short, stigma not only pushes individuals deeper into the struggles they may develop, it also lessens the likelihood they will pursue or successfully engage in the resources that could free them from the exact characteristics or behaviors their culture admonishes. For years, a dominant perspective was that shame and stigma could serve as a motivator, but research suggests stigma is more likely to infuse anxiety and depression into any change made, which in turn can increase substance use over the long run (Kammerer, 2019). As professionals, it is critical to include knowledge about stigma in the ways we understand student behavior and their relationships to the university. If, for example, students feel that changing their relationship to alcohol or another drug could risk their belonging, why would they ask for help?

It is important to note these dynamics also impact professionals. While this topic warrants a larger discussion than can be contained in this chapter, it is important to quickly consider the assumed baseline for professional substance use and the dynamics that enforce it. Similar to what students experience, professional culture develops a similar "rule book" of expectations around when and how colleagues will engage in substance use. Professional networks can be expanded and deepened at gatherings after hours over drinks. Partnerships and donations can be brokered through the art of "wining and dining." In this context, could regularly turning down opportunities to consume alcohol with peers be detrimental to one's career or professional standing? Additionally, if a professional developed a substance use disorder (as one in six people in the United States do) what may prevent them from seeking help (SAMHSA, 2022)?

Stigma in Recovery

While there are many examples of how stigma shows up on campus, a unique and even surprising place where the complexities of stigma are evident is within the ways campuses support or fail to support students in recovery from issues like addiction. Through identifying as in recovery, these students indicate they have overcome, or are in the process of overcoming, the substance use and behavioral concerns that are so heavily stigmatized. Analyzing the growth, or lack thereof, in these recovery-supportive student spaces can help shed light on the ways stigma can shape campus attitudes and response.

Collegiate recovery is a 40-year-old, yet still emerging, practice and functional area of Student Affairs (Greenagel, 2016).[4] This work seeks to serve students in recovery from an addiction, often primarily focusing on substance use disorders, and the many unique needs they experience while navigating colleges and universities. The first collegiate recovery program was established in 1977, around the same time identity-affirming centers on college campuses were increasing in popularity. Identity-affirming centers on college campuses, like Black Student Unions or

[4] For more information about collegiate recovery, and how to establish a collegiate recovery program on your campus, visit the Association for Recovery in Higher Education (ARHE) at www.collegiaterecovery.org.

LGBTQIA+ Centers, are rooted in the student-led struggle to hold institutions of higher education accountable. Considering a multitude of microaggressions from predominantly White and predominantly male spaces, identity-affirming centers act as counter-spaces and a haven from hostile territory (Yosso & Lopez, 2010). Identity-affirming centers are not monolithic, but collegiate recovery communities do share some similarities to identity-affirming centers in that they can provide relief from hostility in the broader campus community. Notably, identity-affirming centers serve as powerful symbols of the institution's commitment to diversity and support for students from a certain identity group: they signify an investment of resources (e.g., space, staff, budget) and a recognition that the group belongs to the campus community (Magolda & Baxter Magolda, 2011).

Despite more than 20 million people in the United States reporting being in recovery from a substance use challenge (SAMHSA, 2022), fewer than 5% of campuses have ever had structured programming to support students who share this experience. While many campuses do not establish collegiate recovery support due to a lack of funding and staffing, the systemic lack of resources signals the complex stigma present in US culture and on college campuses. If identity centers signal belonging on campus, the absence of these programs at many institutions may be interpreted by students as rejection or exclusion. It is important to consider: what may lead students in recovery to be relatively invisible at so many institutions of higher education?

One of the most common responses collegiate recovery advocates receive when promoting recovery programming to campus leaders is the curt, "We don't have students in recovery here." According to the National Collegiate Health Assessment, 2.2% of college students in the United States identify as in recovery from their relationship with alcohol and drugs, yet it seems on most campuses these students remain underserved and underrecognized (American College Health Association, 2023). The history of anonymity in the recovery world is complex, but it is still worth asking why so many leaders on campus report never having met or worked with a student in recovery. While stigma is a reasonable answer here, the circularity of stigma illustrates just how difficult these issues can be to understand.

First, stigma encourages silence and shame. However, this invisibility of students in recovery illustrates how deep stigma strikes into the hearts and identities of those impacted, and the way we think about individuals we mark with stigma. Recovery represents a complex and deeply transformational process of positive change. Students pursuing recovery often reclaim healthy and productive lives after experiencing significant consequences from their behavior of concern. Yet, even after these students have dedicated significant parts of their daily lives toward this change, embodying the ideals universities seek within their student body such as grit, resilience, service, and discipline, our campus cultures often silence rather than celebrate this journey. As collegiate recovery programs and communities are established on campuses, these students thrive and serve the campus in many ways once their existence and belonging are affirmed (Laudet et al., 2014). Still, these students report navigating not just the stigma of addiction, but students whose recovery entails abstinence also report campuses being "abstinence hostile." Meaning, the act of abstaining from substances signals to peers and staff that these students might be different, and therefore incompatible with the traditional college experience and the relationships campuses create. These students recognize they are not a priority when traditions and norms center substance use (often in the form of alcohol consumption) as a rite of passage. Despite representing campuses so well, students in recovery are held responsible for multiple layers of stigma: they are outsiders because they sought help or change; they are outsiders for not engaging in substance use in the same ways as their peers; and they are outsiders because of the assumptions we make about addiction, such as a lack of trustworthiness or self-control.

Lessons Learned Navigating Substance Use Stigma

While there are countless examples of how stigma emerges on campus, and stories from students in recovery regarding stigma within their educational experience, there are also emerging trends professionals might consider for mitigating stigma. Two of the most powerful themes the authors of this chapter have found and placed at the center of this work are: offering tools for students and affirming their life experiences. Both lessons center respect for students as decision-makers. In this section, we will discuss these lessons before reflecting on how they could impact the field of student affairs overall.

You Can't Do a Don't

Professionals who have participated in educational outreach regarding topics such as mental health and substance use are often met with scoffs, eye rolls, and giggles as they seek to attract students to their tables and programming. While these experiences can be frustrating and clearly indicative of stigma, there is a truth that students are communicating: they don't want what they expect to receive. Typically, students expect lectures and scare tactics mirroring the lectures they have been given their whole lives. Past generations of substance use prevention work in the United States have underlined stigma through fearmongering and campaigns promoting refusal skills to protect oneself from becoming "like the others." While the field of prevention has moved on from "this is your brain on drugs" and "just say no," the core values of those campaigns frequently resurface in the messages students receive. The challenge and greatest failure of these approaches come the moment someone uses substances without significant consequences, or when they want to be an effective bystander for those who do use. Respecting the dignity of emerging adults, even if it is preferable that students do not engage in substance use, begs the question: "If you do use, how can you mitigate risk?"

For well over a decade, harm reduction through programs such as BASICS, the Alcohol Skills Training Program, Choices, and others have replaced the "oughts and shoulds" of moralistic prevention while maintaining necessary policies and legal compliance on our campuses (Dimeff, 1999; Miller et al., 2001; Parks & Woodford, 2005).[5] Evidence suggests the current generation of students is ready for the same approach to drugs other than alcohol. While cannabis and other psychedelic substances reclaim legal status or become decriminalized, students take notice of the culture around them that has led to those changes. As opioid overdose rates rise, students wonder why their campuses stand idly by. Despite a dedication to developing leaders who can change the world, many institutions still rely on outdated prevention approaches grounded in binary thinking and compliance through lecture and policy enforcement. One solution is to offer options for developing bystander skills and increasing students' capacity to make healthier and safer choices, even if the calculus includes substance use. Institutions can mitigate overdose by providing students with tools, such as drug testing resources (where laws allow) and naloxone, so they might respond if they find someone in need. Research also points to the efficacy of hotlines, like the Never Use Alone hotline, that connect people who use substances with a peer who can request medical intervention if callers become unresponsive.[6] Another way an institution can highlight and communicate the possibility of substance use behavior change is to support a vibrant community of students in recovery. Any attempt to tell students what not to do should be replaced or quickly flanked with alternative options, choices, or ways to be an effective bystander that allows students the ability to make choices that align with their values and goals. In short, "you can't do a don't": that is, you can't measure, assess, or track growth toward a goal if the goal is simply in a negative.[7]

Disarming with Affirmations

Psychologists have confirmed what so many know intuitively: that humans, particularly emerging adults, do not want to be told what to do. When we feel a threat to our ability to choose for ourselves, we can rebel, feel anxious, annoyed, or angry. This is called psychological reactance (Cleveland Clinic, 2023). During pivotal times, we need to believe we have made decisions about ourselves, for ourselves.

---

[5] To learn more about these programs and resources, visit CollegeAIM. CollegeAIM—the College Alcohol Intervention Matrix—is a resource that assists universities select from dozens of alcohol intervention options available through a comparative analysis of research and evaluation. Learn more at: https://www.collegedrinkingprevention.gov/.

[6] One of the greatest risk factors for fatal overdose is using substances without bystanders present who can intervene in an emergency with naloxone and medical care. https://neverusealone.com/ and their Opioid Overdose Lifeline (877-696-1996) is a toll-free national overdose prevention, detection, life-saving crisis response and medical intervention service for people who use drugs while alone.

[7] SAFE Project provides cost-free technical assistance to collegiate staff seeking to implement recovery support, harm reduction, and anti-stigma approaches such as those shared throughout this chapter. For more information, visit www.safeproject.us.

When having developmental dialogues with students, campus professionals must be mindful of what opposing reactions they could inspire. It becomes quickly evident that respecting the autonomy and dignity of students must be integral in any conversation about student substance use, particularly when increased or initiated use could be a response. When professionals fail to center student dignity, students may shut down completely. Conversely, students may "comply" by sharing dishonest or sanitized opinions rather than their true beliefs to avoid discomfort or to end the conversation. Professionals can instead help students make sustainable change by engaging them in reflective decision-making processes that reach conclusions based on the student's own values rather than a predetermined ideal outcome. This approach requires a high degree of respect for affirmative support, empathy, nonjudgment, and respect for autonomy.

Professionals regularly see the importance of rapport with students, and how powerful it can be to begin a challenging conversation by simply asking students to share and reflect on their own experiences. It can be helpful, therefore, to ask questions about what an individual or group of students get out of their substance use, both positively and negatively. Once professionals develop a greater understanding of a student's interest in or commitment to change, they can better assist the student in the co-creation of a plan to move forward with or without particular substances. Many college students can cite positive things alcohol and other drugs can do for them or their peers, as maladaptive as these benefits may sometimes be (Logan et al., 2012). In addition to offering a semblance of inner peace, pain relief, focus, and increased sense of self-worth, substances offer the incentive of escaping the embodied experience of being uncomfortable and isolated in one's own skin (Maté, 2022). Most students will just as readily share the experiences and trends that are not so positive. Respecting a student means acknowledging that often a person will do whatever they feel they need to in order to survive and thrive, including misusing substances, especially if these are among the only tools they think they have access to or are aware of. According to the principles of motivational interviewing, empathy is a key aspect of human behavior change (Miller & Rollnick, 2023). Students must feel as though staff, faculty, and administration on campus hear them, see them, and can understand why they make the decisions they do. Ultimately, the goals of students and university staff are the same: for students to holistically thrive and have the tools required to do so. When all players see themselves as on the same team, the challenge of student substance use and the stigma associated with it begins to dissipate. The "them" problem can be more usefully navigated as an "us" problem.

The power of an affirmative and empathetic approach is that it can soften the foundational belief and motivator of stigma: that using drugs or having a disordered relationship with alcohol is something to hide and be ashamed of. As Brené Brown (2015) often remarks, shame cannot survive being spoken. When practitioners provide cues or suggestions that substance use is a topic that should not be talked about honestly, they feed the stigma preventing students from seeking help when they need it. Instead, we find that students are so used to being talked at about substance use that they are shocked when asked calmly and honestly to chat about the good, the bad, and the ugly. When campus stakeholders engage in overdose prevention and recovery support work that includes student voices, students are often surprised "the adults" in their lives are not only asking for their opinion, but actively listening to their response.

Additionally, professionals utilizing a stance that validates the dignity and experiences of students can flip the traditional power dynamics of prevention and the stigma that may hide there. Many health promotion and prevention practices center education as the primary solution to the substance use concerns students face. The logic implied in this focus on education is, if students knew about the potential harms they would act differently; that they do not act differently indicates they do not know. While this idea can be useful in motivating the sharing of new information, it can easily disregard the knowledge and experiences students bring with them. When support staff concede students are the experts of their own experience, they can transform a relationship of perceived ignorance into one of collaboration and collective learning; a relationship inherently vulnerable and connected, where stigma and shame cannot take hold.

Permission to Evolve: Implications for Student Affairs

Breaking from the Past

Through regularly navigating stigma on campus regarding substance use and mental health, developing tools to destigmatize students and their behaviors, and even while writing this chapter, a few larger implications for the field have revealed themselves. First, all members of our campus communities benefit from, and deeply appreciate, permission to speak openly about the role of substances in their lives. Second, harm reduction is a modern approach to public health that is simply incompatible with stigma. Finally, confronting stigma related to substance use and substance use disorder cuts far deeper than many initially may believe.

One of the most foundational implications of confronting stigma regarding substance use and pursuing programs such as naloxone availability and recovery support is that it allows for a more authentic and honest approach to student development. When providing trainings about harm reduction or substance use education, professionals and students alike will remark, as if we are relieving years of pressure, "Wait, we're really finally allowed to talk about this stuff openly?" Many of us are familiar with our own encounters with addiction, chaotic substance use, or even mundane substance use within our own lives and communities. For generations, stigma has kept discussions and meaning making of these experiences behind closed doors or in whispered side-room chats. We do not often realize how secretive we are expected to be about these discussions until we are truly given permission to consider them openly.

Moving from Moralism to Compassion

In Student Affairs, we believe in the worth of students and seek to be partners in their journeys toward becoming self-authoring humans (Baxter Magolda, 2001). We recognize the inherent value of moving from dualistic thinking to more nuanced ways of understanding (Perry, 1981, 1998). Yet, traditionally, substance use work on college campuses has focused on prevention, education, and policy intervention. Collegiate professionals regularly tell students not to use, explain to students why they should not use, and, if students are caught using, they are punished or provided more information or rationale about why they should not use. Students seeking to be treated with dignity and respect regarding their valid questions and concerns about substance use revert to peers rather than trusted mentors to make sense of the role of substances and drug-related risk in their lives. Of course, campuses must navigate and enforce applicable laws and policies, but these boundaries rarely need to get in the way of discussing and supporting health and safety.

How liberating for students, just as professionals proclaim about themselves, for us to be willing to have nuanced and nonjudgmental conversations about substance use. When we can set aside our own discomforts and stigma, we find opportunities to re-engage with the heart of our work where students are developing adults rather than potential criminals. Then, risk management solutions like naloxone need not be complicated any further than "We're here for you, and we want to keep you alive." Most campuses have readily accepted harm reduction efforts as they relate to safer sex, nicotine cessation, and the adoption of masks for respiratory viruses like COVID-19. For drugs, though, we seem slow to adapt. Students are critical thinkers, see these contradictions, and are eager for us to catch up.

Replacing Judgments with Resources

Among the most challenging yet rewarding parts of anti-stigma work regarding substances and people who use them is that this work is deeply intersectional. For generations, the culture of the United States has utilized substance use stigma as a mask for other types of stigma or discrimination. Cannabis (or marijuana) prohibition was rooted in a deeper anti-Mexican immigrant sentiment and tied to racist tropes around Black musicians. Opium and other opiate prohibition was deeply rooted in anti-Chinese immigrant sentiment, and again later tied to Black musicians. The current fentanyl crisis is being actively tied to anti-Mexican immigration policies as well as anti-Chinese attitudes. The tactics have been to attach certain drugs to a population viewed as an emerging threat to the White, Anglo-Saxon, Protestant "ideal" of the United States and pursue criminalization to a degree rarely informed by, or even reflective of, the true risks involved in the substance (Hari, 2015; Herzberg, 2020). While the initial criminalization is often rooted in stigma and "othering," we continue to see stigma against drug users as a barrier to taking meaningful action toward solving public health crises that have a relationship, real or perceived, to substance use. Concerns such as food insecurity, homelessness, HIV/AIDs, and mental health conditions are regularly deeply intertwined in substance use stigma.

All of this begins to shift when we remove the moral judgments from concerns related to substance use and approach the issue with compassion instead. A critical reframe with incredible implications is to consider why individuals begin to use in the first place. As was previously mentioned regarding the power of an affirmative and empathetic stance toward students, when we are able to remove judgment about substance use, we quickly gain access to deeper social issues students face.

Regularly, as we work with campuses to implement programs such as collegiate recovery support groups or opioid overdose response programs, we find recognition for other support systems naturally emerging or being intertwined. Food pantries, for example, quickly become partners of these initiatives. Without judgment, staff and students connect the dots between social determinants of health and find so many of these issues, like chaotic substance use, housing and food insecurity, general mental health, and many physical health conditions such as chronic illness, are all intertwined. Digging deeper, we find the web of human suffering is also weaved by larger systemic issues such as white supremacy, physical and emotional trauma, ableism, classism, heterosexism, and more. This intersectionality suggests two truths: addressing any one issue quickly reveals the need to begin to creatively address all of them, and true improvement with any one issue can spur improvement for all of them.

While we often focus on struggles, these trends are also reflected in our success stories. As we start to empower students to make positive change and to find sustainable support networks, their stories and successes have rippling effects. We repeatedly find when campuses support students in recovery, these students serve as role models for their peers currently experiencing substance use challenges, those in early recovery, or even students not yet comfortable being public about their own healing journey. Further, these recovering students quickly branch out as leaders and peers seeking to solve additional social and cultural issues. The history of harm reduction has been equally clear; when we share knowledge and tools for folks to navigate risk, they share with each other and even refine the strategies (Szalavitz, 2021).

References

American College Health Association. (2023). *National college health assessment III: Reference group executive summary Spring 2023*. https://www.acha.org/documents/ncha/NCHA-III_SPRING_2023_UNDERGRAD_REFERENCE_GROUP_EXECUTIVE_SUMMARY.pdf

American Psychiatric Association. (2022). *Diagnostic and statistical manual of mental disorders* (5th ed., text rev.). https://doi.org/10.1176/appi.books.9780890425787

Barber, J. P. (2011). If curbing alcohol abuse on college campuses is an impossible dream, why bother with interventions aimed at curbing abuse? Navigating the drinking culture to become productive citizens. In P. M. Magolda & M. B. Baxter Magolda (Eds.), *Contested issues in student affairs: Diverse perspectives & respectful dialogue* (pp. 162–180). Stylus Publishing.

Baxter Magolda, M. B. (2001). *Making their own way: Narratives for transforming higher education to promote self-development*. Stylus Publishing.

Blanco, C., Okuda, M., Wright, C., Hasin, D. S., Grant, B. F., Liu, S. M., & Olfson, M. (2008). Mental health of college students and their non-college-attending peers: Results from the National Epidemiologic Study on alcohol and related conditions. *Archives of General Psychiatry, 65*(12), 1429–1437. https://doi.org/10.1001/archpsyc.65.12.1429

Brown, B. (2015). *Daring greatly: How the courage to be vulnerable transforms the way we live, love, parent, and lead*. Penguin.

Caldeira, K. M., Kasperski, S. J., Sharma, E., Vincent, K. B., O'Grady, K. E., Wish, E. D., & Arria, A. M. (2009). College students rarely seek help despite serious substance use problems. *Journal of Substance Abuse Treatment, 37*(4), 368–378. https://doi.org/10.1016/j.jsat.2009.04.005

Carey, K. B., Durney, S. E., Shepardson, R. L., & Carey, M. P. (2015). Incapacitated and forcible rape of college women: Prevalence across the first year. *Journal of Adolescent Health, 6*(6), 678–680. https://doi.org/10.1016/j.jadohealth.2015.02.018

Cleveland Clinic. (2023, April 21). Why we don't like being told what to do. *Cleveland Clinic*. https://health.clevelandclinic.org/why-we-dont-like-being-told-what-to-do/

Corrigan, P. W., Druss, B. G., & Perlick, D. A. (2014). The impact of mental illness stigma on seeking and participating in mental health care. *Psychological Science in the Public Interest, 15*(2), 37–70. https://doi.org/10.1177/1529100614531398

Cox, M. J., DiBello, A. M., Meisel, M. K., Ott, M. Q., Kenney, S. R., Clark, M. A., & Barnett, N. P. (2019). Do misperceptions of peer drinking influence personal drinking behavior? Results from a complete social network of first-year college students. *Psychology of Addictive Behaviors: Journal of the Society of Psychologists in Addictive Behaviors, 33*(3), 297–303. https://doi.org/10.1037/adb0000455

Custer, B. D., & Kent, R. T. (2018). Understanding the drug-free schools and communities act, then and now. *Journal of College and University Law, 44*(2), 137. https://jcul.law.rutgers.edu/wp-content/uploads/2019/04/understanding-drug-free-schools-community-act-then-now.pdf

Dimeff, L. A. (Ed.). (1999). *Brief alcohol screening and intervention for college students (BASICS): A harm reduction approach*. Guilford Press.

Drug Enforcement Agency. (2020). Prevention with purpose: A strategic planning guide for preventing drug misuse among college students. https://www.dea.gov/sites/default/files/2020-03/Strategic%20Planning%20Guide%20%28Final-Online%29%20%281%29_0.pdf

Drug-Free Schools and Communities Act of 1989. (1989). H.R. 3614, 101st Cong. https://www.congress.gov/bill/101st-congress/house-bill/3614

Friedman, J., Godvin, M., Shover, C. L., Gone, J. P., Hansen, H., & Schriger, D. L. (2022). Trends in drug overdose deaths among US adolescents, January 2010 to June 2021. *Journal of American Medicine, 327*(14), 1398–1400. https://doi.org/10.1001/jama.2022.2847

Goffman, E. (1963). *Stigma: Notes on the management of spoiled identity*. Simon & Schuster.

Greenagel, F. (2016). History of collegiate recovery programs. *Hazelden Betty Ford*. https://www.hazeldenbettyford.org/articles/greenagel/history-of-collegiate-recovery-programs

Hari, J. (2015). *Chasing the scream: The first and last days of the war on drugs*. Bloomsbury USA.

Herzberg, D. (2020). *White market drugs: Big pharma and the hidden history of addiction in America*. The University of Chicago Press.

Hingson, R., Heeren, T., Winter, M., & Weschler, H. (2005). Magnitude of alcohol-related mortality and morbidity among U.S. college students ages 18–24: Changes from 1998 to 2001. *Annual Review of Public Health, 26*, 259–279. https://doi.org/10.1146/annurev.publhealth.26.021304.144652

Kammerer, A. (2019, August 9). The scientific underpinnings and impact of shame. *Scientific American*. https://www.scientificamerican.com/article/the-scientific-underpinnings-and-impacts-of-shame

Ketterer, S. (2022, October 7). UT's narcan program can't keep up with student demand. *Houston Chronicle*. https://www.houstonchronicle.com/news/houston-texas/education/article/UT-Austin-has-made-Narcan-available-across-17492295.php

Knox, L. (2022, August 16). Narcan is increasingly common on college campuses. *Inside Higher Ed.* https://www.insidehighered.com/news/2022/08/15/narcan-increasingly-common-college-campuses

Krieger, H., Young, C. M., Anthenien, A. M., & Neighbors, C. (2018). The epidemiology of binge drinking among college-age individuals in the United States. *Alcohol Research: Current Reviews, 39*(1), 23–30. https://pubmed.ncbi.nlm.nih.gov/30557145/

Laudet, A. B., Harris, K., Kimball, T., Winters, K. C., & Moberg, D. P. (2014). Collegiate recovery communities programs: What do we know and what do we need to know? *Journal of Social Work Practice in the Addictions, 14*(1), 84–100. https://doi.org/10.1080/1533256X.2014.872015

Lawyer, S., Resnick, H., Bakanic, V., Burkett, T., & Kilpatrick, D. (2010). Forcible, drug-facilitated, and incapacitated rape and sexual assault among undergraduate women. *Journal of American College Health, 58*(5), 453–460. https://doi.org/10.1080/07448480903540515

Logan, D. E., Henry, T., Vaughn, M., Luk, J. W., & King, K. M. (2012). Rose-colored beer goggles: The relationship between experiencing consequences and perceived likelihood and valence. *Psychology of Addictive Behaviors, 26*, 311–317. https://doi.org/10.1037/a0024126

Magolda, P. M., & Baxter Magolda, M. B. (2011). *Contested issues in student affairs: Diverse perspectives and respectful dialogue* (1st ed.). Stylus Pub.

Marconi, A., Washington, R., Reeves, M., Bradley, Q., Ayala, A., & Griggs, C. (2022). Examining racial microaggressions and alcohol use among marginalized populations at a predominately white institution. *Journal of American College Health*, 1–10. https://doi.org/10.1080/07448481.2022.2098027

Maté, G. (2022). *The myth of normal: Trauma, illness, and healing in a toxic culture*. Penguin.

Miller, E. T., Kilmer, J. R., Kim, E. L., Weingardt, K. R., & Marlatt, G. A. (2001). Alcohol skills training for college students. In P. M. Monti, S. M. Colby, & T. A. O'Leary (Eds.), *Adolescents, alcohol, and substance abuse: Reaching teens through brief interventions* (pp. 183–215). Guilford Press.

Miller, W. R., & Rollnick, S. (2023). *Motivational interviewing: Helping people change*. Guilford Press.

Munk, O. (2014). Beer at Harvard. *The Harvard Crimson*. https://www.thecrimson.com/article/2014/10/9/timeline-beer-at-harvard/

National Safety Council. (n.d.). Deaths by demographics: Age and cause. *NSC Injury Facts*. https://injuryfacts.nsc.org/all-injuries/deaths-by-demographics/deaths-by-age/

Parks, G. A., & Woodford, M. S. (2005). CHOICES about alcohol: A brief alcohol abuse prevention and harm reduction program for college students. In G. R. Walz & R. K. Yep (Eds.), *VISTAS: Compelling perspectives on counseling, 2005* (pp. 171–174). American Counseling Association.

Perry, W. G. (1981). Cognitive and ethical growth: The making of meaning. In A. W. Chickering et al. (Eds.), *The Modern American College* (pp. 76–116). Jossey-Bass.

Perry, W. G. (1998). *Forms of intellectual and ethical development in the college years: A scheme*. Jossey-Bass.

Russell, A. M., Patterson, M. S., & Barry, A. E. (2021). College students' perceptions of peer alcohol use: A social network analytic approach. *Substance Use & Misuse, 56*(1), 46–53. https://doi.org/10.1080/10826084.2020.1833929

Substance Abuse and Mental Health Services Administration. (2022). Key substance use and mental health indicators in the United States: Results from the 2021 National Survey on Drug Use and Health (HHS Publication No. PEP22-07-01-005, NSDUH Series H-57). *Center for Behavioral Health Statistics and Quality, Substance Abuse and Mental Health Services Administration*. https://www.samhsa.gov/data/report/2021-nsduh-annual-national-report

Szalavitz, M. (2021). *Undoing drugs: The untold story of harm reduction and the future of addiction*. Hachette Go.

U.S. Department of Health and Human Services. (n.d.). Stigma: Overcoming a barrier to pain treatment and addiction recovery. *National Institutes of Health*. https://heal.nih.gov/news/stories/stigma

Volkow, N. D. (2020). Stigma and the toll of addiction. *The New England Journal of Medicine, 382*(14), 1289–1290. https://www.nejm.org/doi/full/10.1056/NEJMp1917360

Yosso, T. J., & Lopez, C. B. (2010). Counterspaces in a hostile place: A critical race theory analysis of campus culture centers. In L. D. Patton (Ed.), *Culture centers in higher education* (pp. 83–104). Routledge.

Dylan Dunn, MS, senior director of SAFE Campuses, has dedicated his career in student affairs to transforming student support through the lenses of recovery and harm reduction. While a graduate student at Colorado State University, Dunn re-established a collegiate recovery initiative before taking his first professional role at University of Denver where he founded collegiate recovery, recovery housing, overdose prevention, and recovery allyship programs for students, staff, and faculty. Dunn serves on the SAFE Campuses team where he has impacted nearly 500 campuses through public speaking, training, technical assistance, and overdose prevention and response programs.

Kimberly Boulden, Ph.D., director of operations at MATTERS Network, brings over 10 years of experience in higher education and community-serving nonprofits to her current role. Previously, Boulden served as the associate director of admissions for the collegiate recovery program at Augsburg University prior to joining SAFE Project to lead the SAFE Campuses national portfolio until 2025. Boulden's practice centers decolonization in the assessment and evaluation of teaching, learning and the integration of social justice and sustainability initiatives. She has also worked on publications regarding university partnerships, research on diversity in university marketing, and grant-funded initiatives to decolonize computer science and engineering education.

Sydney Cheifetz, MPH, deputy director of SAFE Campuses, has extensive experience in international public health, collegiate recovery, health education, and disease prevention. Sydney oversees SAFE Project's student development programs, including the Collegiate Recovery Leadership Academy and the National Internship Program. Previously, Cheifetz served as health promotion specialist at Gonzaga University, where she led prevention, harm reduction, and recovery programs. Cheifetz holds a master's degree in public health and epidemiology from Oregon State University and a bachelor's degree in political science from Northern Arizona University. She is certified in motivational interviewing, recovery coaching, and ethical public health research.

Chapter 11
College Athletes: Stigma Around Mental Health Concerns and Related Support Systems

Amie Macbeth and Ryann N. Shelton

Abstract College athletes continue to experience mental health crises, as depression, anxiety, high-risk behaviors, and suicide are widely reported across levels of play. The National Collegiate Athletic Association (NCAA) recently provided guidelines for colleges and universities which emphasize athletes need continued mental health support. There is evidence of support for athletes who seek help for mental health concerns, but stigma and hesitation in mental health-seeking persist. Stigma prevents many people from seeking or maintaining mental health care, even when they know they could benefit from it; college athletes are less likely to seek help due to multiple stigmas around self-determination and athletic identity. In this chapter, we focus on the college athlete experience, mental health, stigma related to seeking mental health care, and research-based recommendations for college athlete mental health support.

Keywords College athletes · Mental health · Stigma · Treatment-seeking · Athletic departments · Recommendations

Years of research have focused on the mental health of college athletes, who continue to experience mental health crises (Anchuri et al., 2020; Armstrong et al., 2015; Bissett & Tamminen, 2022; Fogaca, 2021; Mansell, 2021; Putukian, 2016; Rice et al., 2016; Sauvé et al., 2022; Sutcliffe & Greenberger, 2020; Vidic et al.,

---

The authors have no conflicts of interest to declare that are relevant to the content of this chapter.

A. Macbeth (✉)
Dorchester County Public Schools, Cambridge, MD, USA
e-mail: amie_macbeth1@alumni.baylor.edu

R. N. Shelton
School of Education, Baylor University, Waco, TX, USA

© The Author(s), under exclusive license to Springer Nature Switzerland AG 2025

K. M. Brennan, K. S. Gorman (eds.), *A University-Wide Approach to Changing Campus Cultures of Mental Illness Stigma*, Knowledge Studies in Higher Education 18, https://doi.org/10.1007/978-3-031-86496-4_11

2017; Wu et al., 2021). Depression, anxiety, high-risk behaviors, and suicide are widely reported across levels of play (Anchuri et al., 2020; Armstrong et al., 2015; Fogaca, 2021), with suicide as the second leading cause of death among college athletes (Whelan et al., 2024). The National Collegiate Athletic Association (NCAA) recently provided guidelines for colleges and universities that emphasize the need for continued mental health support for athletes (NCAA Sport Science Institute, 2020). Colleges and universities need to be aware of and address the pervasive mental health stigma within the athletic community to encourage college athletes to use available help (Bauman, 2016; Eisenberg et al., 2009; Fogaca, 2021; Glick & Horsfall, 2009; Gulliver et al., 2012; Kaier et al., 2015; Reardon & Factor, 2010). This chapter focuses on the college athlete experience, mental health, stigma related to seeking mental health care, and research-based recommendations for mental health support.

The College Athlete Experience

The college athlete experience is unique. College athletes have many obligations that demand their time and add stressors to their mental well-being; they not only attend regular practices but also often have private training, strength training, and sports-related psychotherapy (Anchuri et al., 2020; Chen et al., 2010; Gulliver et al., 2012; Putukian, 2016; Sauvé et al., 2022; Vidic et al., 2017; Watson, 2005; Wu et al., 2021). Their elite athlete status creates positive and negative self-perceptions tied to self-worth and athletic identity (Griffith & Johnson, 2002).

Researchers have identified numerous positive attributes of being a college athlete. College athletes transfer the work ethic needed to succeed at a high-level of competition to their everyday life experiences (Chen et al., 2010). Improved health, self-restraint, character building, self-esteem, and self-empowerment are notable identity characteristics of the elite athlete (Chen et al., 2010). Additionally, mindfulness, mental toughness, and psychological skills such as motivation, attention, and confidence are found to be critical attributes of successful college athletes (Wu et al., 2021). Other skills associated with optimal athletic performance include coping ability, motivation, self-confidence, concentration, and stress adjustment (Anchuri et al., 2020; Brewer & Petitpas, 2017; Miller & Hoffman, 2009; Sauvé et al., 2022; Wu et al., 2021). These positive attributes buffer college athletes' mental health from environmental stressors. Athletic participation also provides a sense of belonging to a community, meaningful relationships, self-efficacy, and individual accomplishment (Kroshus, 2016; Miller & Hoffman, 2009; Rao et al., 2015). College athletes' lower rates of depression are likely due to positive social bonds and relationships with teammates or other on-campus athletes (Armstrong et al., 2015).

However, the burden of the athletic identity can be too much for some athletes (Brewer & Petitpas, 2017; Miller & Hoffman, 2009). As Taylor (2014) noted, "Players become masters at keeping their game faces on all the time, often until it's too late" (p. 2). Mental toughness may perpetuate the notion that athletes are not impacted by stress and may add to the stigma around seeking mental health support; this comes at a cost for some. Researchers have explored the degree to which the athletic identity affects college athletes' personal beliefs about themselves, their role on the college campus, and the potential for mental health issues (Brewer & Petitpas, 2017; Griffith & Johnson, 2002; Miller & Hoffman, 2009). Brewer and Petitpas (2017) revealed the buffering effect of participating in sports could be negated by focusing on one goal for an extended time. This athletic identity foreclosure can add to the stigma around seeking mental health support; it also can create risk for injury and poor play (Bauman, 2016; Moore, 2017). Athletes who focus on one sport often believe their friends and family like them because of their athleticism, so they may not explore other interests and subsequently are at risk of not developing their full personalities. Individuals with strong athletic identities may also be more likely to participate in risk-taking behaviors, especially those involving alcohol and drugs, to mitigate the accompanying stress (Brewer & Petitpas, 2017; Putukian, 2016; Sauvé et al., 2022).

In addition to managing these self-perceptions, college athletes have numerous stressors, including academics, team obligations, and personal pressure to perform, which contribute to mental health strain. Beyond these stressors, they face increased scrutiny from external factors like social media, coaches, teammates, and team doctors (Armstrong et al., 2015). Other mental health aggravators include distance and time away from family and other support systems, worry about critiques from social media, and relationship problems (Breslin et al., 2017). Rice et al.'s (2016) systematic review found injury, mistakes on the playing field or court; fatigue; and school, team, or organization climate are everyday sources of stress for athletes. Additionally, athletes are less likely to seek support compared to other college students when presenting with symptoms of stress or anxiety (Armstrong et al., 2015). In short, the idealization of athletes has impeded progress related to effectively addressing their mental health concerns and deepened the stigma that they need not seek support for mental health aggravators.

College Athlete Mental Health

The various obligations related to being a college athlete put them at risk for mental health concerns. Chronic stress and uncertainty are created by the unpredictable nature of sports and a player's role in changing the outcome of a game or match; this uncertainty and pressure can lead to stress-induced anxiety, depression, and a propensity toward high-risk behaviors (Beauchemin, 2014; Mansell, 2021). Researchers have found that nearly one in four college athletes have self-reported depression (Sutcliffe & Greenberger, 2020; Wolanin et al., 2015) and nearly one in three report anxiety (Sutcliffe & Greenberger, 2020). Reardon and Factor's (2010) list of common disorders amongst college athletes included mood disorders, suicide, social anxiety disorder, compulsive disorders, eating disorders, ADHD, addictive disorders (alcohol, stimulants, steroids), gambling, and concussion. Further, nearly half have clinical needs warranting counseling intervention, but many underreport their symptoms for fear of falling out of favor with their coaches or teammates (Wolanin et al., 2015). The prevalence of these mental health struggles warrants an examination of targeted support by college athletics.

Many college athletes participate in alarming high-risk behaviors, including binge drinking, gambling, hazing, performance-enhancing drugs, substance misuse, interpersonal violence, disordered eating, and overtraining (Anchuri et al., 2020; Armstrong et al., 2015; Chen et al., 2010; Glick & Horsfall, 2009; Greenleaf et al., 2009; Joy et al., 2004; Sønderlund et al., 2014; Yang et al., 2007). High-risk behaviors are a coping skill developed to avoid treatment or support, and to cover up depression, anxiety, or uncomfortable emotions (Glick & Horsfall, 2009). Examining high-risk behaviors is essential because they point to possible depression (Anchuri et al., 2020; Armstrong et al., 2015; Chen et al., 2010; Putukian, 2016; Reardon & Factor, 2010), which has a direct link to suicidal ideation and attempts (Rao et al., 2015).

College athlete mental health is more complex when there is an injury. How they perceive their injury and their chance to return to play is a factor in how they cope (Putukian, 2016). Some injuries trigger a grief response; the response depends on the college athletes' self-worth and extrinsic factors, such as the severity of the injury, mental health support, and length of recovery time (Armstrong et al., 2015). Other responses to injuries, including irritability, sleep disturbance, anger, and depression, can result in engagement in high-risk behaviors, including substance misuse (Putukian, 2016).

Mental health also plays a role in injury prevention, as a college athlete's response to stress can lead to biological changes that affect coordination or muscle tension, increasing the chance of injury (Putukian, 2016). Further, stress can cause injury because high cortisol rates lead to muscle tension and coordination issues. Injury recovery can be hindered by stress for the same chemical reasons, leading to a spiral that can heighten depression or depressive tendencies (Putukian, 2016). A two-year study of 330 American college football players discovered that athletes who reported depression symptoms were 10% more likely to get injured; however, those who reported anxiety did not (Yang et al., 2014). Injury prevention protocols must include strategies targeting psychological risk factors (Yang et al., 2014). Access to mental health support and services is essential to meet the holistic needs of college athletes.

The Stigma Related to College Athletes Seeking Mental Health Care

Colleges and universities have a unique opportunity to intercede during a critical time in a young adult's life, but stigma surrounding mental health support creates athletes' resistance toward using the support available to them (Reardon & Factor, 2010). The athletic world values mentally tough people because perseverance is considered the way to be successful and this toughness is embedded in the college athlete's identity. This toughness becomes a barrier for seeking and receiving help, even when it would be beneficial (Armstrong et al., 2015; Bauman, 2016; Eisenberg et al., 2009; Fogaca, 2021). Kaier et al.'s (2015) study of 304 college athletes from 16 Division I teams identified two commonly accepted types of stigma: public stigma, the belief about others' perceptions of those with mental illness, and personal stigma, one's own beliefs about those with mental illness. The athletes reported significantly more perceived public stigma than personal stigma and at higher rates than their non-athlete peers.

Causes of Stigma

Several studies have focused on the ways mental health care stigma is developed and reinforced in college athletics: social history, the early channeling into a specific sport, high profits in sports organizations, individual pressures, family expectations, media attention, and the team's belief about mental health (Bauman, 2016; Fogaca, 2021; Gulliver et al., 2012; Kaier et al., 2015; Maniar et al., 2001; Watson, 2005). Watson (2005) studied differences in help-seeking behaviors between athletes and non-athletes and discovered that simply offering support services for all college students may not be enough. College athletes have created success for themselves by ignoring physical pain and overcoming obstacles. Their persona, on and off the playing field, is usually tied to believing they must mask discomfort and get the job done, so asking for and receiving help can be difficult. Thus, it seems the stigma for college athletes lies in help-seeking, as they fear the consequences of asking for help, not in the mental health concern itself.

Changes in Help-Seeking

Within this context of stigma, athletic department leaders are noting some changes in mental health support-seeking by college athletes. Athletic directors and trainers who were participants in a recent study spoke to two stigma-related outcomes (Macbeth, 2023). One participant noted stigma around mental health has significantly decreased, but the lack of resources at their school was a problem. A second participant noted there was still a stigma with mental health in the United States but acknowledged there has been a change. This participant described an incident wherein they were shocked when a college athlete was forthcoming with their struggles and high-risk behaviors; this participant believed the willingness to talk about struggles is the biggest recent shift related to stigma. Based on Macbeth's (2023) study, we share a fictional vignette to illustrate one type of stigma related to college athletes' mental health concerns and related support systems.

Vignette

In a recent department meeting, an athletic director and several athletic trainers were discussing student concerns and questions:

Trainer 1: One of our soccer players needed to be held for a mental health concern today.

Trainer 2: Yes, she announced it to the team during morning lift.

Athletic Director: She announced it to the team? It seems like personal information.

Trainer 1: I think we are working with a different generation here. I am following the required steps to connect her with university support systems.

Trainer 2: I wasn't sure how to respond when she shared it with everyone. How should we respond in this situation in the future?

Athletic Director: I think it is personal and shouldn't be shared.

As noted in the fictional vignette and as shared by some athletic department leaders in Macbeth's (2023) study, college athletes seem to be more comfortable discussing mental health and mental health support than department staff. According to athletic department leaders, some college athletes are speaking out for more mental health support through non-profit groups and student representative opportunities (Macbeth, 2023). It is important for colleges and universities to hear and support these voices.

Existing mental health supports for college athletes vary depending on school size, athletic division, and barriers to access. If they do seek help, college athletes prefer those within the athletic department as they believe people outside of it are potentially unable to understand their unique situation (Beauchemin, 2014; Glick & Horsfall, 2009; Gulliver et al., 2012; Maniar et al., 2001; Sauvé et al., 2022). Given their critical role in supporting well-being, athletes prefer to seek help from their coaches first. The second support sought is from a sport-titled professional, and then, if necessary, a counselor or psychologist (Beauchemin, 2014). As such, college athletes underutilize college and university counseling services and instead seek help within the athletic department which is typically only charged with supporting their academic and physical well-being (Watson, 2005).

The Role of the National Collegiate Athletic Association

The NCAA (2024) recommends schools provide targeted mental health services, such as available support services and educational materials, to college athletes because of the added stressors accompanying their roles as students and athletes, but it does not require standardized screening and monitoring (Conley et al., 2014; Joy et al., 2004; National Athletic Trainer's Association [NATA], 2013; NCAA Sport Science Institute, 2024). While they admit increased stress and pressures placed on athletes can lead to depression (Armstrong et al., 2015), the NCAA only provides guidelines for schools to follow and a list of resources to find funding. According to the NCAA Sport Science Institute (2024), "Student-athlete mental well-being is best served through a collaborative process of engaging the full complement of available campus and community resources, which may include athletics, campus health, counseling services, disability services, and community agencies" (p. 6). The NCAA's four recommendations for schools are to create an environment that supports mental health, create a procedure for identifying mental health symptoms and disorders, create an action plan for referral for college athletes, and hire or consult with licensed providers to oversee college athlete mental health care (NCAA Sport Science Institute, 2024).

There is loose oversight around mental well-being for college athletes despite the guidelines suggested by the NCAA; there is no standard practice for college athlete mental health screening and support. This gives schools freedom to focus on what they want to do and can do. Some schools are limited by resources, others by interest. As noted in the fictional vignette, there are different levels of understanding about mental health within the athletic department. The lack of guidelines about how to address mental health within the department may lead to further stigma, which may create barriers to help-seeking. Division I schools have more significant and different funding sources that impact the resources they can offer and are more likely to have a written plan for mental health screening (Kroshus, 2016). This screening is a first opportunity to acknowledge the existence of mental health challenges for athletes and is important given sports and the development of athletes too often focus on improving an athlete's biomechanics and injury prevention while rarely working on mental health or performance psychology (Bauman, 2016). Having a focused plan in place to address stigma and to support athlete mental health is important.

Research-Based Recommendations for College Athlete Mental Health Support

College athletes, NATA, coaches, and other athletic department leaders have contributed to the following recommendations regarding how to provide support for this population (Conley et al., 2014; Glick & Horsfall, 2009; Joy et al., 2004;

Kroshus, 2016; NATA, 2013; Neal et al., 2013). As this is an emergent field, best practices are still left to individual colleges and universities. This section highlights three research-based recommendations to support college athletes' mental health and to challenge stigma in college athletics: improve the annual preparticipation evaluation process, provide college athletes with access to a psychological support team with an emphasis on ensuring all related personnel can recommend athletes to this support option, and offer athletes context-specific holistic support.

Include Mental Health Screening in the Preparticipation Evaluation

The current practice of an annual preparticipation evaluation (PPE) is the sole medical evaluation for a large majority of college athletes. Currently, most schools use the PPE to detect emergency or life-threatening physical symptoms that should prevent an athlete from participating. Kroshus (2016) conducted a study of 365 schools and found that less than one-third of schools required a PPE for returning students. Further, about four in 10 schools had a written plan to identify college athlete mental health concerns. School screening rates for specific types of mental health concerns included: 44.5% for disordered eating, 32.3% for depression, and 30.7% for anxiety (Kroshus, 2016). Nearly, one-third of schools do not screen for any of the six NCAA-identified mental health concerns: anxiety, depression, disordered eating, alcohol misuse, prescription drug misuse, or illegal drug misuse (Kroshus, 2016).

A more inclusive PPE could identify more physical and mental health concerns than it does (Conley et al., 2014; Macbeth, 2023; NATA, 2013). Using concussion protocols as inspiration, NATA (2013) suggested mental health baselines and histories be taken yearly. They also suggested frequent check-ups with immediate, as-needed support services much like the attention given to injuries. NATA (2013) created a list of PPE recommendations, including many body-centered tests for general health, medication use, nutritional assessment, and mental health assessment. Because stigma may inhibit college athletes from coming forward without specific prompting to do so, a standardized and specific mental health screening in the PPE process could potentially provide early intervention by connecting them to necessary mental health support. Athletic trainers and team physicians can then monitor behaviors for patterns or changes and address them.

Require Department Training on the Referral Process to a Psychological Support Team

The referral process to connect an athlete with a psychological support team on campus should be clear, easy, and swift. The coach, athletic trainer, and team physician should know how to refer and encourage referrals (Neal et al., 2013). Athletes rely heavily on trainers as their support persons, especially after an injury (Neal et al., 2013), so trainers should be trained to notice and report mental health concerns. As seen in the fictional vignette in this chapter, trainers must be ready to discuss mental health because they are often the first in the department to hear about these concerns. Athletic trainers should have options to help college athletes find the mental health support they need (Armstrong et al., 2015).

Proper training for all athletic department members in responding to mental health disclosures is essential to provide the best possible support. As demonstrated in the fictional vignette, not everyone in the department is prepared to respond to an athlete in need. Physicians and other medical personnel interacting with athletes should also have training on and understand sports and teams dynamics. Glick and Horsfall (2009) noted that support personnel who understand team dynamics help college athletes seek and continue mental health support. Departments should offer training about the impact of stigma. At the same time, this care team must be aware of their role in reducing stigma efforts, as these efforts are the first step to reducing personally held stigmatizing attitudes and increasing the help-seeking behaviors of college students (Eisenberg et al., 2009). Training those closest to college athletes to help them seek mental health support when needed helps reduce the stigma, as it normalizes conversation and provides another trusted layer of support.

Provide Tailored Support

It is critical to consider the specific context of the college athlete to construct a multi-modal, holistic approach to reduce mental health related stigma. It is important to address mental health concerns in a way conducive to college athletes' identity and specific needs. They carry with them a perception of mental toughness and have developed trusted relationships with some, but not all, of the athletic department members. Ideally, a combination of sports psychologist and athletic trainer interventions can provide essential messaging to athletes about mental health. This multi-modal support system can help mitigate the effects of stigma on help-seeking behaviors (Fogaca, 2021; Neal et al., 2013; Parcover et al., 2009; Putukian, 2016). Athletes are more willing and able to participate in integrated stress reduction and coping skill learning as part of holistic support (Fogaca, 2021). Purposeful teaching of techniques to manage emotions, awareness, and coping strategies can assist them in learning to manage stress when it arises (Lazarus & Folkman, 1984). In working with college athletes, the environment and expectations inevitably become stressors out of the athlete's control. Therefore, providing college athletes healthy outlets for coping is critical to their mental health. These conversations are another way that the department can demonstrate its commitment to mental health and are a means of challenging the stigma by intentionally addressing these topics.

Conclusion

Interest in mental health, specifically in college athlete mental health, continues to grow. College athletes have a unique experience that requires specialized interventions and support. Depression, anxiety, high-risk behaviors, and suicide all impact this tight-knit community (Anchuri et al., 2020; Armstrong et al., 2015; Fogaca, 2021; NCAA Sport Science Institute, 2020). Continued efforts to research and build support systems for college athletes are needed. While the forward momentum by the NCAA continues the conversation about mental health, the systems of support in place for college athletes must continue to fight the stigma around mental health support-seeking embedded into the athletic culture.

Acknowledgments The material in this chapter is developed from the lead author's problem of practice dissertation: Macbeth, A. M. (2023). *Beyond talk: A multiple case study exploring athletic directors' and trainers' perceptions of mental health support systems in college athletics* [Ed.D. Problem of Practice Dissertation]. Baylor University.

References

Anchuri, K., Davoren, A. K., Shanahan, A., Torres, M., & Wilcox, H. C. (2020). Nonsuicidal self-injury, suicidal ideation, and suicide attempt among collegiate athletes: Findings from the National College Health Assessment. *Journal of American College Health, 68*(8), 815–823. https://doi.org/10.1080/07448481.2019.1616743

Armstrong, S. N., Burcin, M. M., Bjerke, W. S., & Early, J. (2015). Depression in student athletes: A particularly at-risk group? A systematic review of the literature. *Athletic Insight, 7*(2), 177–193. https://digitalcommons.sacredheart.edu/cgi/viewcontent.cgi?article=1186&context=pthms_fac

Bauman, N. J. (2016). The stigma of mental health in athletes: Are mental toughness and mental health seen as contradictory in elite sport? *British Journal of Sports Medicine, 50*(3), 135–136. https://doi.org/10.1136/bjsports-2015-095570

Beauchemin, J. (2014). College student-athlete wellness: An integrative outreach model. *College Student Journal, 48*(2), 268–280.

Bissett, J. E., & Tamminen, K. A. (2022). Student-athlete disclosures of psychological distress: Exploring the experiences of university coaches and athletes. *Journal of Applied Sport Psychology, 34*(2), 363–383. https://doi.org/10.1080/10413200.2020.1753263

Breslin, G., Shannon, S., Haughey, T., Donnelly, P., & Leavey, G. (2017). A systematic review of interventions to increase awareness of mental health and well-being in athletes, coaches, and officials. *Systematic Reviews, 6*(1), Article 177. https://doi.org/10.1186/s13643-017-0568-6

Brewer, B. W., & Petitpas, A. J. (2017). Athletic identity foreclosure. *Current Opinion in Psychology, 16*, 118–122. https://doi.org/10.1016/j.copsyc.2017.05.004

Chen, S., Snyder, S., & Magner, M. (2010). The effects of sports participation on student-athletes' and non-athlete students' social life and identity. *Journal of Issues in Intercollegiate Athletics, 3*, 176–193. https://scholarcommons.sc.edu/jiia/vol3/iss1/10/

Conley, K. M., Bolin, D. J., Carek, P. J., Konin, J. G., Neal, T. L., & Violette, D. (2014). National Athletic Trainers' Association position statement: Preparticipation physical examinations and disqualifying conditions. *Journal of Athletic Training, 49*(1), 102–120. https://doi.org/10.4085/1062-6050-48.6.05

Eisenberg, D., Downs, M. F., Golberstein, E., & Zivin, K. (2009). Stigma and help seeking for mental health among college students. *Medical Care Research and Review, 66*(5), 522–541. https://doi.org/10.1177/1077558709335173

Fogaca, J. L. (2021). Combining mental health and performance interventions: Coping and social support for student-athletes. *Journal of Applied Sport Psychology, 33*(1), 4–19. https://doi.org/10.1080/10413200.2019.1648326

Glick, I. D., & Horsfall, J. L. (2009). Psychiatric conditions in sports: Diagnosis, treatment, and quality of life. *The Physician and Sportsmedicine, 37*(3), 29–34. https://doi.org/10.3810/psm.2009.10.1726

Greenleaf, C., Petrie, T. A., Carter, J., & Reel, J. J. (2009). Female collegiate athletes: Prevalence of eating disorders and disordered eating behaviors. *Journal of American College Health, 57*(5), 489–496. https://doi.org/10.3200/JACH.57.5.489-496

Griffith, K. A., & Johnson, K. A. (2002). Athletic identity and life roles of Division I and Division III collegiate athletes. *Journal of Undergraduate Research, 5*(1), 225–231. https://www.uwlax.edu/globalassets/offices-services/urc/jur-online/pdf/2002/griffith_and_johnson.pdf

Gulliver, A., Griffiths, K. M., & Christensen, H. (2012). Barriers and facilitators to mental health help-seeking for young elite athletes: A qualitative study. *BMC Psychiatry, 12*(1), 157. https://doi.org/10.1186/1471-244X-12-157

Joy, E. A., Paisley, T. S., Price, R., Jr., Rassner, L., & Thiese, S. M. (2004). Optimizing the collegiate preparticipation physical evaluation. *Clinical Journal of Sport Medicine, 14*(3), 183–187. https://doi.org/10.1097/00042752-200405000-00012

Kaier, E., Cromer, L. D., Johnson, M. D., Strunk, K., & Davis, J. L. (2015). Perceptions of mental illness stigma: Comparisons of athletes to nonathlete peers. *Journal of College Student Development, 56*(7), 735–739. https://doi.org/10.1353/csd.2015.0079

Kroshus, E. (2016). Variability in institutional screening practices related to collegiate student-athlete mental health. *Journal of Athletic Training, 51*(5), 389–397. https://doi.org/10.4085/1062-6050-51.5.07

Lazarus, R. S., & Folkman, S. (1984). *Stress, appraisal, and coping*. Springer Publishing Company.

Macbeth, A. M. (2023). *Beyond talk: A multiple case study exploring athletic directors' and trainers' perceptions of mental health support systems in college athletics* [Unpublished doctoral dissertation]. Baylor University.

Maniar, S. D., Curry, L. A., Sommers-Flanagan, J., & Walsh, J. A. (2001). Student-athlete preferences in seeking help when confronted with sport performance problems. *Sport Psychologist, 15*(2), 205–223.

Mansell, P. C. (2021). Stress mindset in athletes: Investigating the relationships between beliefs, challenge, and threat with psychological wellbeing. *Psychology of Sport and Exercise, 57*, 102020. https://doi.org/10.1016/j.psychsport.2021.102020

Miller, K. E., & Hoffman, J. H. (2009). Mental well-being and sport-related identities in college students. *Sociology of Sport Journal, 26*(2), 335–356. https://doi.org/10.1123/ssj.26.2.335

Moore, M. (2017). Stepping outside of their comfort zone: Perceptions of seeking behavioral health services amongst college athletes. *Journal of Issues in Intercollegiate Athletics, Special Issue*, 130–144. http://csri-jiia.org/wp-content/uploads/2017/07/JIIA_2017_SI_08.pdf

National Athletic Trainers Association. (2013, September 25). *NATA releases consensus statement for developing a plan to recognize and refer student athletes with*

psychological concerns at the collegiate level. https://www.nata.org/press-release/092513/nata-releases-consensus-statement-developing-plan-recognize-and-refer-student
National Collegiate Athletic Association Sport Science Institute. (2020). *Mental health best practices: Understanding and supporting student-athlete mental awareness*. https://ncaaorg.s3.amazonaws.com/ssi/mental/SSI_MentalHealthBestPractices.pdf
National Collegiate Athletic Association Sport Science Institute. (2024). *Mental health best practices: Understanding and supporting student-athlete mental awareness: Second edition*. https://ncaaorg.s3.amazonaws.com/ssi/mental/SSI_MentalHealthBestPractices.pdf
Neal, T. L., Diamond, A. B., Goldman, S., Klossner, D., Morse, E. D., Pajak, D. E., Putukian, M., Quandt, E. F., Sullivan, J. P., Wallack, C., & Welzant, V. (2013). Inter-association recommendations for developing a plan to recognize and refer student-athletes with psychological concerns at the collegiate level: An executive summary of a consensus statement. *Journal of Athletic Training, 48*(5), 716–720. https://doi.org/10.4085/1062-6050-48.4.13
Parcover, J. A., Mettrick, J., Parcover, C. A. D., & Griffin-Smith, P. (2009). University and college counselors as athletic team consultants: Using a structural family therapy model. *Journal of College Counseling, 12*(2), 149–161. https://doi.org/10.1002/j.2161-1882.2009.tb00112.x
Putukian, M. (2016). The psychological response to injury in student athletes: A narrative review with a focus on mental health. *British Journal of Sports Medicine, 50*(3), 145–148. https://doi.org/10.1136/bjsports-2015-095586
Rao, A. L., Asif, I. M., Drezner, J. A., Toresdahl, B. G., & Harmon, K. G. (2015). Suicide in National Collegiate Athletic Association athletes: A 9-year analysis of the NCAA resolutions database. *Sports Health, 7*(5), 452–457. https://doi.org/10.1177/1941738115587675
Reardon, C. L., & Factor, R. M. (2010). Sport psychiatry: A systematic review of diagnosis and medical treatment of mental illness in athletes. *Sports Medicine, 40*(11), 961–980. https://doi.org/10.2165/11536580-000000000-00000
Rice, S. M., Purcell, R., De Silva, S., Mawren, D., McGorry, P. D., & Parker, A. G. (2016). The mental health of elite athletes: A narrative systematic review. *Sports Medicine, 46*(9), 1333–1353. https://doi.org/10.1007/s40279-016-0492-2
Sauvé, J. L., O'Rourke, J. J., Wilson, B., Bundon, A., & Beauchamp, M. R. (2022). Looking back to move forward: Recently retired Olympians' perspectives of factors that contribute to and undermine athlete well-being. *Sport, Exercise, and Performance Psychology, 11*(1), 44–60. https://doi.org/10.1037/spy0000273
Sønderlund, A. L., O'Brien, K., Kremer, P., Rowland, B., De Groot, F., Staiger, P., Zinkiewicz, L., & Miller, P. G. (2014). The association between sports participation, alcohol use and aggression and violence: A systematic review. *Journal of Science and Medicine in Sport, 17*(1), 2–7. https://doi.org/10.1016/j.jsams.2013.03.011
Sutcliffe, J. H., & Greenberger, P. A. (2020). Identifying psychological difficulties in college athletes. *Journal of Allergy and Clinical Immunology: In Practice, 8*(7), 2216–2219. https://doi.org/10.1016/j.jaip.2020.03.006
Taylor, A. (2014). Game face is not the only face. In G. T. Brown, B. Hainline, E. Kroshus, & M. Wilfert (Eds.), *Mind, body, and sport: Understanding and supporting student-athlete mental wellness* (pp. 2–4). NCAA.
Vidic, Z., Martin, M. S., & Oxhandler, R. (2017). Mindfulness intervention with a U.S. women's NCAA Division I basketball team: Impact on stress, athletic coping skills and perceptions of intervention. *Sport Psychologist, 31*(2), 147–159. https://doi.org/10.1123/tsp.2016-0077
Watson, J. C. (2005). College student-athletes' attitudes toward help-seeking behavior and expectations of counseling services. *Journal of College Student Development, 46*(4), 442–449. https://doi.org/10.1353/csd.2005.0044
Whelan, B. M., Kliethermes, S. A., Schloredt, K. A., Rao, A., Harmon, K. G., & Petek, B. J. (2024). Suicide in National Collegiate Athletic Association athletes: A 20-year analysis. *British Journal of Sports Medicine, 58*, 531–537. https://doi.org/10.1136/bjsports-2023-107509

Wolanin, A., Gross, M., & Hong, E. (2015). Depression in athletes: Prevalence and risk factors. *Current Sports Medicine Reports, 14*(1), 56–60. https://doi.org/10.1249/JSR.0000000000000123

Wu, C. H., Nien, J. T., Lin, C. Y., Nien, Y. H., Kuan, G., Wu, T. Y., Ren, F. F., & Chang, Y. K. (2021). Relationship between mindfulness, psychological skills, and mental toughness in college athletes. *International Journal of Environmental Research and Public Health, 18*(13), 6802. https://doi.org/10.3390/ijerph18136802

Yang, J., Cheng, G., Zhang, Y., Covassin, T., Heiden, E. O., & Peek-Asa, C. (2014). Influence of symptoms of depression and anxiety on injury hazard among collegiate American football players. *Research in Sports Medicine, 22*(2), 147–160. https://doi.org/10.1080/15438627.2014.881818

Yang, J., Peek-Asa, C. P., Corlette, J. D. M., Cheng, G. M., Foster, D. T., & Albright, J. P. (2007). Prevalence of and risk factors associated with symptoms of depression in competitive collegiate student athletes. *Clinical Journal of Sport Medicine, 17*(6), 481–487. https://doi.org/10.1097/JSM.0b013e31815aed6b

Amie Macbeth, Ed.D., is an assistant principal for the Dorchester County Public Schools in Maryland. She has previously taught English and designed curriculum for middle school and high school programs. Her research interests include mental health support for college athletes, mental health support programs, and equity and access in education.

Ryann N. Shelton, Ph.D., is a lecturer for the online Ed.D. in Learning and Organizational Change program in the School of Education at Baylor University. She teaches graduate-level courses in instructional design and advises students in the dissertation process. Her research interests include mathematics education, teacher education, and instructional design.

Chapter 12
It Takes All of Us: A Comprehensive Community Approach to Challenging Campus Stigma

Kimberly S. Gorman and Kathleen M. Brennan

Abstract It is important to bring attention to the ways mental illness stigma is entrenched in the fabric of the campus culture to usher in a change. The voices represented in this volume were those who heeded our call to illuminate the need for a collaborative approach to this very real problem and provide evidence that the solutions for addressing increased distress and challenging mental illness stigma is not just the responsibility of one area on campus. There are several themes in this volume that emerged as important points to address stigma. This chapter provides a summary of those suggestions to assist readers in developing strategies to use on their campuses.

Keywords Higher education · Mental illness · Stigma · Campus collaboration

This volume was born from a desire to amplify the conversation about mental illness stigma on campuses, given the existing literature examining mental illness stigma within the university focuses mainly on the ways stigma is held by and impacts students who live and study on our campuses. Our research has found evidence that the "backbone of stigma" present in international communities (Pescosolido et al., 2013) is reproduced within a university sample (Brennan & Gorman, 2022) and is negatively associated with desirable outcomes, including mental health treatment seeking (Brennan & Gorman, 2022; Gorman & Brennan,

---

The authors have no conflicts of interest to declare that are relevant to the content of this chapter.

K. S. Gorman (✉)
Division of Student Affairs, Western Carolina University, Cullowhee, NC, USA
e-mail: ksgorman@wcu.edu

K. M. Brennan
Department of Anthropology and Sociology, Western Carolina University, Cullowhee, NC, USA

© The Author(s), under exclusive license to Springer Nature Switzerland AG 2025

K. M. Brennan, K. S. Gorman (eds.), *A University-Wide Approach to Changing Campus Cultures of Mental Illness Stigma*, Knowledge Studies in Higher Education 18, https://doi.org/10.1007/978-3-031-86496-4_12

2023a), which we have found to positively influence student retention and completion on the same campus (Gorman & Brennan, 2023b). We have not found a similarly robust conversation in the literature regarding the way mental illness stigma is entrenched in the policies, practices, and programs we participate in, nor how it is impacting the faculty and staff who work on our campuses.

Encounters with Mental Illness Stigma

We know talking about campus cultures of mental illness stigma is necessary because of the myriad ways we have personally encountered it in our research, teaching, and administrative roles. We hear students use the word "crazy" to describe a wide variety of behavioral issues that may or may not involve mental illness. We hear a student make a joke to a friend, "you really need that!" when passing by a table for counseling services. We hear faculty disregard a larger pattern of academic difficulty because of mental illness by placing blame on the student for their struggles. We hear students conflate daily distress with mental illness, thereby invalidating the experiences of those with mental illness challenges. We hear students say they fear they will be "institutionalized" (sic) for sharing their struggles with suicidality. We hear faculty say the same student experiencing suicidality should be removed from a class. We don't hear administrators sharing their experiences with mental illness because of concerns of how that would be viewed by others on campus.

We see students disappear from classes without any communication to faculty because they do not know how to discuss mental health concerns with faculty and because they are afraid they will be penalized. We see faculty refusing to accommodate students with mental illness, even when the students maintain good communication. We see staff members rushing a student to the counseling center whenever a student indicates they are distressed rather than sitting with that student for a minute to simply listen to them. We see family members scoff at a table advertising counseling services at new student orientation.

We continue to challenge the belief that a student needs to be removed from a classroom because they have disclosed suicidal thoughts. We encourage treatment seeking for students who are hesitant to do so. We emphasize on-campus counseling services for those who hold marginalized identities. We remind faculty and staff of the importance of caring for their own mental health. We add more resources for faculty and staff and talk about these resources in different departmental and university-wide meetings.

Yes, mental illness stigma is present on our campuses. Those of us who study it are acutely aware of how it is expressed daily. However, the covert nature of mental illness stigma results in many campus community members not noticing it. We need to pay better attention.

Looking Outside of the Counseling Center

We have heard the mantra that higher utilization of university counseling centers is an indication of decreasing mental illness stigma (Center for Collegiate Mental Health [CCMH], 2017; Lipson et al., 2019) despite broad research evidence that public stigma is still present in (e.g., Best & Arseniev-Koehler, 2023; Pescosolido et al., 2021) and outside (e.g., Faleti & Akinlotan, 2024; Krendl & Pescosolido, 2020; Schomerus et al., 2022; Subramaniam et al., 2017) the United States, as well as in international university samples (e.g., Brennan & Gorman, 2022; Dare et al., 2023; Gaddis et al., 2018; Lipson et al., 2019; Ruiz et al., 2022). Jumping to this conclusion ignores the reality and complexity of the ways stigma operates in the university context. We cannot say stigma has been reduced when faculty, staff, and students are concerned about jeopardizing a career with a disclosure about mental illness. Nor can we say we have done a good job addressing stigma when campuses continue to construct and/or maintain barriers for individuals who hold marginalized identities. We must contend with the fact that increasing utilization of counseling services might not be because of reduced stigma; it may be our cultures are manufacturing and reinforcing distress for which counseling is more immediately needed. These trends of distress for students arriving on campus in the 2020s have so far been well documented by researchers and attributed to, among other factors, the influences of social media (e.g., Haidt, 2024; Twenge, 2023) and racial injustice (e.g., CCMH, 2024; Jochman et al., 2019). Of note, these factors provide fertile soil for stigma as they allow for multiple ways of othering to occur. Suggesting counseling center utilization has increased because stigma has decreased is a dangerous assumption and could deflect the need for very real attention to how stigma is operating in the hallways of our buildings and the pathways across our campuses.

We believe it is important to bring attention to the ways mental illness stigma is entrenched in the fabric of the campus culture to usher in a change. The voices represented in this volume were those who heeded our call to illuminate the need for a collaborative approach to this very real problem. The various disciplines represented—communication, education, health, higher education, marketing, psychology, sociology, and student affairs—suggest the myriad ways mental illness stigma is embedded in the approaches to our work as well as in the campus culture itself. Of note, there are voices, important ones, that did not respond. The absence of the administrator's voice in this volume is a very real reflection of how stigma is operative such that those who hold power are typically not at the forefront of efforts to change it. The reasons for this absence are not well studied but may relate to heavy workload, lack of awareness or understanding of the issue, risk of self-disclosure of mental illness, or support for stigmatizing systems. We must acknowledge the key role university leaders play in actively dismantling stigmatizing practices and systemic power imbalances that allow stigma to persist. The voices in this volume provide evidence that the solution for addressing increased distress and challenging mental illness stigma is not just the responsibility of the counseling center (e.g.,

Gorman et al., 2024) or of the wellness promotion office on campus: It will indeed take all of us.

A community approach is significant for many reasons. One impact of mental illness stigma discussed in this volume is the alienation and isolation it causes. Isolation and loneliness has garnered attention of late, especially as an outcome of the COVID-19 pandemic (e.g., Ernst et al., 2022). US Surgeon General Vivek Murthy (2020) focused his office's efforts on bringing awareness to the devastating impact that isolation and loneliness has on both our psychological and physical health. This has been a timely alert given the research that highlights the growing disconnection and isolation among youth, not just in the United States but worldwide (Twenge, 2023). For students, this disconnection impacts their help-seeking behavior (Brennan & Gorman, 2023) and ability to graduate from college (Gorman & Brennan, 2023b) with long-term consequences regarding lifetime career earnings (Eisenberg et al., 2009). Eliminating, or at the very least decreasing, mental illness stigma allows us to focus on creating healthy communities in which all individuals can thrive. Only when we take a focused and honest look at what is going on in our community can we eradicate barriers to success and ensure all feel valued.

Suggestions for a Campus Community Approach to Addressing Mental Illness Stigma

The very real solutions of how to implement efforts to change mental illness stigma on campus is an important part of this volume. While each of the authors in this volume suggest approaches which can provide important changes for a campus, we iterate the importance of using multiple and duplicative efforts to exact widespread and hopefully lasting change to the culture and subcultures of mental illness stigma. There were several themes that emerged as important points for this work. We offer this summary of the suggestions herein to assist readers in developing strategies to use on their campuses.

We start our suggestions with the naming and forming of a task force. We are aware of the critiques of such actions, namely, that university-wide committees like this reinforce a heuristic that greater awareness (e.g., of stigma) is enough to address complex problems (Stein, 2019) and this could be a way of diffusing responsibility for a negative climate operative on campus (Abrica et al., 2023). Thus, a task force focused on stigma could easily fall into this trap of believing the work is complete; naming the task force names the presence of stigma on campus. We are offering that a task force focused on stigma can be a way to challenge the general narrative about task forces. As discussed throughout this volume, power is an important factor in the perpetuation of stigma; a university-wide committee provides an opportunity for those in power to recognize who benefits, and who is harmed, from the perpetuation of stigmatizing values and norms. If those in power commit to hearing these concerns and addressing them in the multiple ways that a campus-wide committee suggests, the university has a very real opportunity to create an inclusive community for everyone. A final point before reviewing the different steps of the plan: The creation of a task force should not absolve individual departments nor individuals from participating in this important work. This volume includes suggestions that are directed at certain populations within the university and can be implemented within individual departments and by invested individuals.

The university-wide task force must include faculty, staff, administrators, and students. At least some of the constituents should hold power to make decisions about implementing decisions and directions made by the task force. To reduce the burden on those who are involved, and to reduce the tendency to exploit those whose experiences are likely to make them interested and invested in this work, it is important that task force members be compensated for their work in a manner appropriate for their campus role, and the task force duties must not reflect a work overload. Additionally, the task force must have access to dedicated funds to use to implement programs and efforts that evolve from the decisions made by its members. Finally, the task force needs to have dedicated administrative staff support for the duration of their work.

The task force should focus efforts on first reviewing and identifying the multiple places where stigma exists. Thus, the task force should consider both the instances where stigma is present and places where the understanding of stigma impact is absent. For instance, the task force could create guidelines for policy review that focuses on stigmatizing language used in policies and actions suggested by policies that disadvantage those who experience mental illness. The task force should also focus efforts on educating the various campus constituents about what mental illness stigma is and why it matters that we know about it. Finally, the task force should focus on actionable steps the university community can take that are focused on stigma reduction.

Students must be a part of the task force membership, ideally with students representing leadership positions with potency on the task force. Additionally, the task force needs to involve students in the development and implementation of all stigma-focused programs. Ideally, students will lead this effort in contexts involving students. It is vitally important to involve students who hold marginalized identities. And it is important to involve students who are a part of the subcultures mentioned in this volume (e.g., graduate students, mental health trainees, athletes, and individuals who misuse substances). Involving these students is critical so that programs are reflective of the experiences and needs of all students. An additional benefit for involving them is this effort provides community for these students to decrease the sense of alienation and isolation they may be experiencing. Finally, doing so provides these students with opportunities to ally with others in their efforts to decrease stigma. These students should also be compensated for their time and work.

The task force should create and then use a comprehensive and strategic plan. This plan should have short- and long-term goals and initiatives. The plan should involve ideas for marketing as well as methods for program development and implementation. Additionally, the plan should consider how turnover and staffing changes at the university, along with the graduation of key students, will impact efforts. The task force should discuss at the outset of the work how results will be disseminated. Additionally, the messaging about the work will need to be routinely communicated throughout the university so those who are new to the university are aware of the efforts.

As the initiatives and programs are developed, it is important to make sure to review language used. Given the multigenerational representation of those who live and work on campus, the language used in programs, policies, and advertisements should be accessible, understandable, and meaningful for all.

The task force should develop a plan to implement an assessment of the work. This assessment should be done routinely and systematically. The feedback offered should be heeded to address needed areas. These assessment efforts require asking information of more than those that attend programs. For instance, residence life staff could include assessments in their halls; faculty could provide assessments in their classes to make sure that off-campus students have a chance to provide feedback. Department heads could solicit feedback from programs and events during scheduled faculty/staff meetings.

Once the task force has completed its charge, it is important to create an ongoing campus-wide committee to continue to champion these efforts. The role of the committee's leadership (and hopefully for members as well) should be a part of that employee's job description rather than thought of as an additional task to be carved out of an already overfilled schedule. Student membership on the committee should be prioritized through a reserved seat for representatives from student government, Greek life, athletics, and student organizations with additional opportunities for students who would like to join.

This ongoing attention to eradicating mental illness stigma on campus can build on the groundwork done by the task force to understand mental illness stigma present in the university. Notably, the committee can focus on how intersectional factors, such as racial identity, gender identity, and socioeconomic status impact the experience of stigma by university members. This can be done by routinely bringing in new members to the committee, including those who hold marginalized identities, who have lived experience as a person with mental illness, who are a researcher, and/or who are a student. Such an intentional representation allows for a distribution of power based on these different perspectives and experiences and expands the foundation to do more than just create actionable items to combat stigma. This type of committee can help support comprehensive and systemic strategies to build lasting change in the culture of mental illness stigma on a campus. Of course, this step will require the support and active participation of university governance and university administration so that stigma reduction is woven into the policies and procedures throughout the university. One way to keep this at the forefront for administration is to have a committee member holding a reserved seat on the faculty, staff, and student governing bodies.

We recognize this suggestion necessitates a very large initiative and commitment by the campus; this type of work may be, and probably is, daunting for most.

Challenging embedded stigma within any culture is not an easy task and takes an ongoing and concerted effort. Yet, we believe this effort is worthwhile compared to the alternative of continuing to alienate and harm the members of our campus communities. That being said, the very presence of such a committee is indicative of a campus commitment to creating a different culture on campus. But we cannot become complacent with these efforts. The notable gaps in this volume are opportunities to initiate the conversation about the presence of stigma in other areas, including the university's administration, human resources, residential living, Greek life, and student conduct offices, just to name a few. We hope these conversations occur on your campus and that they are eventually represented in the literature as well. Doing so reinforces our efforts to create a community of care to challenge the notion that stigma "doesn't happen here." It can happen here because it has. It is here, now. It is up to all of us to change it.

References

Abrica, E. J., Hatch-Tocaimaza, D., & Rios-Aguilar, C. (2023). On the impossibilities of advancing racial justice in higher education: Research through reliance on the campus climate heuristic. *Journal of Diversity in Higher Education, 16*(2), 144–156. https://doi.org/10.1037/dhe0000323

Best, R. K., & Arseniev-Koehler, A. (2023). The stigma of diseases: Unequal burden, uneven decline. *American Sociological Review, 88*(5), 938–969. https://doi.org/10.1177/00031224231197436

Brennan, K. M., & Gorman, K. S. (2022). Altering the landscape of mental illness stigma on university campuses. *Stigma & Health, 7*(3), 358–369. https://doi.org/10.1037/sah0000398

Brennan, K. M., & Gorman, K. S. (2023). Expanding counseling center use through campus engagement and social norming. *College Student Affairs Journal, 41*(1), 105–122. https://files.eric.ed.gov/fulltext/EJ1375934.pdf

Center for Collegiate Mental Health. (2017, January). *2016 annual report* (Publication no. STA 18–166). https://sites.psu.edu/ccmh/files/2018/01/2017_CCMH_Report-1r3iri4.pdf

Center for Collegiate Mental Health. (2024, January). *2023 annual report* (Publication no. STA 24–147). https://ccmh.psu.edu/assets/docs/2023_Annual%20Report.pdf

Dare, O., Jidong, D. E., & Premkumar, P. (2023). Conceptualising mental illness among university students of African, Caribbean and similar ethnic heritage in the United Kingdom. *Ethnicity & Health, 28*(4), 522–543. https://doi.org/10.1080/13557858.2022.2104817

Eisenberg, D., Golberstein, E., & Hunt, J. B. (2009). Mental health and academic success in college. *The B.E. Journal of Economic Analysis and Policy, 9*(1), Article 40. https://doi.org/10.2202/1935-1682.2191

Ernst, E., Niderer, D., Werner, A. M., Czaja, S. J., Mikton, C., Ong, A. D., Rosen, T., Bräler, E., & Beutel, M. E. (2022). Loneliness before and during the COVID-19 pandemic: A systematic review with meta-analysis. *American Psychologist, 77*(5), 660–677. https://doi.org/10.1037/amp0001005

Faleti, D. D., & Akinlotan, O. (2024). Stigmatisation of mental illness in Africa: A systematic review of qualitative and mixed studies. *Journal of Mental Health*, 1–18. https://doi.org/10.1080/09638237.2024.2426982

Gaddis, S. M., Ramirez, D., & Hernandez, E. L. (2018). Contextualizing public stigma: Endorsing mental health treatment stigma on college and university campuses. *Social Science & Medicine, 197*, 183–191. https://doi.org/10.1016/j.socscimed.2017.11.029

Gorman, K. S., & Brennan, K. M. (2023a). Mental illness public stigma and treatment seeking among university students. *Journal of College Student Psychotherapy, 37*(1), 52–70. https://doi.org/10.1080/87568225.2021.1891006

Gorman, K. S., & Brennan, K. M. (2023b) More sessions make a difference: University counseling centers and student retention. *Journal of Student Affairs Research and Practice*, 1–13. https://doi.org/10.1080/19496591.2023.2201453

Gorman, K. S., Walden, D., Braun, L., & Hotaling, M. (2024). Navigating a path forward for mental health services in higher education. *Journal of College Student Mental Health*, 1–19. https://doi.org/10.1080/28367138.2023.2298647

Haidt, J. (2024). *The anxious generation: How the great rewiring of childhood is causing an epidemic of mental illness*. Penguin Press.

Jochman, J. C., Cheadle, J. E., Goosby, B. J., Tomaso, C., Kozikowski, C., & Nelson, T. (2019). Mental health outcomes of discrimination among college students on a predominately white campus: A prospective study. *Socius, 5*. https://doi.org/10.1177/2378023119842728

Krendl, A. C., & Pescosolido, B. A. (2020). Countries and cultural differences in the stigma of mental illness: The East–West divide. *Journal of Cross-Cultural Psychology, 51*(2), 149–167. https://doi.org/10.1177/0022022119901297

Lipson, S. K., Lattie, E. G., & Eisenberg, D. (2019). Increased rates of mental health service utilization by U.S. college students: 10-year population-level trends (2007-2017). *Psychiatric Services, 70*(1), 60–63. https://doi.org/10.1176/appi.ps.201800332

Murthy, V. H. (2020). *Together: The healing power of human connection in a sometimes lonely world*. Harper.

Pescosolido, B. A., Halpern-Manners, A., Luo, L., & Perry, B. (2021). Trends in public stigma of mental illness in the U.S., 1996-2018. *JAMA Network Open, 4*(12), e2140202. https://doi.org/10.1001/jamanetworkopen.2021.40202

Pescosolido, B. A., Medina, T. R., Martin, J. K., & Long, J. S. (2013). The 'backbone' of stigma: Identifying the global core of public prejudice associated with mental illness. *American Journal of Public Health, 103*(5), 853–860. https://doi.org/10.2105/AJPH.2012.301147

Ruiz, J. C., Fuentes-Durá, I., López-Gilberte, M., Dasí, C., Pardo-García, C., Fuentes-Durán, M. C., Pérez-González, F., Salmeron, L., Soldevila-Matías, P., Vila-Francés, J., & Balanza-Martínez, V. (2022). Public stigma profile toward mental disorders across different university degrees in the University of Valencia (Spain). *Frontiers in Psychiatry, 13*, 951894. https://doi.org/10.3389/fpsyt.2022.951894

Schomerus, G., Schindler, S., Sander, C., Baumann, E., & Angermeyer, M. C. (2022). Changes in mental illness stigma over 30 years - improvement, persistence, or deterioration? *European Psychiatry, 65*(1), e78. https://doi.org/10.1192/j.eurpsy.2022.2337

Stein, S. (2019). Beyond higher education as we know it: Gesturing towards decolonial horizons of possibility. *Studies in Philosophy and Education, 39*(5), 143–161. https://doi.org/10.1007/s11217-018-9622-7

Subramaniam, M., Abdin, E., Picco, L., Pang, S., Shafie, S., Vaingankar, J. A., Kwok, K. W., Verma, K., & Chong, S. A. (2017). Stigma towards people with mental disorders and its components–a perspective from multi-ethnic Singapore. *Epidemiology and Psychiatric Sciences, 26*, 371–382. https://doi.org/10.1017/S2045796016000159

Twenge, J. (2023). *Generations: The real differences between Gen Z, Millennials, Gen X, Boomers, and Silents—And what they mean for America's future*. Atria Books.

Kimberly S. Gorman, Ph.D., is Associate Vice Chancellor for Health & Wellness in the Student Affairs Division at Western Carolina University, USA. Dr. Gorman's primary research interests are related to collegiate mental health and mental illness stigma in the college population. She has co-authored several papers about the impacts of mental illness and its related stigma in college students. She is a licensed psychologist who has worked in the higher education setting for more than two decades. She has served on the governing board of the Association for University and College Counseling Center Directors and on the advisory board for the Center for Collegiate Mental Health.

Kathleen M. Brennan, Ph.D., is Professor of Sociology and Director of the Sociology Program at Western Carolina University, USA. For more than a decade, she has used quantitative methodologies to collaboratively examine mental illness stigma in the context of higher education. She has co-presented these research findings to professional audiences and co-authored papers in higher education, health, and other disciplinary publications. Additionally, she regularly teaches about and provides consultation on the sociology of mental health and illness on campus and in the regional community.

The manufacturer's authorised representative in the EU is Springer Nature Customer Service Centre GmbH, Europaplatz 3, 69115 Heidelberg, Germany. If you have any concerns regarding our products, please contact ProductSafety@springernature.com

Printed and bound by CPI Group (UK) Ltd, Croydon, CR0 4YY
01/10/2026
02225929-0001